INTRODUCING MAJOR THEOLOGIANS

To my dear parents,
I wrote this book for you,
it being all about learning
from previous generations.
I will never cease to be full of
love and gratitude for you.

And my dear Lucy,
I wrote this book for you,
as from one generation to the next.
Of course you are too young for it now,
but maybe someday you can take it down
from some upper shelf, dust it,
and tell me what you think of it.
And if you never do, just remember
what they say in Geneva:
Post tenebras, LUX!

For related resources, visit
www.uniontheology.org

INTRODUCING
MAJOR
THEOLOGIANS

FROM THE APOSTOLIC FATHERS
TO THE TWENTIETH CENTURY

MICHAEL REEVES

Inter-Varsity Press
Norton Street, Nottingham NG7 3HR, England
Email: ivp@ivpbooks.com
Website: www.ivpbooks.com

Chapters 1 to 6 first published 2010 as *The Breeze of the Centuries*.
Chapters 7 to 12 first published 2011 as *On Giants' Shoulders*.

This combined edition with chapter 13 first published 2015.

British Library Cataloguing in Publication Data
A catalogue record for this book is available from the British Library.

ISBN: 978-1-78359-272-2

Set in Garamond 11/13pt
Typeset in Great Britain by CRB Associates, Potterhanworth, Lincolnshire
Printed and bound in Great Britain by Ashford Colour Press Ltd, Gosport,
Hampshire

*Inter-Varsity Press publishes Christian books that are true to the Bible and that communicate
the gospel, develop discipleship and strengthen the church for its mission in the world.*

*Inter-Varsity Press is closely linked with the Universities and Colleges Christian Fellowship,
a student movement connecting Christian Unions in universities and colleges throughout Great
Britain, and a member movement of the International Fellowship of Evangelical Students.
Website: www.uccf.org.uk.*

CONTENTS

ACKNOWLEDGMENTS

Having written such a very unoriginal book, I have a lot of people to thank. In fact, I feel I really ought to thank these theologians I am introducing, given how much I have learnt from them over the years. The other main force behind these volumes, to whom I owe a special word of thanks, is Dr Philip Duce at Inter-Varsity Press, a kind and deft editor without whom I would have been more than normally helpless.

I also want to thank Justin Taylor at Crossway Books, whose wise input made this revised edition possible; Professor John Webster, who inspired the project; Professor Alan Millard, Professor Carl Trueman, Dr Steve Holmes, Dr Steve Nichols and Professor Ron Frost for their kind attempts to improve the manuscript; Dr Domenico Giordano, for his warm assistance and clarification; Dr Paul Melankreos, whose insights into the early post-apostolic church were invaluable; Professor Thomas Williams, who dispensed advice so willingly; Daniel Hames, who kept throwing fuel on the fire; Elizabeth Fraser, who suggested including timelines; Edward Coombs, who believed that heroes of the faith can still teach and inspire a Sunday congregation; and the late Professor Colin Gunton, who taught me so much about time travel. Lucy and Mia made their own very special contribution: I think I am grateful for that. I certainly am for the TULIP boys, who are a constant encouragement – and, in fact, both wise and adept.

But most of all I thank my dear, wonderful wife, Bethan. It is not easy walking with dinosaurs, but she has done it with overflowing love and grace.

INTRODUCTION: SNOBS, BUMPKINS AND DINOSAURS

C. S. Lewis was a self-confessed dinosaur. He knew perfectly well that he simply did not belong in the modern world. Yet, being born out of due time, he was able to spot what the natives could not. And what he saw in modern culture, perhaps more than anything else, was a suffocating enslavement to the beautiful myth of progress, the dream that history is evolving ever onwards and upwards, that newer is better.

It is the sort of belief that sits very comfortably in the subconscious, giving one the warm glow of knowing that we are faster, better, wiser, more advanced and more knowledgeable than our parents and forebears. Yet one of the problems Lewis noticed in the myth was that such superiority tends to produce not wisdom but ignorance. If we assume that the past is inferior, we will not bother consulting it, and will thus find ourselves stranded on the tiny desert island of our moment in time. Or, as Lewis put it, we will become like the country bumpkin, full of

the cocksure conviction of an ignorant adolescent that his own village (which is the only one he knows) is the hub of the universe and does everything in the Only Right Way. For our own age, with all its accepted ideas, stands to the vast extent of historical time much as one village stands to the whole world.[1]

Of course, such 'chronological snobbery' does not like to admit its own existence. No snob likes to be thought of as an ignorant bumpkin. Indeed, the chronological snob will often be the first to bedeck himself with historical references. The modern writer will allude to the old. But so often it is simply a case of the living plundering the dead. The cachet of the Augustine, the Luther, the Aquinas is purloined, as sound bites from their writings are torn from their original context and pressed into the service of other arguments, or simply used as weapons in the latest theological street fight.

But what Lewis found – and what reading old books makes very clear – is that every age works with a large set of assumptions that seem to it so self-evident they are never questioned. Like the proverbial frog in the kettle, we find it almost impossible to get a real sense of the water we inhabit, and can thus be blissfully unaware of how faddish our beliefs are. It is very tempting for me now to don the grand airs of a sage cultural critic and attempt to list what our unquestioned assumptions are today. But anyone excavating this book from the dusty bowels of some copyright library in fifty years' time would only chuckle at the profound issues I had overlooked. They are simply part of the air we breathe every day, and as such are quite invisible to us.

What to do? 'The only palliative', said Lewis, 'is to keep the clean sea breeze of the centuries blowing through our minds.'[2] That is, we refuse to imprison ourselves in the stuffy broom cupboard of the present and safely familiar, and open up the doors to the refreshing influences of other times. And practically?

---

1. C. S. Lewis, *Studies in Medieval and Renaissance Literature* (Cambridge: Cambridge University Press, 1966), p. 138.)

2. C. S. Lewis, Introduction to *On the Incarnation* by Athanasius (London: Centenary, 1944; repr. Crestwood, N. Y.: SVS, 1998), p. 5.

It is a good rule, after reading a new book, never to allow yourself another new one till you have read an old one in between. If that is too much for you, you should at least read one old one to every three new ones . . . Not, of course, that there is any magic about the past. People were no cleverer then than they are now; they made as many mistakes as we. But not the *same* mistakes. They will not flatter us in the errors we are already committing; and their own errors, being now open and palpable, will not endanger us. Two heads are better than one, not because either is infallible, but because they are unlikely to go wrong in the same direction. To be sure, the books of the future would be just as good a corrective as the books of the past, but unfortunately we cannot get at them.[3]

Such is the motivation behind *Introducing Major Theologians*. It is that, far from turning us into *irrelevant* dinosaurs, reading old books can rescue us from bumpkinery and enlarge our vision. From other centuries we receive an enrichment we could never have through mere feeding on ourselves. And if that is true for old books in general, it is more so for the books of old theologians. Theology is something to be done corporately, by the church. But if we ignore what the bulk of the church has said down through history, then we act as schismatically as if we ignored the church on earth today. More so, in fact.

Would Lewis not be appalled?

Clearly, then, this is a work built on Lewis's foundations. And yet, is this not exactly the sort of dreary modern book Lewis feared would insulate people from the health-giving breeze? Why write another new book when the aim is to have people read old ones?

But this was just why Lewis wrote so much. The fact is, theologians like Athanasius and Calvin are like famous guests of honour at a party. Most people there would love to have some time with

---

3. Ibid., pp. 4–5.

them, but few dare to approach them without a polite introduction. And providing a few introductions to fascinating but
potentially intimidating celebrity theologians is the aim of these
pages.

In that sense, while there might seem to be an insane arrogance
to the thought of trying to squeeze such titans into so few pages,
this is actually a work that makes no great pretences. Rather, it
seeks to do itself out of a job by leading readers on to better
books than this. For that reason I will not spend time pontificating
on 'Anselm's view of God' or 'Barth's view of Scripture' – to do so
could leave readers just as frightened of approaching the great
men for themselves, perhaps more so. Instead, I will try to intrude
as little as possible, simply letting the reader get to know the
theologians on their own terms. Of course, that will not be entirely
possible – and there will be moments when I will be unable to
restrain myself from commenting – but that is the aim: not to pre-
digest, pillage or spin, but to introduce real people, which means
people whose thoughts are so often a puzzling swirl of glories
and gaffes.

Reading these introductions

Each introduction will begin with a little biography and background – after all, no theology is written in a vacuum, and
somehow, knowing about, say, Athanasius' sense of humour
and his 'Boy's Own' adventures makes Athanasius easier to get into.
Then on to the theology, which will amount to a fast jog through
each theologian's major work(s). Note: this is rather different to
my writing on 'Calvin's doctrine of election' or the like; instead, I
will try to walk with readers through Calvin's *Institutes*, getting to
know its structure, feel and argument. Readers interested in
Calvin's doctrine of election should then feel confident enough
to put Reeves on one side and converse with Calvin direct. At the
end of each introduction I will make some suggestions for getting
to know that theologian better, and I will provide a timeline to
help give a snapshot-sense of the order and context of the life in
question.

There is a story that emerges from these pages, and readers who work through one introduction after another should, by the end of the second volume, have glimpsed something of the overall movement and flow of Christian thought through the centuries. However, this is just as much a work to dip in and out of. Its purpose is not so much to tell a grand narrative as to meet and get to know some of the key characters. And those characters are remarkably diverse: some will sound more winning, more trustworthy or more familiar; others may seem quite alien or off-putting. Thus if you find yourself floundering or overly enraged by one theologian, feel happy to move on to the next. He will, assuredly, be quite different.

But why these theologians, and not others? Quite simply, the goal of this work is to make accessible what otherwise seems intimidating, but if the very girth of the volumes was daunting, it would have failed in what it set out to do. I have therefore had to pick and choose theologians to introduce, and that means disappointing those whose heroes are not included. Still, I have not simply come up with a list of personal favourites; I have minor disagreements with every theologian here, and major problems with a few. Nor is this my list of 'great Christians'. Francis of Assisi, John Bunyan and John Wesley will make no appearance, though undoubtedly they were great and influential; it is that their greatness was not so much *as theologians*. Rather, I have tried to choose theologians who are influential or significant especially for the English-speaking world (many of whom, I suspect, are the very ones English-speaking people are most eager to know better). As a result, such mighty names as Origen, Palamas, Gerhard, Turretin and Suárez (the list could go on) are not included. My apologies to any who miss them: accessibility calls.

The last word of introduction really belongs to C. S. Lewis, who grasped so well the point of wrestling with theology:

> For my own part I tend to find the doctrinal books often more helpful in devotion than the devotional books, and I rather suspect that the same experience may await many others. I believe that many who find that 'nothing happens' when they sit down, or kneel down, to a book of devotion, would find that the heart sings unbidden while they are

working their way through a tough bit of theology with a pipe in their teeth and a pencil in their hand.[4]

May it be so for you now.

---

4. Ibid., p. 8.

1. ONLY LET ME REACH JESUS CHRIST!

The Apostolic Fathers

By the end of the first century AD, Jesus' apostles were all dead and Jerusalem and its temple had been destroyed. It was a crucial time of transition for Christianity, made all the more difficult by the hostile notice the Roman Empire began to pay as it saw what looked to it like a subversive new sect in its midst.

The writings of the Apostolic Fathers are the most important books for understanding those first generations after the apostles: how they thought, lived and died. The collection of the Apostolic Fathers consists of about ten authors who wrote from around the end of the first century to the middle of the second, put together by scholars and termed the Apostolic Fathers. However, as a group they are a real mixed bag: some are works by eminent figures of the time such as Polycarp of Smyrna; others are anonymous; they come from different genres (letters, works of apologetics, a sermon, an apocalypse, an account of a martyrdom, instructions on church order); and they represent a wide diversity of theologies. Perhaps the best way to understand them is to see them not as the best theology of the time, but as representative best-sellers of the generation after the apostles. As such they are not only significant but instructive.

We will examine each of the works normally included in the collection in order to see what they say and also to see what they tell us about earliest post-apostolic Christianity and its theology.

Papias

According to tradition, Papias, the bishop of Hierapolis in Asia Minor, was the disciple of the apostle John who actually wrote out John's Gospel as the apostle dictated it. He wrote a five-volume work of his own, *An Exposition of the Sayings of the Lord*, however, today only fragments of his work survive. During the second century, Papias was widely held in high esteem; yet, largely because of his characteristically second-century belief in a literal, future millennium, he fell out of favour with subsequent generations who tended to understand the millennium more symbolically. The great third- to fourth-century church historian Eusebius dismissed Papias for this reason as 'a man of exceedingly small intelligence'.[1]

Papias is valuable today for one reason in particular: he demonstrates for us the importance of oral tradition for early post-apostolic Christianity. It is clear from what survives of his work that an enormous number of oral traditions were in circulation concerning the life and sayings of Jesus and his apostles. It is also clear that such oral traditions were by no means distrusted as mere hearsay; instead, they were valued because they could be probed easily for veracity. For instance, Papias records that John and Philip went to evangelize Asia Minor, Philip settling with his family in Papias' own town of Hierapolis (where, according to tradition, Philip was martyred). John, he tells us, settled in Ephesus, was then exiled for a while to the island of Patmos, was recalled by the emperor Nerva (AD 96–8), whence he returned to Ephesus, there to be killed as the last of the apostles, in fulfilment of Mark

---

1. Eusebius, *Church History* 3.39; quoted from *Nicene and Post-Nicene Fathers*, Second Series, tr. P. Schaff and H. Wace, 14 vols. (Grand Rapids: Eerdmans, 1986–9).

10:38–39. Mark, he tells us, wrote his Gospel based on Peter's testimony (Mark being Peter's disciple and companion in Rome [1 Pet. 5:13]). If true, it adds an exquisite poignancy to Mark's graphic account of Peter's betrayal of Jesus. Papias' most gruesomely fascinating account, though, is of Judas. Papias believed that the two New Testament accounts of Judas' end (Matt. 27:3–10; Acts 1:15–9) could be harmonized by understanding that Judas did not die by hanging himself, but was cut down before he choked to death. Then he lived on, only to die when falling, so bloated that he burst open:

> Judas was a terrible, walking example of ungodliness in this world, his flesh so bloated that he was not able to pass through a place where a wagon passes easily, not even his bloated head by itself. For his eyelids, they say, were so swollen that he could not see the light at all, and his eyes could not be seen, even by a doctor using an optical instrument, so far had they sunk below the outer surface. His genitals appeared more loathsome and larger than anyone else's, and when he relieved himself there passed through it pus and worms from every part of his body, much to his shame. After much agony and punishment, they say, he finally died in his own place, and because of the stench the area is deserted and uninhabitable even now; in fact, to this day one cannot pass that place without holding one's nose, so great was the discharge from his body, and so far did it spread over the ground.[2]

Clement of Rome

1 Clement

Perhaps the oldest complete work in the collection, written around AD 95, is an anonymous letter traditionally attributed to Clement, Paul's co-worker (Phil. 4:3) and the third bishop of Rome after Peter. It was written to the ever-problematic church of Corinth in order to address a number of issues that were causing disquiet

---

2. A fragment of Papias' *Exposition of the Sayings of the Lord*, cited by Apollinaris of Laodicea.

there. One of those issues was still the resurrection of the body: the Corinthians clearly had not taken the message of 1 Corinthians 15 to heart! The main problem, however, was that the old concern of disunity had led to the church's elders being ousted in a church coup and replaced.

1 Clement argues that the takeover was entirely wrong, being motivated by pride and greed, and that the ousted elders must be restored. According to the letter, the move was a rebellion against God, who has appointed a proper ecclesiastical order: God commissioned Christ, who commissioned apostles, who commissioned bishops, who commission deacons.[3] It is arguable whether or not this is a reference to the doctrine of apostolic succession as it would come to be formulated (after all, here the elders were said to have been appointed 'with the consent of the whole church'[4]). What is clear, though, is that the role of the church elder has a significance in *1 Clement* that it does not have in 1 Corinthians: church unity now seems to be sought more in the elders than in the Spirit.

Advocates of Episcopal church government argue that *1 Clement* is evidence of a very early and natural evolution of episcopalism. The fact that Clement was himself bishop of Rome is also used by advocates of papal supremacy to support their theory by suggesting that he wrote with authority to another church because of his position, even though there is no internal evidence in the letter to suggest this.

At the other end of the interpretative spectrum are those who see an almost complete discontinuity between a New Testament radical congregationalism and a monarchical episcopalism in the next generation. On this reading, earliest apostolic Christianity had no concept of eldership, churches being charismatic communities with no need for such leadership, meaning that the pastoral epistles (1 and 2 Timothy and Titus) must be dismissed as later

---

3. *1 Clement* 42.

4. Ibid. 44.3. All Apostolic Fathers quotations from here on are from Michael Holmes's translation, *The Apostolic Fathers in English*, 3rd ed. (Grand Rapids: Baker, 2006).

'deutero-Pauline' books because of their concern for church offices. Stimulating this kind of interpretation was a seminal work published in 1934 by Walter Bauer entitled *Orthodoxy and Heresy in Earliest Christianity*. Bauer's claim was that an originally diverse Christianity soon began to be dominated by just one authoritarian group, found in Rome. The Roman church then rewrote history, setting its own beliefs as the standard of orthodoxy and labelling all dissent as heresy. Bauer's thesis was seriously flawed (if power bought the title 'orthodox', how could those emperors who were Arian be dismissed as heretics?), yet it initiated what is today a prolific trend for describing orthodoxy as mere authoritarianism.[5]

2 Clement

The second letter of Clement is misleadingly titled: it is neither a letter, nor is it by Clement. It is a sermon, quite possibly preached by one of the Corinthian elders who were restored to their offices following Clement's 'first' letter. The sermon has to do with a call to repentance, to think of Christ as God and to believe in the resurrection. Its greatest value for us, though, is probably its treatment of Scripture: it contains the earliest example (outside the New Testament) of a passage from the New Testament being referred to as 'Scripture' alongside the Old Testament.[6] It reveals that there was a clear and early understanding of a New Testament canon of Scripture.

Ignatius of Antioch

One of the most remarkable and memorable figures of the first post-apostolic generation was Ignatius, bishop of Antioch in Syria. Strangely, we know almost nothing about him until he explodes onto the historical scene just a few weeks before his martyrdom in around AD 110. During a citywide persecution, he and some other Christians were arrested and sent to Rome to be thrown to wild

---

5. Bart Ehrman is perhaps the foremost exponent of this view today.
6. *2 Clement* 2.4.

beasts in the arena. En route, under armed guard, he dashed off seven letters to the churches he would pass through: the churches of Ephesus, Magnesia, Tralles, Philadelphia, Smyrna (as well as one to Polycarp, the bishop of Smyrna), and Rome. The letters really were dashed off (their style shows that they were written hastily and under considerable strain); nevertheless, they make for fascinating and illuminating reading. They are the last words of a man with only weeks to live, and yet, to quote Bruce Metzger, are filled with 'such strong faith and overwhelming love of Christ as to make them one of the finest literary expressions of Christianity during the second century'.[7]

As he wrote, Ignatius had three main concerns on his mind. The first was that the churches be unified under their respective bishops. On this issue, Ignatius is so strongly Episcopalian he makes Clement appear positively Congregationalist in contrast. For Ignatius, the church finds its unity through the bishop, and therefore he writes, 'you must not do anything without the bishop and the presbyters'; indeed, it 'is not permissible either to baptize or to hold a love feast without the bishop'.[8] This is because, for Ignatius, the bishop represents Christ to the church, and thus to meet without the bishop would be to fail to be Christ's church: 'For everyone whom the Master of the house sends to manage his own house we must welcome as we would the one who sent him. It is obvious, therefore, that we must regard the bishop as the Lord himself.'[9]

The second concern on Ignatius' mind was the problem of false teaching. In particular, Ignatius had two types of false teachers in mind: Docetists and Judaizers, both of whom denied in their own way that Christ had come in the flesh (cf. 1 John).

The Docetists maintained that Jesus was entirely divine, and that he only *appeared* to be human (the name 'Docetic' comes from the Greek word *dokeō*, meaning 'to seem' or 'to appear'). Perhaps

---

7. B. M. Metzger, *The Canon of the New Testament: Its Origin, Development, and Significance* (Oxford: Clarendon, 1987), p. 44.

8. *Magnesians* 7.1; *Smyrnaeans* 8.2. Quotations are taken from Holmes, *Apostolic Fathers in English*.

9. *Ephesians* 6.1; cf. *Trallians* 3.1; *Ephesians* 5.3; *Smyrnaeans* 6.2.

the most notorious Docetic teacher was Marcion, who taught that the good Saviour-God of the New Testament is a different being to the bad Creator-God of the Old Testament. Jesus thus had nothing to do with the evil Creator-God's physical world, and so could not actually have had a physical body, been born, have eaten, died and so on. In stark opposition, Ignatius would boldly speak of 'the blood of God', for if the divine Christ had not truly assumed our humanity, then he could not have died for our sins.[10] In fact, Ignatius' entire motivation in accepting martyrdom was based upon his belief in the real incarnation of Christ: Ignatius longed for martyrdom because then he would be copying Christ, but if Christ did not really suffer in his body, then Ignatius could not be copying him at all. 'If that is the case, I die for no reason,' he wrote.[11] Instead, Ignatius wanted his life and death to proclaim that 'There is only one physician, who is both flesh and spirit, born and unborn, God in man, true life in death, both from Mary and from God, first subject to suffering and then beyond it, Jesus Christ our Lord.'[12] It is hard to read such material and not be incredulous of the claim that Jesus' full divinity and full humanity is a later, fourth-century invention.

The other type of false teacher Ignatius was eager to arm Christians against (particularly in Magnesia and Philadelphia) was the Judaizer, who taught that Christians must abide by Jewish customs, especially circumcision and the Mosaic Law. For a time when Christianity was only just beginning to be recognized as something distinct from Judaism, this was a most pressing issue. Ignatius argued that the Judaizer's teaching misunderstood the very nature of the Old Testament: 'if we continue to live in accordance with Judaism, we admit that we have not received grace. For the most godly prophets lived in accordance with Christ Jesus.'[13] The mistake of the Judaizers was to fail to see that Old Testament believers were themselves Christians, saved by nothing else than

---

10. *Ephesians* 1.1; cf. *Romans* 6.3.

11. *Trallians* 10.1; cf. *Smyrnaeans* 4.2.

12. *Ephesians* 7.2.

13. *Magnesians* 8.1–2; cf. 9.2.

by trusting in Christ.[14] The Jewish Scriptures existed to proclaim Christ and his gospel. As we will see, this was to be the issue of issues for many Christians of the day, who saw that the entire legitimacy of their faith depended on the Hebrew Scriptures being inherently Christian. If they were not, then Judaism, not Christianity, was true.

Ignatius' third concern as he wrote his letters was, understandably, his own death. This surfaces most clearly in his letter to the Romans. The point of his letter is to beg the Christians in Rome not to try to help him escape death when he arrives, for he is eager to be martyred:

> I implore you: do not be unseasonably kind to me. Let me be food for the wild beasts . . . Bear with me – I know what is best for me. Now at last I am beginning to be a disciple. May nothing visible or invisible envy me, so that I may reach Jesus Christ. Fire and cross and battles with wild beasts, mutilation, mangling, wrenching of bones, the hacking of limbs, the crushing of my whole body, cruel tortures of the devil – let these come upon me, only let me reach Jesus Christ![15]

This enthusiasm of his is so inexplicable to many modern commentators that he is all too often written off as a psychotic. In point of fact, however, he is profoundly realistic, anticipating, for example, that his courage may well fail when the moment comes. Thus he writes, 'if upon my arrival I myself should appeal to you, do not be persuaded by me'.[16] Part of Ignatius' reasoning was that Christians were normally only released upon denying Christ, and this would undoubtedly be what people would assume had happened if Ignatius were released, even if the Roman church really did manage to secure his freedom in another way. He would rather suffer death than that. Far more significantly, though, Ignatius believed that the best way for him to follow Christ was through the same kind of violent death Christ had suffered. In this way he would

---

14. *Philadelphians* 9.1.
15. *Romans* 4.1; 5.3.
16. Ibid. 7.2.

become most Christlike, and thus most clearly confess the saving suffering of his God.[17]

Polycarp of Smyrna

Ignatius sent one of his letters to Polycarp, the bishop of Smyrna and former disciple of the apostle John, who is probably the most renowned of all the Apostolic Fathers because of the martyrdom he would also suffer.

The Letter of Polycarp to the Philippians

Polycarp himself wrote a letter to the church of Philippi a few weeks after Ignatius' death in order to tackle some difficulties they were facing. The presenting issue was that one of their elders, Valens, had embezzled some of the church funds.[18] However, there was also a problem of false teaching. When Paul wrote to the Philippians sixty or so years earlier, he had had to tackle some Judaizing false teachers (Phil. 3:2–3). By Polycarp's time, the false teaching was more predominately Docetic.[19] What is perhaps most interesting about Polycarp's letter is the mildness of his rebuke to Valens in comparison with his treatment of the false teachers. Valens, who had been immoral, is called to repentance; the false teachers, on the other hand, are anathematized as 'the firstborn of Satan'.[20] What appears to be going on is that Polycarp viewed theological belief as the impetus for behaviour, and thus wrong belief would corrupt and splinter the church. The church in this harassed time needed to stand fast in its doctrine in order to stand fast at all.

The Martyrdom of Polycarp

The eyewitness account of the events leading up to, and including, Polycarp's execution fill out for us our understanding of both

---

17. Ibid. 6.3.
18. *Philippians* 11.1.
19. Ibid. 6.3 – 7.1.
20. Ibid. 11.4; 7.1.

the post-apostolic church's theology of martyrdom, and of why Christians of the time were persecuted.

The account describes Polycarp's martyrdom as the last in a local wave of persecution. Thus it begins with the trials and martyrdoms of other local Christians. Most are said to have been given extraordinary courage in their moment of need. However, one man, Quintus, rashly volunteered himself for martyrdom, only to apostatize when threatened. His behaviour is included as a warning not to volunteer for martyrdom, however good it might be for those on whom it is thrust (like Ignatius).[21]

Polycarp is then sought out, and neither seeks martyrdom nor shies away from it. From then on, numerous parallels between the last hours of Christ and Polycarp show Polycarp to be an exemplary follower of Christ. Like Ignatius, he is being a disciple in facing his martyrdom. The Roman officials try to persuade Polycarp to say 'Caesar is Lord', to offer him incense and to revile Christ. He continually refuses (at which time he utters the immortal words 'eighty-six years I have been his [Christ's] servant, and he has done me no wrong. How can I blaspheme my King who saved me?'[22]), and eventually he is sentenced to be burned at the stake. The fire, however, fails to kill Polycarp, and thus he is stabbed to death.

We can learn a number of things from the account. We see that it was the mob, rather than the government, that instigated a local persecution of the Christians. This was certainly the normal pattern: there were instances when systematic persecution became Roman imperial policy,[23] but by and large persecution was popularly motivated, and thus sporadic and local. We also see that the reason Christians were persecuted was not per se because they were Christian, but because they refused to worship the state gods,

---

21. *Martyrdom* 4.

22. Ibid. 9.3.

23. This happened during the reigns of the emperors Nero (54–68), Trajan (98–117), Marcus Aurelius (161–80), Septimius Severus (193–211), Maximian (235), Decius and Valerian (249–60) and Diocletian and Galerian (303–13).

especially the emperor. To refuse to worship the emperor looked seditious to the Roman mind, for which religion was a highly political concept; to fail to worship the other gods looked dangerously anti-social, for the gods, if not revered, could mete out all manner of punishments from plague to crop failure. For the people, the persecution of such blasphemers was self-protection. It was for this reason that, a generation later, the great African theologian Tertullian wrote:

> If the Tiber rises as high as the city walls, if the Nile does not send its waters up over the fields, if the heavens give no rain, if there is an earthquake, if there is famine or pestilence, straightway the cry is, 'Away with the Christians to the lion!'[24]

The Didache

The Didache (teaching) *of the Apostles* was a work known only by its title until its discovery, amid much media excitement, in a library in Constantinople in 1873. Its discovery caused such a stir because it is such an early (c. AD 100) and detailed discussion of life, practice and beliefs in the early post-apostolic church.

It starts with a section of ethical teaching, explaining that there are two paths for us, the path of life (an extremely strict code of morality) and the path of death (failure to adhere to that code). What is both striking and disturbing is that there is nothing explicitly Christian in that entire section of ethical instruction. Justification and the gospel of grace are poignantly absent, leaving the impression of a life that knows far more of legalism than freedom. Ironically, it feels a very far cry from the actual teaching of the apostles as we have it in the New Testament. Instead, being so early an exhibit of Christian legalism, it serves as a powerful affirmation of the apostle Paul's point, that people can turn with astonishing speed from the grace of Christ to another gospel (Gal. 1:6).

---

24. Tertullian, *Apology* 40.

The next section gives instructions on how to practise baptism, prayer, fasting and the Eucharist, before moving on to deal with what was evidently a growing problem: what to do with itinerant 'apostles and prophets'. Apparently, two types of Christian leader had developed by this time: itinerant prophets who followed the apostle Paul's model of ministry, and local church elders who were permanent members of one church. The problem, however, was that, unlike Paul, some of these prophets had begun to be a burden to local churches by living off them. While respecting the office of the itinerant prophet as of equal value to that of the elder, *The Didache* responds with strict instructions on how to sort out the rogues: if, for example, they stay for more than two days, order meals 'in the spirit' or ask for money, they are to be rejected as false prophets.[25]

The work closes with a brief apocalyptic section, which is just one of many reminders in the Apostolic Fathers that the future return of Christ was an almost shockingly prominent feature in the minds of that generation of Christians. It forcefully moulded not only how they died, but also how they lived.

The Shepherd of Hermas

The most popular and influential of the Apostolic Fathers in its day was the lengthy quasi-apocalyptic book *The Shepherd of Hermas*. In it the author (Hermas) records in floridly religious tones a number of visions he has received concerning the nature and state of the church in his day. For the first half of the book, these visions are interpreted to him by a female figure who represents the church. In the second half of the book it is Hermas' guardian angel who interprets the visions to him while taking the form of a shepherd (hence the title of the book).

Hermas begins the work by writing of a time when he had lusted after a woman he once saw bathing in the river Tiber. His first vision then commences, in which he sees the woman

---

25. *Didache* 11.5–6.

accusing him from heaven. At first, surprisingly, he is surprised, and responds, 'I sinned against you? In what way? Or when have I ever spoken an indecent word to you? Have I not always regarded you as a goddess?' (not the best defence, one might have thought, though he certainly had thought about her like this when he saw her naked in the river).[26] Yet she convinces him that his lust was sin, leaving him to wonder, 'If even this sin is recorded against me, how can I be saved? Or how will I propitiate God for my conscious sins?'[27] This sets the scene for the rest of the book, which is chiefly concerned with the possibility of forgiveness.

Four more visions follow, the most important of which concerns a tower built on water.[28] This represents the church built on baptism and reveals what a high view of baptism had started to emerge in certain Christian circles. It begins to clarify a main concern of the book, and what was clearly a popular concern of the day: is there a possibility of forgiveness after the washing of baptism? The answer given is yes, but only one possibility, for 'there is only one repentance for God's servants'.[29] It was this graceless belief that fuelled the practice of postponing baptism until near death. The sorts of things Hermas sees in the vision are angelic builders removing stones from the tower, indicating the removal of believers for sin, and round stones that do not fit, representing rich believers, who must first have their riches chopped away before they can fit into the tower.[30]

Next come twelve 'commandments', all largely pragmatic and moral. The sixth contains the crudest statement of salvation by works prior to the arch-heretic Pelagius:

'Now hear,' he said, 'about faith. There are two angels with a person, one of righteousness and one of wickedness . . . This commandment explains the things about faith, in order that you may trust the works of the angel

---

26. *Hermas* 1.7.
27. Ibid. 2.1.
28. Ibid. 9–21.
29. Ibid. 29.8; 31.1–7.
30. Ibid. 13.5; 14.5–7.

of righteousness, and that doing them, you may live to God. But believe that the works of the angel of wickedness are dangerous, so that by not doing them you will live to God.'[31]

Surely the oddest commandment, though, is the tenth:

> Clothe yourself, therefore, with cheerfulness, which always finds favor with God and is acceptable to him, and rejoice in it. For all cheerful people do good things and think good things, and despise grief. But sorrowful people always do evil.[32]

One wonders how the apostle Paul would have reacted (cf. Rom. 9:2), for this is nothing like his liberating theology of joy.

The book ends with ten 'parables', or lessons to be learned from trees, vines, stones and so on. These too contain 'wisdom' that seems almost entirely ignorant of salvation not by merit but by grace:

> Keep the Lord's commandments, and you will be pleasing to
> him and will be enrolled among the number of those who keep
> his commandments. But if you do anything good beyond God's
> commandment, you will gain greater glory for yourself, and will be
> more honored in God's sight than you otherwise would have been.[33]

The idea that we can do good works above and beyond what God commands ('works of supererogation') was wholly rejected by Protestants at the time of the Reformation as an arrogant undermining of both man's sinful inability before God, and God's grace.[34]

---

31. Ibid. 36.1, 10.
32. Ibid. 42.1–2.
33. Ibid. 56.2–3.
34. Article 14 of the Church of England's Thirty-Nine Articles, for example, reads, 'Voluntary Works besides, over and above, God's Commandments, which they call Works of Supererogation, cannot be taught without arrogancy and impiety: for by them men do declare, that they do not only render unto God as much as they are bound to do, but

Yet it fits Hermas' understanding that the gospel is a new law from God.[35] On this understanding, it is no wonder that mere faith is insufficient to be justified before God. In this way *The Shepherd of Hermas* is the most stark indication of a popular turn in the early second century from the gospel of grace to a harsh legalism.

Letter to Diognetus

The final two Apostolic Fathers are essentially works of apologetics. They are the *Letter of Barnabas*, a work that seeks to defend Christianity in the face of Judaism, and the *Letter to Diognetus*, a piece that defends Christianity in the face of paganism.

Apologies became a popular form of literature among Christians in the second century, both because of the desire to promote Christianity, and because of the need to defend it from often-violent attack. Other examples include the *Octavius* of Minucius Felix and the works of Justin Martyr. In the *Octavius* we learn that Christians were accused by society at large of gross sexual immorality, incest, cannibalism and murder. Minucius Felix explains that these charges arose out of complete misunderstandings of the facts that Christians were compelled to meet secretly, where they would greet each other as brothers and sisters with the kiss of peace (whence the charges of incest), there to eat the flesh and drink the blood of the Son of God (whence the charges of cannibalism).

The *Letter to Diognetus* is a work nobody seemed to know of until a manuscript was discovered in 1436, being used to wrap fish in a fishmonger's shop in Constantinople![36] It is an anonymous work, though it is possible that it could be either the lost apology of

---

that they do more for his sake, than of bounden duty is required: whereas Christ saith plainly, When ye have done all that are commanded to you, say, We are unprofitable servants.'

35. *Hermas* 69.2.

36. The manuscript fared little better later on; having been transcribed, it was destroyed when the library of Strasbourg, where it had been deposited, was bombed in 1870.

Quadratus spoken of by Eusebius,[37] or by Polycarp. It is addressed to a 'most excellent Diognetus', who could well be the Diognetus who was a tutor to the emperor Marcus Aurelius, making it most likely that the work was intended as an open letter for public consumption by a pagan audience.

Apparently, Diognetus had expressed interest in why Christians worshipped neither the gods of the pagans, nor in the same way as the Jews. The author replies with an attack on idolatry that is reminiscent of Isaiah 44: the gods of wood and stone are deaf, dumb and blind. 'These are the things you call gods; you serve them, you worship them, and in the end you become like them.'[38] It is a mocking but deftly made theological point: we become like the gods we serve.

The Jews, he goes on to argue, are equally mistaken in their understanding of God, for, as pagans make offerings to gods unable to receive them, so Jews make offerings to God when in fact he has no need of them.[39] This argument fits well into an understanding of the gospel that is refreshingly opposed to the legalism of *The Didache* and *The Shepherd of Hermas*. In fact, reading the *Letter to Diognetus* is like reading Luther in comparison. For example, he writes of God that

> when our unrighteousness was fulfilled, and it had been made perfectly
> clear that its wages – punishment and death – were to be expected . . .
> he himself gave up his own Son as a ransom for us, the holy one
> for the lawless, the guiltless for the guilty, the just for the unjust, the
> incorruptible for the corruptible, the immortal for the mortal. For what
> else but his righteousness could have covered our sins? In whom was it
> possible for us, the lawless and ungodly, to be justified, except in the Son
> of God alone? O the sweet exchange, O the incomprehensible work of

---

37. A fragment from the apology of Quadratus, preserved for us by Eusebius
    (*Church History* 4.3.1–2), is sometimes included in the collection of the
    Apostolic Fathers. Some scholars believe that the fragment should be
    fitted into a gap that exists in the text of the *Letter to Diognetus*.

38. *Diognetus* 2.5.

39. Ibid. 3.5.

God, O the unexpected blessings, that the sinfulness of many should be hidden in one righteous person, while the righteousness of one should justify many sinners![40]

His argument continues with a defence of the innocence of Christians. Yet, he maintains, 'what the soul is to the body, Christians are to the world' – that is, as the soul is in the body but not of it, so Christians are in the world, and so, like souls, are despised. And, just as the soul is improved by fasting, so Christians increase when persecuted.[41]

Finally, amid an explanation of how God has shown his love to us sinners in sending Christ for our salvation, the author calls Diognetus to acquire the joyous knowledge of God for himself. 'Then you will admire those who for righteousness' sake endure the transitory fire, and you will consider them blessed, when you comprehend that other fire . . .'[42] Again the author makes it clear that the coming judgment was a prime consolation for the persecuted Christians of the time.

Letter of Barnabas

The last of the Apostolic Fathers is an anonymous letter, allegedly written by the apostle Paul's companion, Barnabas. It is often interpreted as an argument that the Christian church has superseded and replaced the Jewish nation as God's true people. However, it is in fact an argument that, from the very beginning, the faithful always were Christian, even though the majority of the nation of Israel failed to understand their own Scriptures' proclamation of Christ.

Like Ignatius, Barnabas held that the Old Testament was originally intended as a Christian book. Both saw that unless the original authors of the Scriptures had intended to teach the Christian gospel,

---

40. Ibid. 9.2–5.
41. Ibid. 6.
42. Ibid. 10.8.

then Christians could validly be accused by Jews of reading an alien meaning back into those Scriptures. Yet, if a Christological understanding of the Old Testament were possible only with hindsight, Christianity could be neither authentic nor credible. In order to be able to face Judaism and Marcion alike, Barnabas argued that a true understanding of Moses should lead to faith in Christ.[43] Thus he writes, 'Abraham, who first instituted circumcision, looked forward in the spirit to Jesus when he circumcised';[44] Moses, both by stretching out his hands on the hill in Exodus 17, and by lifting up the serpent on the pole in Numbers 21, deliberately showed the people 'a symbol of Jesus'.[45] 'Again, what does Moses say to "Jesus" the son of Nun when he gave him this name, since he was a prophet, for the sole purpose that all the people might hear that the Father was revealing everything about his Son Jesus?'[46] Barnabas' intention is to demonstrate that Moses and the prophets were deliberate in prophesying Jesus' work. For this reason he does not appeal to the New Testament to support his argument (in any case, he could not, given that the New Testament was not yet a fixed canon), but seeks instead to interpret the Old Testament on its own terms so that his reading can be seen to represent the inherent meaning of the Hebrew Scriptures.

After looking at aspects of the sacrificial system, the events of the exodus and so on, Barnabas comes to consider Solomon's temple, and his treatment of it illustrates his entire approach. He argues that the temple in Jerusalem was an earthly copy that existed to proclaim a spiritual reality. The mistake of the Jews who set their hope on the building was to set their gaze on the copy, when they should have learnt about the spiritual reality from it.[47] So it was with circumcision and the entire law: the Jewish mistake

---

43. For a helpful discussion of how this principle functioned in the wider church at the time, see Gerald Bray, *Creeds, Councils and Christ*, 2nd ed. (Fearn: Mentor, 1997), pp. 49–54.

44. *Barnabas* 9.7.

45. Ibid. 12.5–6.

46. Ibid. 12.8.

47. Ibid. 16.

was to confuse the earthly signs with the spiritual realities they represented. In looking only to the earthly, they found themselves enslaved to the ruler of this age and his angels.[48] And thus, by failing to be led to Christ by their own Scriptures, Barnabas maintains that Jews had come to worship a quite different god.

Barnabas' letter may not appear to cover material as urgently significant for the time as, say, a theology of martyrdom; however, what he makes clear is that the battle for Christianity's survival in the hostile second century was as much as anything else the battle for ownership of the Scriptures.

Going on with the Apostolic Fathers

In order to read the Apostolic Fathers themselves, the best place to start is probably with Michael Holmes's excellent modern translation, *The Apostolic Fathers in English*, 3rd ed. (Grand Rapids: Baker, 2006). Holmes also provides brief introductions to each work. After that, Clayton Jefford has provided the two most useful introductions: a shorter one, *The Apostolic Fathers: An Essential Guide* (Nashville: Abingdon, 2006), and a slightly longer one, *Reading the Apostolic Fathers* (Peabody: Hendrickson, 1996).

---

48. Ibid. 18.1–2; 9.4.

Apostolic Fathers timeline

60–135?	Papias
64	Great Fire of Rome
64–8	Nero's punishment of the Christians
70	Destruction of the temple in Jerusalem
70–135	*Letter of Barnabas*
95?	*1 Clement*
96?	*2 Clement*
100?	*The Didache*
100–165	Justin Martyr
110?	Martyrdom of Ignatius
110–40?	*The Shepherd of Hermas*
130–200	Irenaeus of Lyons
150–90	*Letter to Diognetus*
155?	Martyrdom of Polycarp
160–225	Tertullian
303–12	The 'Great Persecution'
312	Conversion of the emperor Constantine to Christianity
325	Council of Nicea

2. TO ARMS

Justin Martyr and Irenaeus

By the second half of the second century AD, Christianity was despised by Judaism, feared by the official paganism of the Roman Empire, and infested with heresies. The need for theologians and apologists of substance was great. Many arose, but perhaps the greatest of these were Justin Martyr and Irenaeus.

Justin Martyr

Justin was born somewhere around AD 100 in Flavia Neapolis, where ancient Shechem had been and where Nablus is today, in Palestine. However, his family were probably Gentile pagans, rather than native Samaritans; certainly, he was given a Greek education. All this was an apt upbringing for a man who would go on to defend Christianity from both Jewish and cultured Greek attacks. Justin himself tells us that his education led him to dabble in some of the main branches of Greek philosophy: Stoicism, Peripateticism and Pythagoreanism, before becoming a settled Platonist.

At some point he moved to Ephesus, which is almost certainly where, struck by how fearlessly Christians died and sensing that here was the true and highest philosophy, he converted to Christianity. For the rest of his life he wore the gown traditionally donned by Greek philosophers in order to present Christianity as the goal of all searches for knowledge. Travelling widely, he visited Rome, where he lived near the Colosseum and founded a school of theology.

Justin wrote a number of works of theology and apologetics; however, today only three remain that scholars agree are authentically his. They are his *First* and *Second Apologies* and his *Dialogue with Trypho*.

First Apology

Justin's *First Apology* was written around AD 153–4 as an open letter to Emperor Antoninus Pius and his two adopted sons who would succeed him, Marcus Aurelius and Lucius Verus. All three were renowned as keen philosophers and just rulers, and it is to these traits that Justin appeals.

The *Apology* opens with a plea for Christians to be judged on the basis of evidence, and for charges against them to be investigated before judgment was passed. Clearly, the reality on the ground was that Christians were being punished on the basis of unsubstantiated rumours, the three main forms of which Justin goes on to counter. First, he states, Christians are not atheists as alleged, for they worship the Father, Son and Spirit. Secondly, Christians are not immoral, but are all prepared to stand proper trial for their conduct. Thirdly, they are not seditious, the kingdom they seek not being of this world. Rather, they are loyal citizens, paying their taxes.

Having thus dealt with the common charges against Christianity, Justin then goes on to show the positive value of Christianity. It is unreasonable to dismiss Christian beliefs, he argues, for they are the most reasonable. Many Christian beliefs, he suggests, share similarities with features of paganism that Romans happily accepted (the Romans believed in an afterlife, in deification [for Caesar at least][1] and in virgin birth [Perseus supposedly was born

---

1. It was common for theologians of the early post-apostolic church to speak of deification as a key aspect of Christian salvation. Quite different

of a virgin]). The difference is, Christians have concrete historical reasons for their belief, whereas pagans have nothing better than unsubstantiated fables.

The main bulk of Justin's argument, though, is taken up with addressing what was in its day perhaps the most fundamental objection to Christianity. In the second century and the centuries around it, antiquity was venerated and novelty despised. Thus Rome was generally tolerant towards the monotheism of Judaism that otherwise jarred so awkwardly with its own pluralism and imperial cult, but was intolerant towards what it saw in Christianity as an upstart sect. Justin's response is to argue that Christianity is, in fact, the oldest of religions. Christ's birth was predicted by Jacob (Gen. 49:10), Isaiah (7:14) and Micah (5:2), among others; his death was predicted by many (e.g. Ps. 22). And since they understood such things, believers such as Abraham were, in fact, Christians. The reason, he argues, why the Jews are not Christian is because they fail to understand their own Scriptures' witness to the Father and the Son, and the promise of Christ's coming. Worse, they even remove from their own Scriptures the verses that most offend them. An example he gives is Psalm 96:10, which he says should read 'the LORD has reigned from the tree', but from which the Jews had cut the words 'from the tree' because of its obvious reference to the cross.[2]

---

things could be meant by it. For theologians of the second century, though, deification was normally seen as being roughly synonymous with adoption; that is, through the Spirit, Christians are made sons of the Most High in the Firstborn Son, Christ (cf. *Dialogue with Trypho* 124). In this way, Christians can be said to enter the eternal fellowship of the Father, Son and Spirit.

2. *1 Apology 41*. No extant Hebrew manuscript has the words 'from the tree' in Psalm 96:10, though it seems unlikely that Justin's argument came from a mere slip of memory (he repeats the claim in his *Dialogue with Trypho* 73). A number of other theologians from the first five centuries AD also believed that Psalm 96:10 should read 'the Lord has reigned from the tree' (cf. Tertullian, *An Answer to the Jews* 10, 13; *Five Books Against Marcion* 3.19; Augustine, Comment on Ps. 96). Two manuscripts of the Psalms in Greek

Justin then goes on to argue that because Christianity is the oldest, rather than the latest, religion, ancient and venerated philosophers stole their best ideas from it. In particular, he argues, Plato plagiarized Moses in composing his philosophy. Moses, for instance, had created the tabernacle according to the heavenly pattern shown him on Mount Sinai; Plato had adapted this idea to suggest that all earthly things are copies of an ideal reality:

> And the physiological discussion concerning the Son of God in the *Timaeus* of Plato, where he says, 'He placed him crosswise in the universe,' he borrowed in like manner from Moses; for in the writings of Moses it is related how at that time, when the Israelites went out of Egypt and were in the wilderness, they fell in with poisonous beasts, both vipers and asps, and every kind of serpent, which slew the people; and that Moses, by the inspiration and influence of God, took brass, and made it into the figure of a cross ... Which things Plato reading, and not accurately understanding, and not apprehending that it was the figure of the cross, but taking it to be a placing crosswise, he said that the power next to the first God was placed crosswise in the universe. And as to his speaking of a third, he did this because he read, as we said above, that which was spoken by Moses, 'that the Spirit of God moved over the waters.' For he gives the second place to the Logos which is with God, who he said was placed crosswise in the universe; and the third place to the Spirit who was said to be borne upon the water.[3]

And it was not just Plato who was guilty of plagiarism, according to Justin. The demons have always aped true religion in their attempt to lure humanity into idolatry. For instance, the idea of Bacchus, the God of wine, born out of the union of a God and a

---

(the Septuagint) have the words, and the equivalent words are also found in the Coptic Sahidic translation of the Psalms probably made in the middle of the third century AD. The words also appear in some copies of the Old Latin translation, the version used by the churches in the West before Jerome made the Latin Vulgate, used by Tertullian and Augustine. It seems most likely, then, that Justin was using a Greek version of the Psalms.

3. *1 Apology* 59.

woman, and honoured in the drinking of wine, was stolen from Moses' prophecies of Christ and perverted.[4]

Furthermore, Christ is the true Logos. All humans, he says, being 'logical' creatures, have something of the Logos in their nature (though he does not explicitly connect this with the image of God). When they speak proper logic, they speak of something the fullness of which is found in Christ. Thus Socrates, in upholding proper logic against all the false gods of classical Athens, could, on this basis, be said to have 'partially known' Christ.[5] Therefore, it is not just a question of plagiarism: the Christ-centred nature of reality, Christ being the Logos, means that human philosophy and mythology must necessarily contain echoes of the truth of the gospel. Yet those echoes are always so garbled, weak and self-contradictory that those who believe them are condemned out of their own mouths, for the echoes in themselves display their own futility.

Christianity, Justin thus concludes, is the true philosophy, and is therefore to be examined, respected and followed, not condemned.

Second Apology

Soon after Justin had finished writing his *First Apology*, three people were beheaded in Rome simply for confessing they were Christians. Justin hastily responded with an appendix to his work. We now refer to this addition as his *Second Apology*, even though it is not really a separate work.

---

4. Ibid. 69. Justin's argument here may seem very alien to us today; however, it is becoming relevant again as the old accusation resurfaces that Christianity has stolen its ideas from older sources. Rob Bell mentions precisely this example of Bacchus/Dionysus when he asks if, hypothetically, 'the virgin birth was really just a bit of mythologizing the Gospel writers threw in to appeal to the followers of the Mithra and Dionysian religious cults that were hugely popular at the time of Jesus, whose gods had virgin births' (*Velvet Elvis: Repainting the Christian Faith* [Grand Rapids: Zondervan, 2005], p. 26). For Justin, the answer is simple: Christianity and the promise of a virgin birth is older than the Mithra and Dionysian cults; if anything, they stole from Christianity, not vice versa.

5. *2 Apology* 10; cf. *1 Apology* 46.

Many of the same themes reappear, but Justin deals with two more popular objections to Christianity: (1) Since Christians seem to love martyrdom so much, why do they not all commit suicide? (2) Why does God not protect Christians? To the first he responds that, while Christians are happy to face death, they live for God's will, which is that they bring life to others. To the second he replies that evil angels cause suffering in the world, but that God allows it to discipline his beloved. He then turns the martyrdom objections into a challenge by arguing that the way Christians die is proof that Christianity has a truth which all the philosophies and super-stitions of men do not have.

Dialogue with Trypho

Justin's last and most substantial work is another apology, this time written to answer the anti-Christian claims of Judaism. It takes the form of a two-day debate with an educated Jew (Trypho), often thought to be the great Rabbi Tarphon mentioned in the Mishnah. It is clearly not a stenographer's account, yet neither does it seem to be a mere literary device, as some more sceptical scholars would have it. It seems to be an account of an actual dialogue between Justin and Trypho.

The *Dialogue* is interesting for a number of reasons. First, we see how strongly trinitarian Justin is: he clearly sees the Father, Son and Spirit as three distinct persons.[6] Secondly, we are clearly shown the stark difference between the rabbinic Jewish reading of Scripture and the early post-apostolic Christian reading. For Trypho, the Hebrew Scriptures prove that Jesus could be neither Christ nor God; for Justin, those same Scriptures prove precisely the opposite!

The work as we have it (some of the original introduction is missing) opens with Trypho approaching Justin because of his

---

6. It is sometimes suggested that Justin was unable to distinguish the Son from the Spirit properly. This is almost certainly unfair, and due partly to his willingness to speak of the eternal Word as 'a spirit', and partly to the fact that, for instance, he believed that the 'holy spirit' that descended on Mary in Luke 1:35 was the Word (*1 Apology* 33). Yet he never fails to differentiate between that 'spirit' and the Spirit.

philosopher's gown. Justin then gives his testimony, of how a 'certain old man' once engaged him in conversation, pulled apart the Platonism he was then devoted to, and told him of how, long before the philosophers, prophets who spoke by the Divine Spirit announced the true God together with his Son. Then 'straightway a flame was kindled in my soul'.[7]

Trypho, hugely disappointed that Justin was not the sophisticated Greek philosopher he had taken him for, tells him that Christians are needlessly suffering for mere fabrications. He also adds that Christians cannot be righteous, because they do not follow the law (especially, they remain uncircumcised). Justin replies that Trypho has interpreted the law carnally (thinking that physical circumcision is of value), whereas he should understand it spiritually (by circumcising the heart). For, if physical circumcision were necessary, Adam would have been created circumcised; yet when declared good, he was uncircumcised. Enoch, Noah and the earliest patriarchs, when found pleasing to God, were not circumcised; nor was Abraham, when he was justified. And what of women, who cannot be circumcised?

Trypho's next complaint is that Jesus was a man cursed in his death by God, not the glorious Son of Man prophesied by Daniel. Justin's response is that Trypho has failed to recognize that Christ was prophesied to come twice, and that Trypho has done so because he misinterprets Scripture. Psalm 110, for instance, cannot be about Hezekiah, as Trypho asserts, for Hezekiah was not a priest for ever; not could Isaiah 7 be about Hezekiah; nor could Psalm 72 be about Solomon, for kings did not bow down to him, nor did he reign to the ends of the earth.

From the question of whether Jesus is the prophesied Christ, Trypho then moves the debate on to whether Jesus is Lord and God:

> you utter many blasphemies, in that you seek to persuade us that this crucified man was with Moses and Aaron, and spoke to them in the pillar of the cloud; then that he became man, was crucified, and ascended up to heaven, and comes again to earth, and ought to be worshipped.[8]

---

7. *Dialogue* 8.
8. Ibid. 38.

Justin is thus drawn in to look at the appearances of God in the Old Testament:

> Then I replied, 'Reverting to the Scriptures, I shall endeavour to persuade you, that He who is said to have appeared to Abraham, and to Jacob, and to Moses, and who is called God, is distinct from Him who made all things, – numerically, I mean, not [distinct] in will.'[9]

Starting with Genesis 18 – 19, he argues that God appeared to Abraham along with two angels, yet from Genesis 19:24 (where the Lord rained down sulphur 'from the LORD') it can be seen that he is distinct from the Lord in the heavens. For there are a 'number of persons associated with one another' who can be called Lord and God (he also refers to Gen. 1:26; 3:22; Pss 45:6–7; 110:1).[10] Because of this, the Lord and God who appeared to Abraham, and who is distinct from the Lord and God in the heavens, can be called the Angel (or 'messenger') of the Lord (he also examines Gen. 31:11–13; 32:22–30 to see more of the Angel). Justin's point is that God the Father is utterly transcendent and invisible in the heavens. However, he is made known by his Logos or Angel, who appeared to make God known to the patriarchs and prophets, and who took flesh for our salvation.

To support his case that Jesus was this Logos or Angel, Justin explains that 'Jesus' is the name of God: God said (in Exod. 23:20–21) that his name would be in the one sent ahead of Israel to lead them into the Promised Land. That one was 'Hoshea', whose name was changed in Numbers 13:16 to 'Joshua', the Hebrew form of 'Jesus'.[11] Jewish failure to notice this, Justin argues, only betrays their wilful ignorance of the Scriptures, for while they carefully study why Abram's name was changed to Abraham, they do not think why Hoshea's name was changed to Joshua.

> Then Trypho remarked, 'Be assured that all our nation waits for Christ; and we admit that all the Scriptures which you have quoted refer to Him.

---

9. Ibid. 56.
10. Ibid. 62.
11. Ibid. 75.

Moreover, I do also admit that the name of Jesus, by which the son of Nave (Nun) was called, has inclined me very strongly to adopt this view. But whether Christ should be so shamefully crucified, this we are in doubt about. For whosoever is crucified is said in the law to be accursed, so that I am exceedingly incredulous on this point.'[12]

To which Justin responds with how the cross is foreshadowed in the Old Testament in such places as Numbers 21 and Psalm 22.

What is so important to notice here is that Justin restricts himself to arguing from the Hebrew Scriptures alone, knowing that the books that make up what we now call the New Testament will carry no weight with Trypho. In this, Trypho and Justin are agreed: the case for Christianity can be made or broken by the Hebrew Scriptures. This can also be seen in Justin's answer to Trypho's next question. Trypho asks if it can be true that Christians believe in a resurrection of the dead; Justin's answer is emphatic: those 'who say there is no resurrection of the dead, and that their souls, when they die, are taken to heaven; do not imagine that they are Christians', but his proof-text for Trypho comes from Isaiah 65![13]

The rest of the dialogue is essentially dedicated to the question of the inclusion of the Gentiles, to which Trypho objects. Yet (referring to Gen. 9:27) Justin insists that since the days of Noah, the inclusion of the Gentiles has been prophesied. Furthermore, Christ, he argues, alluding to Genesis 32, is the true Israel, wrestling with God and being injured in the process, so that those who are his might have God's blessing:

> As therefore from the one man Jacob, who was surnamed Israel, all your nation has been called Jacob and Israel; so we from Christ, who begat us unto God, like Jacob, and Israel, and Judah, and Joseph, and David, are called and are the true sons of God, and keep the commandments of Christ.[14]

---

12. Ibid. 89.

13. Ibid. 80–81.

14. Ibid. 123.

Unlike later church fathers such as Origen and Augustine, Justin does not find much allegory in the Bible; instead, he finds the Old Testament full of types (Moses' bronze serpent being a 'prototype' of the cross; Joshua's circumcision of the Israelites being a type of Jesus' circumcision of the hearts of his people).[15] Yet he does see an allegory relevant to the issue of the Gentiles. Prompted by Paul's allegory of Abraham's two wives, Hagar and Sarah, he sees an allegory in Jacob's two wives: Jacob's first, short-sighted wife, Leah (through whom came Judah) represents old, ethnic Israel; his second, beloved wife, Rachel, represents the new Israel.[16]

Justin sums up his argument with an appeal to Trypho, that if he had read his Scriptures properly, he would have trusted Christ and known these things. This, for Justin, is the heart of the issue: Christians have not read their meaning into the Hebrew Scriptures, but have interpreted them correctly:

> if you knew, Trypho . . . who He is that is called at one time the Angel of great counsel, and a Man by Ezekiel, and like the Son of man by Daniel, and a Child by Isaiah, and Christ and God to be worshipped by David, and Christ and a Stone by many, and Wisdom by Solomon, and Joseph and Judah and a Star by Moses, and the East by Zechariah, and the Suffering One and Jacob and Israel by Isaiah again, and a Rod, and Flower, and Corner-Stone, and Son of God, you would not have blasphemed Him who has now come, and been born, and suffered, and ascended to heaven; who shall also come again, and then your twelve tribes shall mourn. For if you had understood what has been written by the prophets, you would not have denied that He was God, Son of the only, unbegotten, unutterable God.[17]

With a final call from Justin to trust in Christ and believe him instead of the rabbis, Trypho leaves, apparently 'not far from the kingdom of God'.

---

15. Ibid. 114.
16. Ibid. 134.
17. Ibid. 126.

Justin martyred

About five years later, Justin, along with six friends, was brought before the prefect of Rome for refusing to sacrifice to the gods. He confessed he was a Christian, and was summarily flogged and beheaded. Fellow Christians then carefully buried his remains, as had become customary for a people who believed passionately that the bodies of believers have a future beyond death.

Irenaeus of Lyons

Irenaeus once wrote:

> Thou wilt not expect from me, who am resident among the Keltae, and am accustomed for the most part to use a barbarous dialect, any display of rhetoric, which I have never learned, or any excellence of composition, which I have never practised, or any beauty and persuasiveness of style, to which I make no pretensions.[18]

As a result, Irenaeus has become a somewhat forgotten theologian, quickly dismissed as blundering and confused. Certainly, he is difficult to access, and hard-going theologians tend to incite the wrath of the critics. However, Emil Brunner's reassessment of Irenaeus has become increasingly standard:

> In spite of the fact that in the formal sense Irenaeus was not a systematic theologian, yet – like Luther – he was a systematic theologian of the first rank, indeed, the greatest systematic theologian: to perceive connections between truths, and to know which belongs to which. No other thinker was able to weld ideas together which others allowed to slip as he was able to do, not even Augustine or Athanasius.[19]

Who was Irenaeus, then?

---

18. *Against Heresies* 1.preface.3.

19. E. Brunner, *The Mediator: A Study of the Central Doctrine of the Christian Faith*, tr. O. Wyon (London: Lutterworth, 1934), p. 262.

He was born somewhere around AD 130 and grew up in Smyrna in Asia Minor, where the then bishop, Polycarp, became his mentor and passed on his memories of the apostle John and others who had seen the Lord. It was to be extremely important to Irenaeus that he had such a direct link back to the apostles. It is possible that he went with Polycarp to Rome – at any rate, both visited Rome. There Irenaeus seems to have learned from men such as Justin (he clearly borrowed much from him), as well as seeing how endemic the problem of heresy was there. He then travelled to Gaul and settled where a church had been founded quite recently in the capital city of Lugdunum (Lyons).

Then in 177 he was sent back as the church's delegate to Eleutherus, then bishop of Rome, perhaps to discuss the problem of false teaching in Gaul. At any rate, while he was away, a ferociously violent wave of persecution swept through Lyons; many of Irenaeus' friends and fellow-believers were horrifically tortured and killed, including the old bishop, Pothinus. When Irenaeus returned, he was chosen to succeed Pothinus as bishop.

After that, the only thing we know of his life is his intervention in the Paschal controversy. Victor, Eleutherus' successor as bishop of Rome, had threatened to excommunicate the churches of Irenaeus' native Asia Minor for celebrating Pascha (later called Easter) on 14 Nisan, rather than the following Sunday, as they did in Rome. Irenaeus wrote irenically to Victor and the bishops of the Asian churches, urging them that on such secondary matters both parties should be free to celebrate according to their own tradition. It was an important little incident, for it showed that, despite all Irenaeus' emphasis on unity in the apostolic tradition, he did not countenance unconditional submission to the bishop of Rome, and could allow for different practices in the church.

Irenaeus wrote a number of works of theology; today, though, apart from a number of fragments from his writings, we have only two complete works of his: *Detection and Refutation of What Is Falsely Called 'Knowledge'*, usually known simply as *Against Heresies*, and his much shorter *Demonstration of the Apostolic Preaching*. In these works we see the first serious attempts to formulate Christian doctrine into a coherent structure. Irenaeus is thus a key architect of Christian thought. As such it is unsurprising that his influence spread so rapidly and so far (a fragment of *Against Heresies*, dating from when Irenaeus was still alive, has been found at Oxyrhynchus in Egypt, the other side of the known world from where he wrote the work).

We actually have no idea when or how Irenaeus died, though later tradition has it that he was martyred on 28 June 202.

Against Heresies

By the middle of the second century a collection of sects we now lump together and call Gnosticism had infected much of the church with various odd mutations of Oriental and Greek philosophies. One branch in particular seemed to be thriving: Valentinianism. Its leading light, Valentinus, once expected to become the next bishop of Rome, was an influential, gifted and persuasive theologian who managed to draw a number of disciples to his peculiar beliefs. Quite a number in the church in Lyons had been won over. Irenaeus saw this Gnosticism as a many-headed monster, threatening his flock. And, a pastor at heart, through his great five-volume work *Against Heresies* he set out to protect the Christians, convert the Gnostics from their error and bring them to saving knowledge and, ultimately, kill the monster. Certainly, *Against Heresies* struck Gnosticism a mortal blow.[20]

Book 1: The many-headed monster

Irenaeus begins with a description of the beast. According to Valentinianism, everything began with a collection of thirty angelic beings (known as 'aeons') who together made up the spiritual realm. Then one of the more junior aeons had a wicked thought. This wicked thought had to be removed from the perfect, spiritual realm, whereupon it became the basis for the physical cosmos.

---

20. However, the fact that Gnosticism never quite died out is one reason why Irenaeus remains relevant today. Irenaeus believed that Valentinus had managed to come up with the definitive heresy that summed up and encapsulated all heresies. If there is any truth to that, it should be no surprise that we live today in a culture increasingly fed on a diet of rewarmed Gnosticism (witness the essential Gnostic themes of Dan Brown's *The Da Vinci Code* and Philip Pullman's *His Dark Materials* trilogy).

The logic of Genesis was thus reversed, with creation following a fall.

In so teaching, Gnosticism directly challenged the heart of the Christian gospel, for the creation, in such a model, was not good but bad. The human body was thus a despicable tomb for the valuable spirit and soul. And if that were the case, what of the incarnation? For Gnosticism, the incarnation was impossible. Instead, 'Christ passed through Mary just as water flows through a tube' (in other words, without taking on real flesh).[21] As a result, many Gnostics believed that Christ could not have died, but instead that another was made to look like him and was crucified in his place. Others believed that the cross was the moment when the divine being, Christ, left the man, Jesus (hence Jesus' cry, 'My God, my God why have you forsaken me?').

In any case, in Gnosticism there was not much need for Christ to die, because the problem was not sin but having a body. Thus, for the Gnostic, 'salvation' was not about having faith in Jesus, but looking within to know the precious spark of the divine that would one day be liberated from the body. This being the case, Gnostic practice was always prone to lurch between two opposite extremes. On the one hand, the radical split between the body and the spirit allowed some Gnostics to indulge their flesh in the comforting knowledge that the spirit, like a pearl in the mud, would remain entirely unspoiled. On the other hand, their hatred for the body turned other Gnostics into radical ascetics, for although they were of the world, they had no desire to be in it.

What was Jesus about, then? For Valentinus, all of Jesus' life was a code, in which he symbolically acted out and so revealed what had taken place within the spiritual realm. The thirty years of his 'hidden life' before his public ministry spoke of the thirty aeons; the apostasy of Judas, the 'twelfth apostle', spoke of the sin of the twelfth aeon, and so on. That none of this was obvious was precisely the point: Jesus, the Gnostics claimed, had not taught openly, but in parables, only giving the secret knowledge of their

---

21. *Against Heresies* 1.7.2; 3.11.3 (references to *Against Heresies* consist of three numbers, identifying the book, the chapter and the section, respectively).

meaning to his most trusted disciples. This knowledge could not be seen clearly in the apostolic writings acknowledged by the church, but was passed on secretly by oral tradition. This all seems very tendentious to us today, but given how highly oral tradition was valued in the second century, this was a very serious threat to the church.

The Gnostics, then, were those who had this secret tradition of knowledge (the word 'Gnostic' comes from *gnōsis*, the Greek word for 'knowledge') and who sought not salvation in any normal sense, but the knowledge that within themselves lay a spiritual spark of the divine. It was this that Irenaeus sought to oppose in his *Detection and Refutation of What Is Falsely Called 'Knowledge'*.[22]

Book 2: Slaying the dragon

Irenaeus' first objection was that Gnosticism had denied that God is the Creator. For, it argued, the one who had organized a cosmos that by its very existence was evil must himself be evil. Yahweh, the Creator and God of Israel, could not then be the true and supreme God made known in the New Testament; he could only be a wicked angelic pretender to supreme deity. Some, like Marcion, thus sought to distance the God of Jesus as far as possible from Yahweh by rejecting the Hebrew Scriptures and any apostolic writings that connected them. Others, such as the Cainite sect, were more radical and sought to hold up Cain (and all the other characters of the Old Testament who refused to submit to Yahweh) as role models for their wise refusal to submit to the evil impostor-god.

For Irenaeus, their suggestion that there might be a God higher than the Father was precisely their downfall. Believing in such a multiplicity of competing gods, it was no wonder that Gnostic

---

22. For centuries, without much other evidence left of what Gnosticism was like, people wondered how fair Irenaeus had been in his assessment of Gnosticism. Had he simply set up a straw man? Yet in 1945 a collection of Gnostic writings was found at Nag Hammadi in Egypt (the most famous being the so-called *Gospel of Thomas*), giving an unprecedented insight into Gnostic teachings. Judging by these, most scholars now agree that Irenaeus was remarkably accurate in his description of Gnosticism.

thought was so diverse and self-contradictory. In contrast, he holds up the unity of the church's faith, a unity that flows from the fact that one Father, by his one Word, in one Spirit, gives one truth to one church for all.

However, Irenaeus argues, the root of the problem lay in how the Gnostics read Scripture. He suggests that they treated Scripture like a mosaic, taking whichever tiles they liked and rearranging them to come up with whatever image they fancied, so transforming the original picture, of, say, a king, into something entirely different, perhaps that of a dog or fox. They are thus, he says, perverters, abusers and evil interpreters of the Scriptures. Yet how exactly they are so is vital for Irenaeus. The reason they warp Scripture is because they read it based on non-scriptural principles, forcing it to fit into an alien mould. Scripture cannot be so read, according to Irenaeus; rather, Scripture can only be understood by Scripture. No other knowledge, theological system or oral tradition can accurately mediate the true meaning of Scripture.[23]

Book 3: A grand plan

If Irenaeus were to respond properly, he could not limit himself to attacking the so-called 'knowledge' of the Gnostics; he had to present the true knowledge of which they were actually ignorant. From here on, then, Irenaeus sets out to show what a correct interpretation of Scripture looks like.

It all starts with the one God. First, the Father (the Creator) and the Son (the Saviour) are not two different gods but one; secondly, God is one in the sense that the God of the Old Testament is the God of the New Testament (for obvious reasons, Irenaeus, like Justin, seeks to make both points from the Old Testament,

---

23. Cf. *Against Heresies* 3.12.9. This *sola Scriptura* principle at the heart of Irenaeus' theology gives the lie to the misconception that Irenaeus gave a higher authority to apostolic succession and tradition than he did to Scripture. He did value the direct connection between the apostles and their successors, the bishops, in his day; however, that never served as a grid to force Scripture through, but as proof that the plain truth of Scripture had been preserved and not distorted by the church.

using especially Gen. 19:24 and Pss 45, 110 to show the Father and the Son at work together in the Old Testament).

From here he moves to demonstrate that the eternal Word truly became flesh, rather then merely resting on, or pretending to be, a real man called Jesus. Irenaeus saw that if God despised flesh and so refused to become incarnate, there would be no salvation. To deny the incarnation, as the Gnostics did, is thus spiritually murderous. It would also rob Christians of all loyalty to Christ in the face of martyrdom, for if Christ did not really suffer death on the cross, but flew off, leaving another in his place, why should Christians who seek to follow him suffer? Rather, Irenaeus argues, Christians must affirm that Jesus Christ is truly God with us who came in real flesh.

Why, though, would God take on flesh? To answer this, Irenaeus now articulates the theory for which he is most famed: 'recapitulation'. In a nutshell, Irenaeus' idea of recapitulation is that Christ is the second Adam, undoing the evils brought about by the first Adam. Sin and death had entered the world on a bad Friday (Irenaeus placed Gen. 3 in day six of creation), through a tree (the tree of knowledge), through one man eating, aided by a disobedient betrothed virgin (Eve); life and salvation came on Good Friday, through a tree (the cross), through one man fasting (in the desert), aided by an obedient betrothed virgin (Mary).[24]

However, the word 'recapitulation' can be a little misleading (as well as off-putting!), giving the impression that Irenaeus imagined Christ simply reversing the fall to take us back to Eden. Irenaeus was a long way from seeing salvation as a U-turn, though: for him, salvation was about going through death to a perfection never possible in Eden. Irenaeus believed that Adam and Eve were never God's goal; they were only children, and the project of salvation was about humanity being brought to maturity. This was achieved in Christ, who came as an infant and grew to full

---

24. For Irenaeus, Mary was necessary to salvation in a similar way to how Joseph and Judas were necessary (though clearly she was more important, Jesus inheriting his humanity solely from her). However, the role Irenaeus gave Mary played a part in the rise of the theory that Mary is 'co-redemptrix' alongside Christ.

maturity for us.[25] Adam was a 'pattern of the one to come' (Rom. 5:14); an image of the true Image of God, Jesus Christ; filled with breath as a type of the one filled with the Spirit.

Humanity, from the moment of its creation, then, was destined for Spirit-filled maturity in Christ. Yet if Christ were to bring the humanity that was created to its goal, he could not 'pass through Mary as water through a tube', or take a body afresh from the earth as Adam had been; he needed an umbilical cord of continuity with the race of Adam. Only by taking the actual flesh of Adam's race (through Mary) could Adam's flesh be saved. In this way the humanity that had been created would be redeemed.

From this it looks like Irenaeus is moving towards saying that humanity was created *in order* to be saved, which raises some profound questions: Would Christ have come if Adam had not sinned? Did Adam fall, or was he pushed? Irenaeus puts it like this: just as God appointed a monster to swallow Jonah for a time, so he ordained Satan to swallow up humanity in death for a time. But humanity was subjected to death in hope, so that God might have mercy, and the apparent victory of Satan gave way to the true and final victory of Christ.[26] Death, then, was brought about as an act of judgment; but there was mercy in the judgment, for death prevented man from being immortal in his state of naked alienation from God. Through death humanity would be brought to be more than mere creatures, as they were created; through death man would become God.

At this point Irenaeus really does start to sound quite strange, and it is easy to leap to wrong conclusions. Yet Irenaeus is emphatic: man was created so that, ultimately, he might become God. Irenaeus is not suggesting that, somehow, we will one day transcend and shed our humanity. Far from it: just as when God became man he remained completely God, so when man becomes

---

25. It was partly for this reason that Irenaeus believed that Christ's incarnate ministry lasted from the age of thirty to fifty (the career length of the Levitical priests), Jesus dying in his early fifties as (what was for the second century) a mature old man (*Against Heresies* 2.22).

26. Ibid. 3.20.1.

God he remains completely man. What Irenaeus means is that the hope of humankind is not merely that we might be declared 'not guilty', or even that we might know God from afar; the hope of humankind is to participate in the being of God, sharing in the Triune life of God as we are loved by the Father through the Son as adopted children in the eternal fellowship of the Spirit. God is glorified and man reaches his goal when man is brought to share God's life and glory. That, according to Irenaeus, is the grand plan of creation, that man might be included in the glory of God.

Book 4: One God, one Word, one plan
Of course, Irenaeus' whole description of God's grand plan depended on Marcion's being wrong, on the fact that it is the one same God who creates, reveals and redeems. It is this that Irenaeus now goes on to demonstrate. The one true God, he asserts, has only one great project because he only ever arranges anything through his Word, and with reference to him. That is, the Father always makes himself known and achieves his purposes through his Son, meaning that the Old and New Testaments have exactly the same purpose:

> the law never hindered them from believing in the Son of God; nay, but it even exhorted them so to do, saying that men can be saved in no other way from the old wound of the serpent than by believing in Him who, in the likeness of sinful flesh, is lifted up from the earth upon the tree of martyrdom, and draws all things to Himself, and vivifies the dead.[27]

Thus Old Testament believers did not worship a different God, but had the same faith as Christians, for through the Word they knew the Father, and through the Spirit foresaw the coming of the Son. In fact, Irenaeus often refers to the Word simply as 'the one who spoke with Moses', because he believed that the Word spoke with Moses and the other prophets and patriarchs to proclaim to them the salvation he would bring, and hence draw them to his Father.[28]

---

27. Ibid. 4.2.7.
28. Ibid. 4.5.2; 4.9.1; 4.10.1; 4.16.3–4.

Thus the content of the apostolic proclamation in Acts was new to Jewish audiences in one respect only: that the same Word that the patriarchs had known had now come in the flesh.

> For nothing else [but baptism] was wanting to him who had been already instructed by the prophets: he was not ignorant of God the Father, nor of the rules as to the [proper] manner of life, but was merely ignorant of the advent of the Son of God.[29]

It was a powerful affirmation against Marcion that the Old Testament is Christian Scripture. For Irenaeus there could be no fundamental difference between the Old and New Testaments: the Father is always known through the Son. Yet if that is so, what was the point of the incarnation? It is to that question that Irenaeus turns in the final book.

Book 5: The salvation of the flesh

In the first few lines of Book 5, Irenaeus sums up his understanding of the incarnation in the famous words 'our Lord Jesus Christ, did, through His transcendent love, become what we are, that He might bring us to be even what He is Himself'.[30] Incarnation, then, is nothing like a mere theophany in Irenaeus' mind. Incarnation is the salvation of the flesh that the Old Testament believers looked forward to. Irenaeus believed that Jesus Christ, the Word of God, is the true Image of God. Adam was created in his image. And, as Adam was filled with breath, so Jesus Christ is eternally filled with the Spirit, whom Irenaeus also calls the 'Wisdom of God' and the 'Likeness of God'.[31] What happened in the incarnation was that the Image of God took human flesh so that that flesh might at last be filled with the Spirit with which the Image had always been filled. Thus flesh is taken into the Image of God and filled with the Likeness of God:

---

29. Ibid. 4.23.2.
30. Ibid. 5.preface.
31. The early post-apostolic church almost universally believed that the figure of Wisdom in Prov. 8 is the pre-incarnate Christ. Irenaeus believed instead that Wisdom is the Spirit.

humanity then truly becomes *Homo sapiens*, filled with the *Sapientia* (Wisdom) of God. Incarnation is thus the essential key to God's grand plan of bringing the fleshly humanity he created to its goal.

The reason Irenaeus finishes his work on this topic is because Gnosticism denied that the flesh could be saved or have any hope beyond death. In stark contrast to Christianity, the Gnostic hope was for a resurrection of the spirit, not the flesh, such that, once the body had died, the spirit alone would live on in heaven. To make their point, the Valentinians in Lyons loved to quote 1 Corinthians 15:50 ('flesh and blood cannot inherit the kingdom of God'). For Irenaeus, this was to deny salvation itself. Instead, seeing that the resurrected Jesus had flesh (Luke 24:39), Irenaeus explained that the apostle Paul's argument moved in completely the opposite direction. Flesh on its own cannot inherit the kingdom of God; however, through the incarnation, the Spirit is joined to flesh so that the flesh might be saved. Whereas in Gnosticism, spirit and flesh must go their separate ways after the sweet release of death, Irenaeus saw salvation being about the marriage of flesh and Spirit. In the incarnation Christ joined the Spirit to human flesh so that human flesh might have a future. Thus the resurrection hope of a spiritual body is not to be less bodily, but to be more truly and completely so, the Spirit coming not to rob but to redeem man from all that impoverishes and undermines him, and bring him to the end for which his flesh was created.

Perhaps, above all, the Eucharist was Irenaeus' crowning proof of the salvation of the flesh: mere bread becomes more than what it once was. The bread is not replaced by something different (just so, the flesh is not replaced by the Spirit in the resurrection); yet the bread is more than mere bread. And, more simply, the Eucharist is all about physical things: bread, wine, body, blood. That being the case, Irenaeus simply could not see how Gnostics, who despised the physical, could take the material elements with any degree of consistency.

Irenaeus rounds off with another 'recapitulation' – as Christ gathers up and brings all human history to a head, so the Antichrist will gather up and bring all evil to a head. Then, as was common in the second century, Irenaeus expected the righteous would enjoy a thousand years of Sabbath rest before the wicked were resurrected to final judgment.

The Demonstration of the Apostolic Preaching

While for a long time it was known that Irenaeus had written a work called *The Demonstration of the Apostolic Preaching*, the work itself had vanished long ago. Then, in 1904, a manuscript was discovered in a church library in Erevan in Armenia. Its publication (in 1907) was eagerly awaited, because this was the earliest Christian work written explicitly to summarize the faith.

Written shortly after *Against Heresies*, the *Demonstration* sets out to give one Marcianus a brief summary of Christian teaching so that he might 'understand all the members of the body of truth'. As the title suggests, it also seeks to demonstrate that the apostolic preaching is the true message of the Old Testament. Irenaeus starts off by giving the content of the apostles' message. It must begin, he says, with the one God, who is the Creator, his Word and Spirit; and from baptism on, the Father, Son and Spirit become the structure of our faith. He then swoops down, through an observation of the creation of the heavens, to how humanity was created to walk and talk with the Word of God in paradise, and how we fell. From there he races through the Old Testament to show how the incarnation and the inclusion of the Gentiles were foretold.

In the second half of the work Irenaeus aims to demonstrate that the whole content of the apostolic preaching comes from the Old Testament. First he shows that Jesus is the eternal Word of God, known by patriarchs and prophets; that he was in the beginning with the Father; that he appeared to Abraham and Jacob, and spoke to Moses from the bush. Next he explains how the fact that the eternal Word has now become God with us, in our flesh, born of a virgin, was also promised in the Old Testament. From virgin birth he moves to prophecies of the life, miracles, sufferings, crucifixion, resurrection and ascension of the incarnate Christ, as well as of the calling of the Gentiles (which was still an issue for dialogue with Jews).

Irenaeus concludes with a warning to avoid all heresies, of which, he says, there are three basic types: the first denies the Father and imagines another God; the second denies the Son and imagines there was no incarnation, and thus no love of God for humanity or our flesh; the third denies the Spirit and despises the true prophecy of Scripture. Instead of falling into such errors, Irenaeus bids the reader to hold to the oldest and truest preaching, that of the true God, the coming of his Son and the gift of his Spirit.

Going on with Justin and Irenaeus

Justin and Irenaeus are always in danger of being confined to the mental museum as mere historical curiosities, and yet the issues they deal with are all still vital: How should Scripture be interpreted? Who is God? What is salvation? However, reading them can be hard. Starting out with a theologian of the second century often feels like arriving on a different planet, for, unsurprisingly, the further one is removed in time from an author, the more alien he tends to feel. As a result, modern readers have to exercise special patience not to force second-century beliefs into more familiar patterns of thought that can be more rapidly digested or rejected.

Unfortunately, mountains of books and articles on these early theologians are guilty of exactly that, and so readers must be careful not to rely blithely on the secondary literature. The fact is, we do not have that much original material to work from, which means it is often quicker and easier to go straight to the horse's mouth.

Sadly for Justin, readers without languages or pots of cash have to rely on some rather rickety old nineteenth-century translations, but all his extant works are easily available online (at <http://www.ccel.org>) or in the *Ante-Nicene Fathers* series (vol. 1). His *Dialogue with Trypho* is probably the best place to start for an all-round feel of Justin's thought.

Irenaeus' *Against Heresies* is also available online (at <http://www.ccel.org>) and in the *Ante-Nicene Fathers* series in the same translation (also vol. 1). It is well worth a few hours' time, though a warning to the reader: unless you are very keen to learn about second-century Gnosticism, skip the first two books! For those who just want a taster of Irenaeus, John Behr's translation of *The Demonstration of the Apostolic Preaching* (Crestwood, N. Y.: SVS, 1997) is excellent, and comes with very helpful notes and introduction, highly recommended. For anyone interested in following up Irenaeus' main themes of incarnation and recapitulation, one outstanding introduction is worth mentioning: Gustaf Wingren, *Man and the Incarnation: A Study in the Biblical Theology of Irenaeus* (Edinburgh: Oliver & Boyd, 1959).

Justin Martyr and Irenaeus timeline

100?	Justin born
100–160?	Marcion
100–160?	Valentinus
130?	Irenaeus born
153–5	Justin's *First and Second Apologies*
155?	Martyrdom of Polycarp
160?	*Dialogue with Trypho*
160–225	Tertullian
165?	Justin martyred
175–89	*Against Heresies* and *The Demonstration of the Apostolic Preaching*
177	Persecution in Lugdunum (Lyons); Irenaeus sent to Rome, returns to become bishop
185–254	Origen
195?	Paschal controversy
202	Wave of persecution instigated by the emperor Septimius Severus. Irenaeus martyred?
303–12	The 'Great Persecution'
312	Conversion of the emperor Constantine to Christianity
325	Council of Nicea

3. AGAINST THE WORLD

Athanasius

Athanasius' name means 'immortal', and could hardly be more fitting. His life of high action and derring-do, his rapier-like mind, his ready smile and the sheer force of his personality all make him entirely unforgettable. Yet there is a greater reason why Athanasius deserves a place in any Christian hall of fame. As C. S. Lewis put it:

> His epitaph is *Athanasius contra mundum*, 'Athanasius against the world.' We are proud that our own country has more than once stood against the world. Athanasius did the same. He stood for the Trinitarian doctrine, 'whole and undefiled,' when it looked as if all the civilised world was slipping back from Christianity into the religion of Arius – into one of those 'sensible' synthetic religions which are so strongly recommended today and which, then as now, included among their devotees many highly cultivated clergymen. It is his glory that he did not move with the times; it is his reward that he now remains when those times, as all times do, have moved away.[1]

---

1. C. S. Lewis, Introduction to *On the Incarnation* by Athanasius (reprint, Crestwood, N. Y.: SVS, 1998), p. 9.

Athanasius' life

Athanasius was born somewhere around AD 296–8, and after that
we know virtually nothing certain about his youth or appearance.
Admirers said he had angelic good looks; opponents called him a
'black dwarf' due to his diminutive stature, the one physical trait
we can be sure of. At quite a young age, though, he seems to have
been talent-spotted by Alexander, the bishop of the bustling
metropolis of Alexandria in Egypt, who provided him with a
first-rate theological education. During his early years, the young
Athanasius would also have seen, sweeping through the city, some
of the most intense waves of persecution that the Roman imperial
authorities had ever mustered, killing off many of the most
prominent Christians of the generation above him.

Then in 318, Arius, a presbyter of the church in Alexandria,
began to accuse Alexander of failing to distinguish properly
between the Father, the Son and the Spirit.[2] Instead, Arius began
teaching that the Son was actually a created being, made by the
Father to go on and create the universe. A brilliant propagandist,
Arius put his theology into ditties, set them to well-known tunes,
and quickly whipped-up popular support for his views.[3] Mobs
were soon marching through the city chanting the slogans of Arius'
theology. Alexander responded by gathering just over a hundred
bishops to Alexandria to examine Arius' views. They quickly condemned the new teaching as heresy, removed Arius as a presbyter,
and forced him to leave the city. Far from putting a lid on the
problem, that just spread it: Arius fled to Nicomedia (near modern

---

2. Arius had received his theological training in Antioch, and so
   approached theology from a rather different angle to the theologians
   of Alexandria.
3. Singing their theology remained an effective Arian tactic for many years.
   Arian choirs used to sing through the night in the streets of
   Constantinople until the bishop, John Chrysostom, set against them
   choirs singing orthodox hymns (a showdown that, somewhat inevitably,
   ended up with the rival choirs in a street battle, after which the practice
   was made illegal for the Arians).

Istanbul), where the bishop, Eusebius, was supportive.[4] Eusebius used his powerful influence to help wage a campaign to win over any bishops who had not condemned Arius at Alexandria.

Not long after, Constantine, who had been a Christian and emperor of the western half of the Roman Empire for a little over a decade, added the eastern half to his domain. Perhaps because he saw Christianity as a potential force for unity, the next year (325) he invited bishops from across the empire – and some from without – to a general council at Nicea (also near modern Istanbul) to resolve the matter of Arius' teaching. Some three hundred came, including Alexander of Alexandria with his young secretary, Athanasius. How the bishops must have pinched themselves! But a few years earlier, the Roman Emperor had been the instigator of persecution, and some of the bishops themselves had been mutilated and scarred in the days of trial. Yet here they were, discussing theology in front of the emperor and being feasted by him!

The small Arian contingent fared badly, though: when they expressed their view of the Son of God they simply horrified the other bishops, some of whom covered their ears while others lost control and started a scuffle. The outcome of the council was the Nicene Creed, which contained the core anti-Arian affirmation that the Son was 'begotten, not made, of the same being of the Father' (*homoousion tō Patri*).[5] They would be words to which the young secretary, Athanasius, would devote his life as he defended them and drew from them the most profound theology.

Three years later Alexander died, and despite his youth Athanasius was appointed bishop of Alexandria. It was not long before the fickle emperor ordered him to reinstate Arius as a presbyter. Athanasius refused, unless Arius would sign the Nicene Creed. And so the troubles began. His opponents saw an opportunity and began circulating dark rumours: Athanasius had bought

---

4. Eusebius of Nicomedia should not be confused with his contemporary Eusebius of Caesarea, the great church historian.

5. The Greek word *homoousios* comes from *homo*, meaning 'same', and *ousia*, meaning 'being'.

the bishopric, had murdered and dismembered another bishop called Arsenius, and was using his severed hand for black magic. There was even a 'hand of Arsenius' doing the rounds to prove the point. Athanasius was summoned to a council at Tyre to answer for himself, and the hand was produced as evidence.

What had actually happened was that Arsenius had gone into hiding to get Athanasius convicted; however, he was tracked down, seized and spirited to Tyre. Then Athanasius had him brought in, wrapped in a cloak. Turning up the cloak he revealed one hand intact, paused dramatically, and then revealed the other hand intact before asking whence the third hand had been cut. Astonishingly, the council was so packed with Arians that Athanasius was still found guilty; and so he fled to Constantinople to appeal to the emperor. However, Athanasius was now such a figure of division that Constantine had little choice but to exile him to his imperial residence in Gaul (Treveri, now Trier, just to the west of Luxembourg). In Alexandria they rioted in protest.

While Athanasius was in exile, Arius died (though his cause was only growing) and Athanasius used the opportunity to warn the western half of the empire about the evils of Arianism. It was perhaps at this time that he also wrote his great double-barrelled work *Against the Heathen* and *On the Incarnation*.

Then, in 337, Constantine died and Athanasius was permitted to return to Alexandria, where he was met by cheering crowds. Yet within just two years new charges of irregularity were brought against him by the Arians and the situation in Alexandria became so dangerous that Athanasius was forced to leave for Rome. This time he had seven years in exile before he could return. When he did, it was to a golden decade of unhampered ministry.

But it was not the end of his troubles. Constantine's son, Constantius, the new emperor, was an Arian, and determined to root out all that Nicea had accomplished. That meant silencing Athanasius, who had become the figurehead of the orthodox Nicene party against the Arians. And so, in 356, five thousand Roman soldiers launched a surprise attack on the church where Athanasius was leading a vigil: the doors were burst open and the soldiers rushed in, swords drawn and arrows flying into the congregation. Athanasius ordered the people to leave so that nobody else might get hurt. However, in the mêlée his monks just grabbed him and smuggled him out through the confusion.

A price was put on his head, and even the desert was scoured; but Athanasius was kept concealed by an army of loyal monks who simply moved him on when any imperial search party got too close. Sometimes he was hidden in a dry cistern, sometimes a cemetery – he even managed to go back and live under cover in Alexandria itself for a while. Yet Constantius' attack on the church, an attack meant to decapitate the Nicene party, only rebounded on him, for Athanasius used his exile to fashion the weapons that would bury Arianism, in particular his masterpiece *Against the Arians*. All in all, it was an astoundingly productive time in the desert: not only did he fire a deadly volley against the Arians; he also managed to produce a masterful defence of the Holy Spirit's deity in his letters to Serapion and, inspired by the desert monks, wrote his *Life of Antony*, a work that would be the fertilizer for the monastic movement.

After a few years Constantius died and was succeeded by Julian, the first (and last) pagan emperor since Constantine. Seeing Athanasius as a controversial catalyst for Christian disunity, he allowed him to return to his bishopric. Immediately, Athanasius had to face a new theology that had come on the scene while he was in hiding. It argued that the Nicene Creed's affirmation that the Son is 'of the *same* being (**homo**ousios) of the Father' led rather too easily to a belief that the Father and the Son are not really distinguishable at all, but are, simply, the same. Instead, it was suggested, it would be better to speak of the Son as 'of a *similar* being (**homoi**ousios) to the Father'.[6]

Athanasius summoned a council to meet in Alexandria, where he rejected both the idea that the Father and the Son are not really distinguishable, and the word *homoiousios*. Instead, he argued, the

---

6. Unhelpfully and unfairly, this position came to be called 'semi-Arianism' because of how it gave room to the Arian tendency to make the Son a different sort of being to the Father. However, it originated as an attempt to make clear that the Father and the Son are not to be thought of as mere masks or modes of a single being, but are distinct and distinguishable.

word *homoousios* does guarantee a distinction between the Father and the Son, for it makes clear that there are two that must be compared; on the other hand, it keeps shut the door that the word *homoiousios* would open to the Arians.

At this point, readers may feel that Athanasius had, like a fussy grammar teacher, got rather too hung up on trivial differences between words. As Edward Gibbon put it, 'the difference between the *Homoousion* and the *Homoiousion* is almost invisible to the nicest theological eye'.[7] Yet, when at the Council of Alexandria the issue was raised whether we should speak of the one *hypostasis* or the one *ousia* of God, Athanasius argued that what mattered was not the words themselves, but their meaning. In so doing, Athanasius showed that he was no theologically trigger-happy scrapper, but a sensitive and realistic pastor. He opposed the word *homoiousios*, not because of the 'i' in the middle, but because it allowed the Son to be seen as something less than truly God, a being merely 'similar' to God.

It took only eight months for the emperor Julian, fearing Athanasius' influence, to exile him once more. Athanasius headed up the Nile to rejoin the desert monks, but even then retained his usual sparkle: finding that he was being tracked, he turned the boat around and soon came alongside that of the pursuers. Asked if he had seen Athanasius, he replied with a twinkle in his eye, 'He is not far off,' before drifting back down the river to steal into Alexandria while the pursuers went on.

Briefly restored by the next emperor, he was, with a certain degree of predictability, ordered to be seized in a night raid by another, just the next year (365). Warned in time, Athanasius fled into his fifth and last period of exile. By this time, however, Athanasius was so influential that Egypt simply was not stable with him in exile. And so he was recalled to live out his final years as bishop. So popular had he become that when an anti-Nicene bishop arrived in Alexandria in these years, he needed a military escort for fear of attack. Many had hated Athanasius for his extraordinary tenacity in defending the real deity of the Son and

---

7. E. Gibbon, *The Decline and Fall of the Roman Empire*, ch. 21, n. 155.

the Spirit, but the majority in Alexandria made it clear that precisely what many hated, they themselves loved. Athanasius died in 373, revered, but also victorious: his theology had triumphed over Arianism and would be canonized eight years later at the Council of Constantinople.

Against the Heathen *and* On the Incarnation

What was this triumphant theology? It is probably best captured by focusing our attention on Athanasius' main works: *Against the Heathen, On the Incarnation, Against the Arians* and *Life of Antony*.

Against the Heathen and *On the Incarnation* are really the titles of the two volumes of a single work. We do not know when it was written, but today it is thought to have been written around 335–6. Its agendum, though, is quite clear: it was written for a recent convert called Macarius as a basic introduction to the faith. From the start, then, this is pastorally concerned theology.

Against the Heathen

The first volume is a piercing theological critique of paganism and idolatry, focused on creation and the nature of sin and evil.

Athanasius starts with Jesus Christ, the Image of God the Father. Only by starting there, Athanasius suggests, can the true nature and purpose of creation be understood aright. Underpinning what it means for Christ to be the Image of the Father, he says, is the fact that Christ perfectly knows and enjoys communion with his Father (only thus can he truly 'image' him to the world). Humanity is then created in the image of Christ. The idea of 'image' having already been shown to be built upon personal knowledge and fellowship, this means that at the heart of human identity is the purpose to know and enjoy communion with Christ, in whose image we are made; and since he is the Image of the Father, through him we know the Father. That knowledge and communion is eternal life.

However, having been created with that purpose, humanity 'fell into lust of themselves, preferring what was their own to the contemplation of what belonged to God'.[8] Made to know and

---

8. *Against the Heathen* 3.2.

contemplate God, they turned away, turning in to contemplate only themselves. But in so doing, humankind became addicted to the self and its bodily pleasures, an addiction that instantly flooded them with the fear of having those pleasures ripped away by death. Instead of knowing Christ the Word and Image of God, humanity now knew anxiety and despair. In that state they imagined other gods, but the only gods they could imagine were anxiety- and despair-inducing gods.

With this, Athanasius provides a glaringly different account of the origin of evil to those given by non-Christian alternatives, especially that of Greek philosophy. In pagan Greek thought, evil exists because matter exists, for matter is inherently imperfect. In Athanasius' scheme, evil arises out of a perverse use of human freedom. Evil comes from sin. As for what sin is, Athanasius argues that it is, at root, a relational problem, a turning away from God. But since God is the ground of all being, to turn away from God is to turn into nothingness. To walk into sin is to walk into unbeing. Sin is anti-being, which is why it never delivers the happiness it promises, for it is the very opposite of being. As for the gods manufactured by the sinful imagination, they too are anti-being and so corrosive of all that humanity was created to be.

From Christ as the Image of God, Athanasius then shifts to focus on Christ as the Word (*Logos*) of God, first, in relation to the soul. The soul, designed to know the *Logos*, is created logical. However, by turning away from the *Logos*, humankind has become illogical. The consequences are ugly, for just as the *Logos* controls the world, so we were given logic to control our bodies; but by abandoning that logic we allow our bodies to rule us, rather than vice versa. Thus the created order is inverted, meaning that the beauty, order and peace of knowing the *Logos* are exchanged for an imprisoning self-obsession that only delivers ugly disorder and fear.

Yet there is good news still to be found in the *Logos* of God. First, this is because of the Word's relation to creation. Creation, Athanasius says, was not only brought into being through the Word, but also, it continues to exist only as it is sustained each moment by the Word. Creation has no inherent ability to maintain itself in existence, but would simply cease to be without the Word.

By this Athanasius wants to show two things: (1) that the Word of God is not a creature, but the one on whom all creaturely being depends; and (2) that the Word is not distant from creation, but intimately related to it, sustaining its every moment.

That starts to look significant when Athanasius goes on to explain the Word's relation to the Father. That is, while the Word is distinct from the Father, he is so intimately related to him that he can be the Father's true 'Interpreter' and 'Angel' (or 'Messenger'). The result is that, while the Father is the Creator, there is no infinite abyss between him and creation as in Greek thought. Rather, he is intimately related to the Word, and the Word is intimately related to creation. If the Word were some third party called into being to bridge a gap between the Father and the creation, then of course the Father would remain infinitely distant from us and ultimately unknowable. However, because of his relation to the Word and the Word's relation to creation, the Father is 'not far from each one of us' (Acts 17:27).

Athanasius is making a bold claim about God's revelation of himself. It is that, because of the Word, there is no darkness or hidden aloofness in God, but an unrestrained self-giving. In the Word, God himself comes to us so that we may contemplate again the very being of God. To see and encounter the Word is to see and encounter God. It was precisely this good news that Arius had stolen away by denying the Word's relation to the Father. For Arius, there could be no true revelation of God; all the Word could reveal could only be a pale imitation of what God is really like. But, sighs Athanasius, to turn away from and deny the Word who reveals the Father to us is the very essence of the tragedy of sin. It is for just that reason that the Image of God, in whose image we were made, must come and remake humankind in his image and so remake fellowship with God.

On the Incarnation

In this second volume Athanasius moves from looking at the Word as *creator* to looking at the Word as *redeemer*; yet while the focus has shifted from creation to the redemption of creation, the subject is the same: the Word of God. The two volumes are emphatically about Jesus Christ, and understanding that helps to make clear the central assertion of the second volume, that '*the renewal of creation has been wrought by the Self-same Word Who made it in the beginning*'.[9] However, the feel of *On the Incarnation* is quite different to that of *Against the Heathen*: here the dark themes of sin, evil and idolatry are driven out by the Word's redemption, making *On the Incarnation* (as C. S. Lewis put it) 'a sappy and golden book, full of buoyancy and confidence'.[10] And it is important to feel that difference (important, though not hard: Athanasius' punchy rhetoric is stirring stuff), for *On the Incarnation* is characterized by the idea of a happy, surprising overturning. Even the revelation of God through the Word is utterly surprising: 'The things which they, as men, rule out as impossible, He plainly shows to be possible . . . and things which these wiseacres laugh at as "human" He by His inherent might declares divine.'[11]

Athanasius starts with the creation of Adam and Eve, explaining that they were created good, but corruptible. Of course, they were then corrupted (one almost senses Athanasius suggesting that that was inevitably going to happen, for God's great purpose was to unite humankind to his own incorruptibility, so giving them incorruptible life). Once they were corrupted, though, what was God to do? Athanasius is adamant that it would not be worthy of God's goodness to allow humanity to be utterly destroyed. Yet destruction was exactly what was happening to humanity, for while the Word had called non-being into being in creation, through sin humankind was slipping back into non-being. What was needed was for the Word to come and recreate humanity.

It was not an entirely different humanity the Word was going to create from nothing, though. That would be no rescue; that would not resolve the problem of humanity's slide into darkness. Rather, he took on *our* humanity, and he took it from a virgin, so as not to inherit the taint of corruption. His was to be a pure humanity, not one that would itself die naturally.

Vitally, the only one who could come and recreate humanity

---

9. *On the Incarnation* §1, p. 26; italics original to translation.

10. Lewis, Introduction to *On the Incarnation*, p. 9.

11. *On the Incarnation* §1, p. 25.

was the Word and Image of God. First, because humanity was
originally created in his image. Athanasius illustrates the point by
comparing humanity made in the image of God to a portrait that
has been defaced; rather than throwing it away, the subject of the
portrait comes and sits again, so that his likeness can be redrawn.
Humanity, then, can only be truly renewed by the self-same Image
according to whom humanity was created. Secondly, Athanasius
has already explained that being created in the image of God
means being designed for personal knowledge of God, and this is
something that only the Word of God can bring. The knowledge
of God that the Word of God brings is precisely what humanity
turned away from in sin as they turned inward and so turned into
non-being. But when the Word of God restores knowledge of
God, he saves humankind from corruption and non-being, from
all 'this dehumanising of mankind'.[12] Only the Word and Image of
God could rehumanize us.

Next comes the cross, 'the very centre of our faith': 'Death
there had to be, and death for all, so that the due of all might be
paid.'[13] Christ could not die just any death, though. First, he had to
be executed. There was no cause for death within his spotless self,
and so he would not have died had death not come from without,
from the sin-filled world. Secondly, he had to be executed on a
tree so as to become a curse for us (Gal. 3:13), and with his arms
outstretched to draw and summon all men to himself. Thirdly, he
had to be lifted up in the air, for 'the air is the sphere of the devil'
(Eph. 2:2), and 'the Lord came to overthrow the devil and purify
the air'.[14] Clearly, the killing of corruption in man (the root of all
evil) would mean not only triumph over the devil, but also the
healing and purification of the cosmos itself.

Then, on the third day, when his body should have corrupted,
Christ was raised in victory over all corruption. In that moment,
for the first time humanity enjoyed the incorruptibility beyond all
death that God had planned for it. And we can be sure that Christ

---

12. Ibid. §13, p. 40.
13. Ibid. §19, p. 48; §20, p. 49.
14. Ibid. §25, p. 55.

is truly alive and victor over death, Athanasius argues, because only a living Christ could topple the old gods of paganism as he seemed to be doing all around, and only a living Christ could daily keep drawing so many to faith in himself. (This was clearly an apologetic that worked best in the years after the emperor Constantine had converted to Christianity.) Athanasius' other proof that Christ has conquered death is equally revealing of the age: it is that Christians, like children who make fun of a dead lion, 'despise death' and 'mock at it now as a dead thing robbed of all strength'.[15] Evidently, Athanasius had witnessed extraordinary courage in Christians facing martyrdom.

From there, he goes on to arguments that seek to persuade unbelieving Jews and Gentiles. First, the Jews: Athanasius rattles through the Old Testament to show how clearly it prophesied the coming of Christ, even including Daniel 9:24–25 to show that it is vain still to wait for the Christ to come, for Daniel specified when he would come, which is why no more prophets, priests or kings appeared in Israel after Jesus' day. Then he turns to the Gentiles, by which he means the Greeks, who thought it foolish to imagine that the Word could ever become flesh. Athanasius rejects their sneer as mere inconsistency, for, he says, they acknowledge a Word or *Logos* of God who is united to the cosmos as a whole (and even speak of the cosmos as the 'body' of the Word); yet if the Word can be united to all the cosmos, why is it foolish to say that he has united himself to a part of it? And Christ, he says, is the Word of God, not a mere man: how else, Athanasius asks, could he have defeated the gods? Nor is he a mere magician: he has destroyed magic. Nor is he a demon, for he drives out demons.

Some of the apologetic arguments near the end of the work strike us today as less than convincing, even if they are revealing of the times. But when he finally returns to the main argument, he becomes magisterial again. That is: why the incarnation? 'He, indeed, assumed humanity that we might become God.'[16] Clearly, Athanasius is not speaking of our becoming God in the sense of

---

15. Ibid. §27, p. 57.
16. Ibid. §54, p. 93.

leaving our humanity behind. That would conflict with everything he has argued for about the recreation of humanity. Rather, he is speaking of being brought into the intimate communion of God, knowing the Father just as Christ knows the Father.

Just as Athanasius made a bold claim about God's revelation, this now is a bold claim about God's salvation. Salvation, according to Athanasius, is not about being given a 'saved' status or a catalogue of blessings by a distant God; it is about entering the very communion of the Father and the Son. And again, this was precisely what Arius had taken away: by making the Son a mere creature, however exalted, he had denied the Son's real communion with the Father. In Arius' mind, then, the Son would be entirely unable to bestow communion with the Father, for the Son never knew it himself. Thus for Arius there could be no true communion with God.

Two criticisms are commonly levelled at Athanasius' theology, especially that of *On the Incarnation*: that he has left out the Spirit, and that he never allows the Word to become fully and truly human.

First, the absence of the Spirit. It is quite true that in these earlier works, Athanasius did not give much space to the Spirit (in that, while he repeatedly mentions the Spirit as one of the divine Three, he never unpacks the Spirit's role). It is entirely understandable, given that Arius' denial of the Son's deity was the pressing concern of the time, yet one misses the added richness that might have been there. That said, it would be entirely unfair to say that this was an ongoing problem in Athanasius' theology. During Athanasius' third exile, his good friend and fellow bishop Serapion wrote to ask for his advice on how to respond to those who denied the deity of the Spirit. Athanasius replied with four letters arguing that the Spirit is *homoousios* with the Father and the Son; indeed, if the Spirit is the one who comes to us to knit us into the Godhead, he must be God.

As for his Christology, the charge is that Athanasius imagines the Word not truly becoming human, but wearing his humanity like a detachable outer skin or, in modern terms, a kind of space-suit. For many years this has been the accepted line on Athanasius, and is based on how, a number of times, Athanasius refers to Jesus' body as the 'instrument' the Word 'uses'. Connected to this is the suggestion that Athanasius was so ensnared by a philosophical notion of God's absolute immutability that he could never imagine God 'becoming' anything, let alone flesh. Thus, the line goes, the Word kept himself safely detached from the spacesuit of his humanity and thus preserved his completely unchanging nature.

The argument, however, has been efficiently shredded in recent years.[17] First, the idea that Athanasius' Christology was driven by such a philosophy of God's immutability is an argument from silence. Instead, it seems that what Athanasius meant is that, when the Word became man, he still remained himself; he had not metamorphosed from being the Word into something entirely different (a man). He was still the Word, but now *also* a man. As for his language of the Word using his humanity as an 'instrument', what was meant was not that his humanity was like an external object he could pick up and put down at will; it is quite simply that his humanity was the means by which he saved humanity. 'He, indeed, assumed humanity that we might become God.' In fact, in some less-studied letters of his, Athanasius is as explicit as he could be that Christ's humanity was no husk, but complete.[18] It had to be, he argued, if Christ was ever to heal humanity completely.

Against the Arians
It was during his third exile, in the desert, on the run from the emperor's search parties, that Athanasius wrote this, the work that would ensure the immortality of his name more than anything else he did. It would do so since his discourses *Against the Arians* turned out to be *the* seminal defence of the Son's eternal deity and the stake through the heart of Arius' theology.

Discourse 1
The opening words show how seriously Athanasius took the Arian threat: 'Of all other heresies which have departed from the truth it

---

17. This is largely the work of Khaled Anatolios, whose arguments are summarized in his superb *Athanasius: The Coherence of his Thought* (New York: Routledge, 1998), pp. 70–72.
18. *Letter to the People of Antioch* 7; Letter 59.7.

is acknowledged that they have but devised a madness . . . whereas one heresy, and that the last . . . has now risen as harbinger of Antichrist, the Arian.' There would be no amicable agreement to disagree here!

First, Athanasius sets up his target by explaining what Arianism is. Arius had started with a philosophical presupposition of what God must be like: God by nature was 'ungenerated' or uncaused; in fact, he held, 'ungenerate' served as about the most basic definition of God. It follows, then, that since the Son is begotten or generated by the Father, he cannot truly be God. Rather, being begotten, he must have an origin: he must have come into being at some point and must therefore be a creature. Thus the eternal Son disappeared in a puff of philosophy – unsurprisingly, for Arianism was rationalist monotheism incarnate, 'one of those "sensible" synthetic religions which are so strongly recommended today and which, then as now, included among their devotees many highly cultivated clergymen' (as C. S. Lewis put it).

According to Arius, then, the Son of God is utterly unlike God; exalted, perhaps, but a mere creature, made so that he might make a creation that the Father was always too transcendent to have anything to do with. As such, it is not that we were created for the Son; rather, the Son was created for us and allowed to participate in certain divine characteristics as a gift. Thus, while he can be spoken of as 'God', he is not actually God, nor does he really know God, but is 'God' to us.

Athanasius' first response is to attack the methodology of the Arians (or 'Ario-maniacs' as he preferred to call them). Essentially, he argues, they get their notion of God from speculation: human sons, they said, start existing at some particular point, when they are begotten; so it must be with the Son of God. 'When they thus speak,' replied Athanasius, 'they should have inquired of an architect, whether he can build without materials; and if he cannot, whether it follows that God could not make the universe without materials.'[19] It is simply not possible, he argued, to work upwards like that towards a real knowledge of God.

---

19. *Against the Arians* 1.23.

Rather, 'it is more pious and more accurate to signify God from the Son and call Him Father, than to name Him from His works only and call Him Unoriginate'.[20] That is, Christians pray to the Father, not to 'the Unoriginate', for Father he is, not merely some abstractly defined 'Unoriginate' being. And it is only possible to know God as Father 'from the Son'. However, if we first define God by something such as being the Creator, we will define God abstractly (as something like 'Unoriginate' or 'ungenerate') and so define the Son out of his deity. And when we do that, we find ourselves worshipping a God who is not a real Father and who does not really have a Son. We have become idolaters. This, Athanasius holds, is the essential Arian problem: by trying to know God other than through the Son, they had come to know an entirely different God. And this was why Athanasius held the deity of the Son to be non-negotiable, for it is only by knowing the Son that any can ever know the God who is.

That said, while the Arians had not got their understanding of God from Scripture, they would use Scripture to support their view. In particular, they liked Hebrews 1, with verses such as 'You are my Son, today I have begotten you' (v. 5) and its references to the exaltation of the Son (an exaltation that seemed to them incompatible with the Son being truly God). Athanasius, citing the Hebrews 1 references to the Son as God on his eternal throne (from Ps. 45) and the Son as creator (from Ps. 102), counters that the Son was always worshipped as Lord in the Old Testament. As for the exaltation/begetting language, Athanasius explains that the Son took on humanity, and that was what was then exalted in Christ's ascension: united to the Son, the humanity was now exalted to the filial status that the Son had always enjoyed. Indeed, that adoption was the purpose of the incarnation.

Discourse 2

In the first discourse, Athanasius had already noted in passing that Arius' God, for all his transcendence, was actually weak and needy, unable to achieve what he wanted without his created helper, the

---

20. Ibid. 1.34.

Son; he was a God 'in process of completion as time goes on'.[21]
Now Athanasius provides the orthodox alternative: God, he says,
must be Father before he could ever be a creator. That is, in order
to be capable of going out in creation, he must be fruitful and life-
giving by nature: such the Father is (being *Father*); such Arius'
lonely 'Unoriginate' was not.

Athanasius thus revealed that his God was an utterly different
being to the God of the Greek philosophy of his day. His God was
not static, but a dynamic, personal being, inherently outgoing and
productive. Athanasius compares the Father to a fountain and a
sun: just as a fountain must pour forth water to be a fountain, and
just as a sun must have a radiance, so the Father must 'pour forth',
'radiate' or beget the Son in order to be who he is, the Father. In
contrast, Arius' talk of a Father without a Son signified a barren
God who was like a dry fountain or a sun that does not shine.

Much of the rest of the second discourse is then taken up with
proving from the Old Testament (and thus from before the
incarnation) that Christ

> is Lord and King everlasting, seeing that Abraham worships Him as
> Lord, and Moses says, 'Then the Lord rained upon Sodom and upon
> Gomorrah brimstone and fire from the Lord out of heaven;' and David
> in the Psalms, 'The Lord said unto my Lord, Sit Thou on My right hand;'
> and, 'Thy Throne, O God, is for ever and ever; a sceptre of
> righteousness is the sceptre of Thy Kingdom;' and, 'Thy Kingdom is an
> everlasting Kingdom;' it is plain that even before He became man, He
> was King and Lord everlasting, being Image and Word of the Father.[22]

In fact, more than any other, it was an Old Testament text,
Proverbs 8:22, that lay at the heart of the exegetical battles
Athanasius had with the Arians, and large swathes of *Against the
Arians* are given over to issues surrounding it. All sides agreed
that Wisdom was a name for Christ, but, unlike the Hebrew text,
the Septuagint (on which both sides relied) had Wisdom being

---

21. Ibid. 1.17.
22. Ibid. 2.13.

'created' in Proverbs 8:22. Athanasius simply treated this as he had treated Hebrews 1, by stating that the 'creation' referred to Christ's humanity, 'created' for him at the incarnation.

This leads Athanasius into an extended discussion of what it means for Christ's humanity to be founded 'before the world'. Athanasius understands that even before creation the Father had his purpose to save through Christ, and this understanding he develops into what is almost certainly the most detailed doctrine of election before Augustine's. It is rather different to Augustine's belief, though, which tended to focus (especially in later years) on individuals being predestined to adoption; instead, Athanasius holds that the Son was the predestined one, and that only in him are we chosen:

> How then has He chosen us, before we came into existence, but that, as he says himself, in Him we were represented beforehand? and how at all, before men were created, did He predestinate us unto adoption, but that the Son Himself was 'founded before the world,' taking on Him that economy which was for our sake? . . . and how did we receive it 'before the world was,' when we were not yet in being, but afterwards in time, but that in Christ was stored the grace which has reached us? Wherefore also in the Judgment, when every one shall receive according to his conduct, He says, 'Come, ye blessed of My Father, inherit the kingdom prepared for you from the foundation of the world.' How then, or in whom, was it prepared before we came to be, save in the Lord who 'before the world' was founded for this purpose.[23]

Discourse 3

Athanasius still did not feel that he had made the relationship between the Father and the Son sufficiently clear, and this he now proceeds to do, with the Nicene formula (that the Son is 'begotten, not made, of the same being of the Father' [*homoousion tō Patri*]) clearly at the forefront of his mind.[24]

---

23. Ibid. 2.76.

24. The Arians' first objection to the word *homoousios* was that it was unscriptural. Yet, as Athanasius effectively demonstrated, not only

Nicea had clarified a distinction between being 'begotten' and being 'made' that had not been sufficiently obvious beforehand, but which would be crucial for Athanasius' doctrine of God (as well as for the church as a whole). That is, a subject can 'beget' only the *same* kind of being as itself; thus men 'beget' men and the Father 'begets' the Son. On the other hand, a subject can only 'make' a *different* kind of being; thus men 'make' doughnuts and God 'makes' the world. Men cannot 'beget' doughnuts, nor God 'beget' the world; just so, men cannot 'make' men, nor God 'make' the Son.

What Nicea had not made clear was what the word 'being' (*ousia*) meant, and it was because of this that some felt the word *homoousios* unhelpfully suggested a lack of distinction between the Father and the Son. Athanasius' whole approach makes it quite apparent, though, that such fears were unfounded. *Homoousios* does not mean that the Father and the Son consist of the same generic material (*ousia*) in the way that two sweets come from the same butterscotch. That would unacceptably imply two Gods. Rather, the Father and the Son are *homoousios* in the sense that they are the same being, the same God.

Athanasius makes clear what he sees as the implication of the Nicene formula by putting the emphasis on the Son's 'same being *of the Father*' (*homoousion **tō Patri***). It is not, then, that there is some third thing, a divine material or 'being' (*ousia*), that the Father and Son share. The Son is not said to be from the being of *God*. The Son is *of the Father*. This means that there is no God-stuff underlying the Father or the Son. The Father's being is not anything more fundamental than that he is the Father. He did not will to become the Father at some point so that we might ask what he was before that and so what he was more fundamentally. Rather, God is the Father begetting the Son, and that begetting is not an add-on to who God is.

---

was the whole Arian approach fundamentally non-scriptural but they themselves also used unscriptural terms – referring to God as 'Ungenerate' and insisting on such phrases as 'there was a time when the Son was not'. The reality was, terms from outside the Bible had to be used to counter the Arian tendency to twist all scriptural terms to fit its non-scriptural philosophical framework.

The Nicene Creed began with the words 'We believe in one God, the Father'. It had not spoken of the 'Ungenerate' but of the 'Father'. What Athanasius sought to establish was that if 'Father' is a real statement about this God's very being, then he cannot have become Father at some point. The Father must have his being begetting the Son. That means that 'when we call God Father, at once with the Father we signify the Son's existence'.[25] Or, to put it another way, if the Father really is eternally Father this means that the Son must be eternal.

And this, Athanasius is able to conclude, becomes the problem for the Arians, for by denying the eternal Son, they had denied the Father's very being and identity and could have no part in him. It is a conclusion that reveals why Athanasius was so unswerving: he saw that he was fighting for the very identity of God, the knowledge of whom is salvation. And if the Arians did not know the Son, then they did not know the Father. They did not know God. The God they had come to believe in through their philosophical presuppositions was a different god.

From those heights, Athanasius then plunges down to tell the story of the Word in his creation. The Word, he says, was often known by the saints of the Old Testament as the Lord's Angel (here he refers to passages such as Gen. 48:15–16; 32:24–30) 'because it is He alone who reveals the Father'.[26] However, something quite different happened when the Word took flesh, and Athanasius is emphatic that we should not think 'that, as in former times the Word was used to come into each of the Saints, so now He sojourned in a man'.[27] Far from merely sojourning in a body, the Word assumed the flesh entirely in order to 'make it Word'. And then (at last!) Athanasius explains that he does this by the Spirit: 'we, apart from the Spirit, are strange and distant from God, and by the participation of the Spirit we are knit into the Godhead'.[28]

---

25. *Against the Arians* 3.6.
26. Ibid. 3.13.
27. Ibid. 3.30.
28. Ibid. 3.24.

Discourse 4

The fourth discourse is actually a different work, grafted onto the first three as an appendix. Nevertheless, it is well worth looking at for how Athanasius now turns his guns from Arianism to modalism, that belief that the Father, Son and Spirit are but mere, interchangeable modes or masks worn by the one God.

How should the modalists be answered? Athanasius does, of course, wheel out a number of Old and New Testament texts to show the Son's real and distinct being, but his main answer is initially cryptic. The modalists, he says, 'must be confuted from the notion of a Son, and the Arians from that of a Father'![29] We have seen how the Arian problem was that, by denying the Son, they denied the Father; now Athanasius inverts the argument for the modalists, saying that their problem is that they do not even acknowledge the existence of a real Son beside the Father. And that, he says, is actually worse than what the Arians did:

> those who say that the Son is only a name, and that the Son of God, that is, the Word of the Father, is unessential and non-subsistent, pretend to be angry with those who say, 'Once He was not.' This is ridiculous also; for they who give Him no being at all are angry with those who at least grant Him to be in time.[30]

Also, he maintains, by murdering the Son, modalism murders belief in a real and good creation, for if the Word simply goes out from God as a mode of his being to bring creation into existence, what will happen when the Word returns to God (in the ascension and final handover of the kingdom to the Father)? It is the Word who sustains creation; but if the Word returns into God and ceases to have any existence of its own, creation will cease to exist. It would be as if creation were a momentary expansion within God, soon to be swallowed back up into nothing.

---

29. Ibid. 4.4.
30. Ibid. 4.8.

Life of Antony

At the same time as he wrote *Against the Arians* while in desert exile among the monks, Athanasius wrote his biography of their renowned leader, the then recently deceased hermit Antony. The work turned out to be enormously popular and influential, playing a key role in the conversion of Augustine and in spreading the monastic ideal.

It is the story of a young Egyptian who hears and applies literally Jesus' words to the rich young man 'If you want to be perfect, go, sell your possessions and give to the poor, and you will have treasure in heaven. Then come, follow me' (Matt. 19:21). Yet getting rid of his possessions clearly antagonized the devil, who, concerned by this zeal, appeared to Antony with new levels of temptation. Antony then decided that he needed to get more serious, and so moved out into the desert to live as a hermit under the strictest of ascetic regimes. There he wrestled with demons, prophesied, had visions, performed miracles and acquired such a reputation for holiness that the sick came out to be healed by him and disciples came out to follow him.

The general feel of the work is surprisingly upbeat, with an exhilarating sense of the victory of Christ over evil and the demonic (which are 'like snakes and scorpions to be trodden underfoot by us Christians').[31] It is characteristic Athanasius, who always managed to imbue the darker themes of Christian suffering and self-denial with a golden sense of light and joy. In a letter that announced the Lenten fast to the Christians of Alexandria, for instance, his focus was not on gloomy thoughts of self-denial, but on entering the fast so as to relish Christ as the true feast. For Athanasius, fasting and self-denial were associated with gratitude, with looking away from the sensual pleasures that foster self-love to contemplate God and find joy in him. Even suffering fitted into this for Athanasius, who counselled Christians to embrace sickness and afflictions in hope and as means to dispel lust of self and conform them joyfully into the image of Christ.

For all that, though, it seems that Athanasius did not actually entirely agree with Antony's asceticism (though, because of his

---

31. *Life of Antony* 24.

profound respect for Antony, he never even comes close to censoring him). Antony's self-denial was always in danger of veering into anti-materialism, something that Athanasius, with his strong doctrine of creation, could never countenance. In a letter to another monk, he warned that it is the devil who suggests 'under the show of purity' that such bodily things as sexuality are inherently evil. Quite the opposite, said Athanasius: 'All things made by God are beautiful and pure, for the Word of God has made nothing useless or impure.'[32]

Going on with Athanasius

Athanasius has a blunt, simple style of writing; however, he can run off on tangents that are quite off-putting for those trying to get to know him for the first time. For that reason, newcomers should probably skip *Against the Heathen*, which is more difficult, and dive straight into *On the Incarnation*, which SVS provides in an easy translation alongside C. S. Lewis's excellent introduction. For those wanting to go a bit deeper, *Against the Arians* should definitely be the next port of call, and can be found online (at <http://www.ccel.org>) or in the *Nicene and Post-Nicene Fathers* (2nd series, vol. 4).

Thomas Weinandy's *Athanasius: A Theological Introduction* (Aldershot: Ashgate, 2007) is probably the best overall introduction, and has the advantage of being up to date with important changes in scholarly opinion. The now classic introduction to the intricacies of the Arian debate is R. P. C. Hanson's *The Search for the Christian Doctrine of God: The Arian Controversy 318–381* (Edinburgh: T. & T. Clark, 1988). Its scholarship is a little dated and it is quite opinionated, yet it remains the standard.

---

32. Letter 48, *To Amun*.

Athanasius timeline

251?	Antony born
256?	Arius born
296–8	Athanasius born in Alexandria, Egypt
303–5	Emperor Diocletian's 'Great Persecution' of Christianity
311	Renewed persecution in Egypt
312	Conversion of the emperor Constantine to Christianity
318	Arius begins to teach that there was a time when the Son was not
325	Council of Nicea
328	Athanasius appointed bishop of Alexandria
335–7	Athanasius' first exile; writes *Against the Heathen* and *On the Incarnation*?
336	Arius dies
339–46	Athanasius' second exile
354	Augustine born
356?	Antony dies
356–62	Athanasius' third exile; writes *Against the Arians*, letters to Serapion and *Life of Antony*
362	Council of Alexandria
362–4	Athanasius' fourth exile
365–6	Athanasius' fifth exile
373	Athanasius dies

4. LOVING WISDOM

Augustine

The fourth century AD was a tumultuous turning point in history. When it began, the Roman Empire was pagan, and Christians were a persecuted minority. When it ended, Christianity was officially accepted, and pagan sacrifices had been made illegal. It was a century that saw the power of the Roman Empire crumble to such an extent that the next would witness the repeated sackings of once-mighty Rome and the complete collapse of the western half of the empire.

As significant as all this, perhaps, was the birth of Aurelius Augustinus in AD 354. Born of a pagan father, Patricius, and a Christian mother, Monica, he was a true child of his times. His life and writings were inseparable from the events around him. Like Rome, he converted from paganism to Christianity. He soon became a bishop, and thus an official of the empire. And his end, like Rome's, came as the barbarian hordes surrounded the city in which he lay dying.

For almost all his life he lived in a provincial backwater of the empire in North Africa. The city of which he was bishop, Hippo Regius (a seaport on what is now the Algerian coast), was otherwise obscure. Yet, in spite of this, Augustine remains perhaps the most influential Christian thinker outside the Bible. His impact on the West, at least, can scarcely be exaggerated. The Reformation in the sixteenth century, for instance, was in many ways a debate within Augustine's head. Both Rome and the Reformers argued that they were the true heirs of Augustine, and both cited him extensively to prove it. Both Luther and Erasmus were once Augustinian monks. And his influence extends well beyond theology, to psychology and philosophy, to shape the very way in which we in the West tend to think of ourselves. Augustine is deep in our blood; and with many of the ideas that he faced still operating today, it seems that he will continue to be of vital importance.

Unsurprisingly, a mind as titanic as Augustine's was extremely prolific. He produced more than two hundred books and treatises on theological, philosophical and pastoral issues, as well as many hundreds of letters and sermons. Yet the combination of over-whelming profundity and so much material (as well as his cultural distance from us) makes Augustine too daunting a prospect for most readers. This need not be. His style is easy and readable, his thought well expressed. All that is needed as a springboard to engagement with him is a rough sketch of the context and contours of his thought.

The place to start is undoubtedly Augustine's *Confessions*, in which the man himself describes his own early life and his early theological and spiritual journey. That introduces Augustine the man and so many of the key points of his thought. With them in place we can complete the picture by working (in rough chrono-logical order) through the major issues he faced in the second half of his life, after having completed the *Confessions*.

Confessions

Augustine wrote his *Confessions* halfway through his life, as a book about his youth. It is not quite an autobiography, however, at least not in the modern sense. For one thing, there is nothing self-congratulatory about it. And, unlike autobiographies, it is written as a prayer. That (coupled with the title) reveals what kind of book it is. It is a confession to God, both of his own sin, and of God's grace to him. It is his testimony. The unusual feature of this testimony, however, is that after nine 'books' or chapters dealing with his life up until just after his conversion, Augustine then finishes the work with four 'books' on memory, time, biblical interpretation and an exegesis of Genesis 1. No wonder the ending so often leaves readers feeling rather thrown! But how these last four 'books' relate to the first nine is vital to understanding Augustine's purpose.

Book 1

Augustine opens the *Confessions* with a paragraph that really encapsulates the whole work:

> Great are you, O Lord, and greatly to be praised; great is your power, and of your wisdom there is no end. Man, being a part of your creation, longs to praise you. He carries his mortality with him, the sign of his sin, the proof that you thwart the proud. Yet man, as part of your creation, still longs to praise you. You arouse us to delight in praising you, for you have made us for yourself, and our hearts are restless until they find rest in you.[1]

Thus Augustine introduces his central theme, which is to be his and all humanity's journey towards rest in God. It is a deeply Christian paragraph (alluding to Pss 145:3; 147:5; 1 Pet. 5:5; Rom. 10:14), but it is also strongly Neoplatonic. The Neoplatonist tradition (which we will examine below) placed a premium on the notion of the soul's movement towards such rest, and was filled with works written as prayers to God. And having noticed the presence of both traditions here, we have noticed something vital about the mature Augustine who wrote the *Confessions*, whose mind was precisely such a mixture of Christian and Neoplatonic thought.

---

1. *Confessions* 1.1.1. Quotations from the *Confessions* are my translation, although no translation seems able to capture the excitement and vivacity of Augustine's Latin.

Augustine then begins his story with a reflection on his infancy. It is not that he can actually remember it, but he writes of it so that he can start things by proving the sinful guilt of even newborn babies from their radical selfishness. In fact, his description of his entire childhood, of how he would lie, hate, cheat and steal, serves not only as a confession of his own wickedness and self-obsession, but as a refutation of the concept of childhood innocence.

Guilty and sinful he might have been; nevertheless, Augustine believed that even at this early stage his journey towards God was beginning. As a child he loved classical Latin literature. In fact, in many ways his life as described in the *Confessions* is a story of encounters with books. His favourite as a child was Virgil's *Aeneid*, the story of the Trojan hero Aeneas' wanderings after the fall of Troy, and of how he came to Carthage before going on to found what would become Rome. It becomes the model for Augustine's own life, the *Confessions* being his own spiritual version of the *Aeneid* as he describes his own spiritual wanderings, which would also take him from Carthage to Rome.

Book 2

Augustine then pursues the theme of his sinful youth, describing in a highly resonant, compelling and convicting way what it is like to sin. The major event of the book is a minor incident from when he was sixteen, but he uses it as both an example and an opportunity to examine the nature of sin. Along with some friends he stole some pears from a neighbour's tree. It may have been a petty crime, but he later felt it displayed his real self. Here he was, another Adam, stealing forbidden fruit. And why did he do it? It was not that he actually wanted the pears themselves (he cannot remember if he even ate any of them); he simply enjoyed doing something illicit. As he sees it, it perfectly illustrates the human condition: sin uses the law as an opportunity for displaying its natural desire to rebel against the Lord (Rom. 7:7–11). The irony he notices is that, while at the time he thought he was making himself divinely free and happy in putting himself above the law, the reality was that he was doing it only to fit in with and follow his friends, and that it did not, after all, bring happiness.

Book 3

In order to continue his education, he then moved, like Aeneas, to Carthage (now Tunis). And, like Aeneas, he found love there. For Aeneas it had been a woman, Queen Dido. Not for Augustine: during his studies he read the *Hortensius*, by the great Roman orator and philosopher Cicero, and was greatly attracted by his noble style of communication. The *Hortensius* is an exhortation to philosophy (literally, the 'love of wisdom') in which Cicero encourages the reader to find eternal wisdom. The book turned Augustine into a philosopher, one who loved wisdom (a love that was truly heartfelt for Augustine, meaning that philosophy, for him, could never be a purely cerebral affair). And so, writing the *Confessions* many years later, looking back as a Christian who believed that Christ is Wisdom (1 Cor. 1:24), he felt that, though he had not known it at the time, at that moment he had begun his search for Christ. Therefore he writes of Cicero's *Hortensius*, 'This book changed my affections, and turned my prayers to you, O Lord.'[2]

Because of his mother's Christianity he began to look for the wisdom he sought in the Bible. Yet, next to Cicero's rhetorical panache, the poor Latin translation he used seemed woefully clunky, and its content (especially the story of Adam and Eve) just struck him as naive. He had major questions to ask, especially concerning the nature and body of God and the origin of evil (questions that would remain key for him throughout his life), but at that time Christianity did not appear to have any satisfactory answers.

Instead, he turned to the sinister and feared sect of the Manichees, who had a more obvious answer to the problem of evil. The Manichees were followers of the third-century Persian prophet Mani, a man who believed himself to be the Paraclete promised by Jesus in John 14 – 16. They saw themselves as basically Christian, though they were strict dualists, holding the body to be evil and the soul good. As a result, they could not accept the Creator as being the true and good God, for he had brought all that was bad (matter) into existence. This meant rejecting the

---

2. Ibid. 3.4.7.

Old Testament and large parts of the New. Furthermore, they could not believe that Jesus was truly human, or that he had been truly crucified, for it would be impossible to nail a spirit to wood. Instead, they viewed the cross as a symbol for the poor plight of all humanity. Their answer to Augustine's problem of evil, however, was attractively simple: evil exists because matter exists. It was almost as attractive as the fact that, according to their teaching, his soul could remain untarnished by the physical relationship he soon began with a concubine.

Book 4

Augustine's latest ideas were soon put to the test with the death of a dear Manichaean friend. This friend had fallen ill and, while unconscious, had been baptized by some rather sneaky Christians (such things were known to happen in North Africa in those days). When he recovered consciousness, Augustine teased him about this baptism, assuming his friend would find it amusing. Instead, he found that his friend had genuinely been converted, and so, instead of laughing along with Augustine, sternly rebuked him. Soon after, the friend died, leaving Augustine shocked and grieving. Yet when he reflected on his grief, Augustine saw that it stemmed from his error of treating the friendship as if it had been an immortal one, of trying to satisfy himself with his friend instead of with God.

Book 5

Shaken, the bright young Augustine soon began to ask questions that the local Manichees were unable to answer. When this happened, they invariably seemed to advise him to speak to a revered Manichee leader called Faustus, when he next came to town. Yet when Faustus finally arrived and Augustine set about questioning him, Augustine found Faustus was equally unable to provide him with satisfactory answers. With disillusionment in Manichaeism setting in, Augustine moved to Rome in the hope of finding more educated people to question (as well as better students to enhance his career of teaching rhetoric). For the same reasons he then moved on quickly from Rome to Milan, which had become the real seat of the Roman Empire in the west.

In Italy he began to engage with minds of a different calibre to those he had known in provincial North Africa. This led him to a much more sophisticated philosophy than Manichaeism: Neoplatonism. In the third century AD the philosopher Plotinus had offered the Roman world an interpretation of Plato that was picked up by Plotinus' disciple Porphyry as a weapon with which to defend paganism against the rising force of Christianity. (Today the movement is called 'Neoplatonism', though they saw themselves simply as Platonists.) In stark contrast to Manichaean dualism, Neoplatonism was monist. It taught that there is a hierarchy of being, at the top of which is a divine triad: the One, Mind and Soul. These are the most real beings, the most non-bodily and the most good. From them emanates all being. Evil is what lies at the other end of the spectrum. It is, as it were, where light, goodness and being run out, leaving dark, evil nothingness. Evil, in Neoplatonic thought, is a lack of being and goodness.

Despite its pagan and even anti-Christian pedigree, many Christians in the fourth century began to be attracted to this philosophical movement, in that it spoke intelligently of a reality 'not of this world'. One such Christian was Ambrose, the eminent bishop of Milan.

Book 6

As a teacher of rhetoric, Augustine first went to hear Ambrose preach because of the bishop's outstanding reputation as an orator. Soon, however, it was the content and not just the presentation of Ambrose's message that began to impress Augustine. In particular, Ambrose taught that many biblical stories, especially those from the Old Testament, were to be taken symbolically and not literally. With this he was able to give them a sophisticated application that appealed to Augustine. From then on, Augustine was to have a fondness for allegorical readings of literature, a tendency that clearly affects how he means the *Confessions* to be read (for instance, wanting his young act of theft from the pear tree to be interpreted as symbolic of the fall).

Being infinitely more refined than the Christians of North Africa, Ambrose soon began to give Christianity a new appeal in Augustine's eyes. In large part, no doubt, Ambrose was able to

make Christianity credible to Augustine because of his own affin-
ity with the Neoplatonism that had begun to fascinate Augustine.
He presented a Christianity that looked easily compatible with
Plotinus' philosophy.

Book 7

In this intriguing central book of the *Confessions*, Augustine
becomes certain of the intellectual superiority of Christianity.
What is strange is that he is convinced of it by reading Neoplatonist
philosophy. He believed that Neoplatonism had understood all the
essential elements of Christianity, with the exception of the incarnation and atonement. It was because of those doctrines that
Christianity was the superior philosophy. Thus, just as he believed
Cicero had first pointed him towards God, so here he argues that
the Neoplatonists taught him about the Word of God.

All this is important for understanding Augustine's theological
method, for of course the Neoplatonists had come to their philosophy by reason, not revelation. It also exposes some of the biases
and gaps in his theology. Soon after the events of Book 7 he wrote
his *Soliloquies*, in which he stated that all he wanted to know was
nothing more than 'God and the soul'.[3] Yet what of Christ, of his
incarnation and crucifixion? What of the very world? Augustine
needed to (and would) become more explicitly Christian in his interests. Yet Neoplatonism would never cease to exercise a strong grip
on his mind. His last recorded words were a quotation from Plotinus.[4]

Book 8

In this book Augustine recounts the climax of his long mental,
spiritual and moral journey from Cicero to Mani to Plotinus, and
finally to Christ. What he makes clear at the beginning of this
book is the moral dimension. Through it all he had battled with an
addiction to sex that had led to two mistresses and a child. 'Lord

---

3. *Soliloquies* 1.7.

4. 'He is no great man who thinks it a great thing that sticks and stones
should fall, and that men, who must die, should die' (cited in P. Brown,
Augustine of Hippo [London: Faber & Faber, 1967], pp. 425–426).

give me continence, but not yet' was his famous prayer.[5] He realized that he could not even want what he wanted, so enslaved was
he to his passions.

Then he describes the moment of his conversion in the garden
of his house in Milan. As he had earlier displayed his rebellion
against God under a pear tree in a garden, so now he describes his
reconciliation to God under a fig tree in a garden. Walking in the
garden (hear the symbolism), crying at his captivity to sin, he heard a
voice repeating the words *Tolle lege* (Take and read). Understanding
this to be a divine command to read the Scriptures, he picked up his
copy of Paul's letters and read the first passage his eye fell on: 'not in
orgies and drunkenness, not in sexual immorality and debauchery,
not in dissension and jealousy. Rather, clothe yourselves with the
Lord Jesus Christ, and do not think about how to gratify the desires
of the sinful nature.'[6] At this, he says, all the darkness of doubt left
him, and his heart was changed towards God.

Book 9

Augustine is then baptized along with a close friend and his own
son. Soon afterwards, however, his mother (who had followed him
to Italy), his son and two close friends all die. This causes him to
write in some detail about Monica, who had been such a dominating figure in his life. As well as having been a formidable and rather
clingy mother, she had been a staunch Christian who had rejoiced
at the events she had so long prayed for: the conversion and
baptism of her son. Yet here Augustine reveals the surprising fact
that Monica had for years been something of an alcoholic, before
finally managing to deal with her addiction by total abstention. This
enables him to examine addiction to habits.

It may also shed light on a common accusation thrown at
Augustine, that he is 'anti-sex'. It is true that he is generally
unhelpfully negative regarding sex, seeing it as the conduit for
original sin. Yet to a great extent Augustine was reacting to his
own addiction to sex in the same way as Monica had reacted to

---

5. *Confessions* 8.7.17.
6. Rom. 13:13–14.

her wine habit – with total abstinence. Moreover, for a fourth-century Christian his views were actually quite moderate. It is his prominence more than his stance that has made him appear to be the main perpetrator of all prudery in the West.

Book 10

The narrative section of the work over, Augustine proceeds to describe himself in the present. Up to this point his focus has been on his own life, written as a small mirror image of the story of creation as it is brought back to God from its fallenness. In the last four books he broadens his vision more explicitly to speak of the bigger picture his life had reflected.

He begins with a discussion of human identity as understood through the concept of *memory* (an appropriate starting point, given how much he has recalled in the first nine books). He sees memory as the very root of the self's identity – how it stays itself from moment to moment. The other key elements of the inner self he believed to be the *intellect* and the *will*. He therefore argued that each human mind is composed of an internal triad analogous to the Trinity (he compares memory to God the Father; intellect [logic] to the Son [the Logos]; and will to the Spirit).

At around the same time as writing the *Confessions*, Augustine began composing his seminal work *On the Trinity*. In that work he also illustrated his understanding of the Trinity by comparing the Father, Son and Spirit to (among other things) the different aspects of an individual human mind.

Book 11

From memory Augustine progresses quite naturally to the question of *time* (analysed through an exegesis of Gen. 1 that will occupy the remainder of the work). He acknowledges that time is an especially profound mystery: 'What, then, is time? If no one ask of me, I know; if I wish to explain to him who asks, I know not.'[7] Yet he is impatient with the joke answer to the question 'what was God doing before creation?' ('Preparing hell for those who pry into such

---

7. *Confessions* 11.14.17.

mysteries'). He wanted to take the question seriously. Instead, his answer is that, since time is a part of creation, there was no time 'before' creation. There was no 'before' creation at all. Thus he argued for a model essentially identical to Plato's sharp distinction between time and a timeless eternity. This was clearly appealing for an audience influenced by Neoplatonism; how well it fits with the biblical model is a question that still divides theologians.

Book 12

Having narrated a story of encounters with books (Virgil's *Aeneid*, Cicero's *Hortensius*, the books of the Platonists and finally the Bible), Augustine now begins to work more systematically through Genesis 1. Here he presents the Bible as the book of books, the true classic that stands above all the revered works of Homer and Virgil, the sum and true presentation of wisdom. In one sense Book 12 is Augustine's guide to biblical interpretation (in a word, to 'allegorize'). In another sense it is a refutation of both Platonism and Manichaeism. Against all forms of Platonism, the Bible shows creation being produced by God out of nothing (rather than out of some pre-existing material); against Manichaeism, creation speaks against dualism and all hatred of the physical.

This is probably the point at which to mention Augustine's mature understanding of evil, which so brilliantly denies Manichaean dualism. Augustine asserted that evil cannot be a thing, for every thing has been created by God, and God's creation is good. Instead, evil is a lack of being, like a hole in something, spoiling it, but not having any independent, substantial existence.

Book 13

Augustine ends his *Confessions* by interpreting Genesis 1 as an allegory of the church (e.g. the creation of the firmament on day two he reads as an allegory of Scripture being placed over the church).[8] This leads him through the creation week to finish the *Confessions*

---

8. This particular allegory is a good example of how variegated even single lines of Augustine's thought can be: the theological conclusion sounds categorically Protestant; the exegesis that gets him there is absolutely not.

where he had started it: with the theme of rest. His heart had found rest in God, and now he looks forward to the promised rest of the eternal Sabbath.

Life and theology after the *Confessions*

Two years after his conversion Augustine went back to Africa. Returning as an exceptionally able convert from Manichaeism, Augustine was welcomed as an essential asset in the North African church's fight against the sect. As such he was soon forcibly ordained as a presbyter in Hippo (like stealth baptisms, a practice not uncommon in the region at the time). His dreams of a life of philosophical contemplation were shattered. Instead, his new role compelled him to do theology in the service of the church.

Since his conversion he had lived a monastic life, which, until his ordination, had meant ivory-towered isolation. He would remain for the rest of his life in a monastery, living out an austere monastic rule. From that time on, however, the monastery was to serve as a seminary for Africa. Especially after Augustine was consecrated Bishop of Hippo, four years later, he succeeded in importing a constellation of highly talented young men who were then planted as bishops across the province.

Against the Donatists

The church in Hippo faced not only the Manichees, but also the Donatist sect. In fact, the Donatists outnumbered the Catholics in Hippo ('Catholic' at this point simply meant 'orthodox', the opposite, not of Protestantism, but heresy). Donatism owed its existence to events of nearly a century before. Prior to Constantine's conversion to Christianity, the emperor Diocletian had instigated a particularly thorough programme for the persecution of Christianity from 303 to 305. Bishops were asked to hand over copies of the Bible to be burnt, and some complied. And so the troubles began. Some Christians believed that such treachery meant that the guilty bishops were no longer worthy of being bishops; their authority in the church was voided. As a result, those they ordained were not truly ordained and those they baptized were not truly baptized. All their churches were polluted. In response, 'pure' rival bishops were elected, one of whom, in Carthage, was called Donatus. The church in Africa had thus been torn into two halves: the 'ultra-pure' followers of Donatus with their rival bishops, and the 'corrupted' Catholic rump.

As the ablest theologian in the region, Augustine was saddled with the task of responding to the claims made by the Donatists. At one level his reply was deliberately unscholarly. 'His polemic against the Donatists betrays un unsuspected flair for journalism . . . He sensed the popular tone of the controversy, and exploited it with gusto. He will begin his campaign by writing a popular song.'[9] At another level his response to the 'pure ecclesiology' of the Donatists was a theology of the church and sacraments that is still determinative today.

Augustine argued that the church is not a pure society, but must consist of both wheat and tares until Christ himself separates them at the end of the age. There is no salvation outside the church, but the unsaved can also be found inside the church. He agreed that the true church and the outward church can be distinguished, but maintained that the two cannot be separated by crude human division, as the Donatists thought, but only by God in final judgment. In this way he denied the possibility of a perfect denomination or church.

As for the sacraments, he argued that a sacrament's validity does not depend on the holiness of the one who administers it. That misunderstands the nature of a sacrament. Sacraments, he suggested, are 'visible words'.[10] Words are a type of sign, pointing us to a reality. Scripture itself, as the word of God, is a sign, pointing us to God. Sacraments are signs of the gift of grace. When we follow the sign by believing it, we receive the reality of the grace it points to. The Donatist's mistake, Augustine argued, was to confuse the sign with the reality.

---

9. Brown, *Augustine of Hippo*, p. 228.
10. *On Christian Doctrine* 2.3.

Within a few years Donatism was officially anathematized, and began to be suppressed. Initially, Augustine was opposed to all compulsion in matters of faith. But when he saw how Donatists crumbled under coercion and rejoined the Catholic church, he revised his position and began writing in defence of the use of force in the subdual of heresy. It was certainly ironic that 'the only Father of the Church to write at length on persecution had himself been a member of a persecuted sect',[11] but then himself began to see force as an instance of much-needed discipline, for 'the LORD disciplines those he loves' (Prov. 3:12).

Augustine's reputation has been severely damaged by the use of his arguments in subsequent church history to sanction all manner of violence against those deemed heretical. However, when, for example, those defending the persecution of the Huguenots in seventeenth-century France appealed to Augustine, they were highly selective in their reading. Augustine's principle commended the loving discipline of a father, and that implied restraint as much as coercion. Torture and capital punishment never applied in his vision.

The City of God

On 24 August 410 Alaric's Visigoths sacked the city of Rome, the symbolic heart of the empire. Culturally, it was a shattering event that left the Romans in a deep state of shock. 'If Rome be lost, where shall we look for help?' wrote Jerome.[12] Suddenly, the province of North Africa was flooded with refugees from Rome, and the people of Hippo were treated to the sight of rich and famous pagan aristocrats walking their streets. Those pagans were vocal in announcing the fact that Rome, which had stood unbreached for 800 years, had fallen swiftly after the official adoption of Christianity. The protection of the old gods had been cast aside, and this, they suggested, was the result. It was a powerful apologetic for a return to classical paganism.

---

11. Brown, *Augustine of Hippo*, p. 242.
12. Letter 123.

In this context Augustine set out his massive counter-apologetic, *The City of God*. The work, however, was far more than a mere reaction or tract for the times. Rather, Augustine used the events of 410 as a platform for a definitive theology of history and politics. His essential point is that the refugees from Rome, living in Africa but hankering to return to the great city, had the right idea. Their mistake was to long for the wrong city: instead, they should long for the heavenly Jerusalem, the City of God. The Christians, he explains, are the ones who understand this, as, like refugees in this world, they ever long for their true heavenly home. It is that heavenly vision that can put the fate of earthly empires like Rome into the correct perspective.

He begins the argument by mercilessly demolishing the theory that the pagan gods had ever offered Rome or their worshippers any protection ('Books' 1–7). He then proceeds to a much more sympathetic discussion of the merits and demerits of Platonism ('Books' 8–10). Then, demolition done, the second half of the work ('Books' 11–22) presents his positive argument for the truth of Christianity. This is done through a chronological overview of all history as described in the Bible, from creation to heaven and hell. Human history, he demonstrates, has from the beginning been a conflict between the City of Man, which is built on love of self, and the City of God, which is built on love of God. This account of the human story was a vital part of the apologetic for Augustine. Roman society had a tendency to venerate antiquity and to be suspicious of novelty, making Christianity unattractive for having appeared so late on the scene. Augustine argued that this was simply not the case: ever since the time of Adam, the City of God had been populated by those who loved God and were saved by the grace of Christ.

The City of God was much more than an apologetic, though. Augustine also wrote it in order to challenge the increasing nominalism of the day. The Christianity he articulated was about political allegiance to the City of God, not political allegiance to the new Christian status quo. And, as relevant today as ever, he wrote to prevent what he called the 'insanity' of confusing any earthly institution with the City of God.

Against the Pelagians

Among the tide of refugees from Rome swept up on the North
African coast at Hippo was an austere but brilliant British
monk called Pelagius. For a number of years he had taught in
Rome, moving in the most exalted circles (circles that included
the pope himself), and leading a protest against the rise of
nominal Christianity and the decline of Christian morality. He did
not remain long in Hippo, but Augustine's ongoing dispute with
him and his followers would be the one for which the bishop
of Hippo would justly be best known. In Pelagius, Augustine
found that he was no longer dealing with the second-rate minds
of local sectarians: here was a theological opponent of an entirely
different calibre.

Pelagius' beliefs were essentially simple. He believed that each
person has the responsibility and the potential to be morally
perfect. Such is God's command, and God would not command
the impossible. Any suggestion that we are in fact incapable of
such perfection he believed would amount to a gross toleration
of sin.

From this basic position sprang a small catalogue of ideas. First,
he argued that death is a simple biological necessity, not a punishment for sin (for all die, even though some, he believed, had
managed to live without sin). Secondly, he maintained that there is
no such thing as inherited guilt. When Adam sinned, he alone was
punished for his sin. In his commentary on Romans 5, Pelagius
took Paul to mean that it is those who copy Adam in his sin who
are punished as he was, not that all Adam's posterity are cursed
and found guilty through being in Adam. For Pelagius believed
we are born innocent, in the same state as Adam before the Fall.
If, then, damnation comes through copying Adam, and not by
inheriting it from him at birth, salvation likewise comes through
copying Christ, and not by receiving it freely from him in a new
birth. That is why God gave the Law, so that through obeying it we
can achieve the perfection God demands and bring back paradise
on earth.

When the theologies of Pelagius and Augustine are compared,
Pelagius is popularly touted as the more appealing of the two

because of his optimism in humanity and his defence of individual human freedom. Promoting a self-help save-the-planet theology, it is no wonder Pelagius receives the better press. Yet in fact it was Pelagius' theology that was the stern and chilling one. He placed a crushing weight of responsibility on the individual: we each must ensure our own, personal perfection.

Ironically, it was an early work by Augustine, *On the Freedom of the Will*, written against Manichaean determinism, that Pelagius frequently turned to for support. However, by the time Pelagius arrived in Hippo, Augustine was settled in his opposition to Pelagius' theology. Perhaps his experience with Donatism had helped, for Augustine detected a similarity between the two heresies: both believed they could manufacture a perfect church. However Augustine did not believe the two to be equal threats: Pelagianism, by replacing God's grace with human effort, effectively preached a message more pagan/Stoic than Christian.

Strangely, Augustine's anti-Pelagian writings are neglected gems. Because of its recurrent importance in church history, the Augustine–Pelagius debate is normally read rather abstractly and timelessly, or with the sixteenth-century Reformers speaking in Augustine's place. The sad result is that the subtlety of the debate and the beauty of Augustine's response is often missed, leaving it all looking rather sterile and formulaic. Yet Augustine's arguments are quite brilliant, and just as much as the question of truth, it is Augustine's grasp of the warmth and attraction of the gospel as against the cold severity of Pelagius' theology that strikes the reader of the anti-Pelagian writings.

Augustine's first main objection to Pelagius was that he was impossibly individualistic. For Pelagius, each person is essentially an island, a self-defining individual whose own efforts determine his or her own destiny. Augustine clearly saw the injustice and cruelty of this, particularly for the handicapped: if defects are not the result of Adam's sin, but sin is interpreted wholly individually, are the handicapped to be blamed for their own disabilities?

His response was that humankind is not a vast throng of separate individuals, but is instead made up of just two persons: *Adam* and *Christ*. Each of us is merely a member of one of their bodies, dependent for our fate not on ourselves, but on the fate of the head of the body of which we are part. Born from and in Adam, we naturally share both his guilt and nature, irrespective of our own acts: 'we all were in that one man when we all were that one man'.[13] Salvation is to be reborn from and in Christ, to be a part of his Body and so share his righteousness.

Augustine's other main objection was that Pelagius did not understand love as the heart of the gospel. This comes out most clearly in what is probably the most important of the anti-Pelagian writings, *On the Spirit and the Letter*. Pelagius believed that living according to the letter of the Law is all that is required for godliness and salvation. Augustine replied that salvation is given to those who love God, which is not at all the same thing. The letter of the Law cannot stimulate love, and thus it can only deliver damnation (2 Cor. 3:6). Instead of the Law, we need the Spirit to give us the capacity to love.

Augustine defined true love as 'the enjoyment of God for His own sake'.[14] God, he held, is an 'insatiable satisfaction',[15] 'sweeter than all pleasure',[16] and thus we love him, desiring to be rewarded with him, and not something else (he had already demonstrated in the *Confessions* the error of trying to enjoy something in the place of God). Augustine thus saw that Pelagius did not love God at all, but only himself: he was using God in order to escape hell and earn heaven for himself (and 'a man who is afraid of sinning because of Hell-fire, is afraid, not of sinning, but of burning'[17]). It is this that provides the all-pervading winsome tenor of Augustine's theology: that he is a theologian of love. From his student days in Carthage, when he fell in love with the idea of

---

13. *City of God* 13.14.
14. *On Christian Doctrine* 3.10.16. The first book of *On Christian Doctrine* is dedicated to the distinction between 'using' and 'enjoying': we 'use' some things (such as a knife and fork) in order to 'enjoy' other things (the roast beef); enjoyment is delighting in something for its own sake. Ultimately, the only object of true enjoyment is God.
15. Sermon 362.28.
16. *Confessions* 9.1.
17. Letter 145.4.

being in love, through all his addiction to sex, his love of friends and, of course, his love of wisdom, it is love that thrilled his heart and shaped his thinking.[18]

One important caveat regarding Augustine's theology of love: for all its strength as a piece of theology, the exegesis in *On the Spirit and the Letter* is not always accurate. 'Justification' he takes to mean 'being made righteous' – it is the pouring or infusing of the love of God into our hearts (Rom. 5:5); it is not an external declaration of our righteous status, independent of the state of our hearts. For Augustine, to be justified is to be made loving, which happens by faith. By noting this feature at the heart of his anti-Pelagian writings, it can be seen how Augustine sowed the seeds for both the Roman Catholic and Protestant theologies of the sixteenth century.

What, next, of Augustine and Pelagius on human free will? Both believed in free will, though by it each meant a very different thing. Pelagius believed that we are able to choose what or whom to love. In contrast, Augustine believed that our will is governed by what we love. Our freedom is that our wills cannot be forced externally. Thus, without the Spirit, we freely choose to love sin, yet we cannot choose otherwise. It takes the Spirit to work internally in us to give us a new object worthy of love and so free our wills to love God.

Augustine's debate with Pelagianism was to occupy much of the last twenty years of his life, and during this time his own stance changed. When writing *On the Spirit and the Letter* (from 412), he believed, for example, that faith is our work. It is not clearly seen as a gift of God. In the last three years of his life he would retract

---

18. Anders Nygren famously attacked Augustine's theology of love in his *Agape and Eros* (London: SPCK, 1938), arguing that it is more Platonist than Christian. Nygren maintained that only the love that gives (*agapē*) is truly Christian; the love that desires (*eros*) is actually sinful. John Burnaby responded with a magisterial defence of Augustine, arguing that Augustine had understood the true nature of Christian love better, that it is a desiring love as well as a giving love (*Amor Dei: A Study in the Religion of St. Augustine* [London: Hodder & Stoughton, 1938]).

this to argue that our initial faith is indeed a gift.[19] This in turn led him to argue that God must choose to give the gift of faith to some and not others. This final move would be yet another major legacy he would leave to the church in the West, for nobody before him had handled election in the way he had with such unique, intricate articulation.

Finally, and most importantly, Augustine's theology officially triumphed over that of Pelagius (though, of course, Pelagius' ghost has never been completely exorcized from the church). At first Augustine had been seen as an isolated provincial quibbling with a cosmopolitan theologian who commanded widespread support. Yet a year after the bishop's death, in 431, Pelagianism was formally condemned at the Council of Ephesus.

Going on with Augustine

Augustine provides a prime example of what it is like to read a great theologian from the past: both grand and alien, both profoundly right and profoundly wrong (often in the same sentence), he challenges in every way. His great temporal distance from us dares our comfortable and well-worn formulas. Even the mistakes we recognize as characteristic of his age force us to ask what mistakes are characteristic of ours.

Where should the beginner go from here? Undoubtedly to the man himself: the secondary literature on Augustine is bewilderingly immense, and generally the man himself is considerably easier to read than his commentators. The first port of call should definitely be the *Confessions*; after that, *The City of God*, *On Christian Doctrine* and his own small 'systematic theology', the *Enchiridion*, are all near 'musts' for the thinking Christian. *Augustine: Later Works*, Library of Christian Classics (London: SCM, 1955), also contains a collection of highly readable shorter works (*On the Spirit and the Letter*, *On the*

---

19. *On Grace and Free Will* 33.18; *Retractions* 1.23; cf. J. Burnaby, Introduction to *On the Spirit and the Letter*, in *Augustine: Later Works*, Library of Christian Classics [London: SCM, 1955], pp. 189–192.

Trinity and *Homilies on the Epistle of John*), accompanied by excellent explanatory notes. The *Homilies on the Epistle of John* are particularly stirring, bite-sized sermons on his theology of love. After that, the best introduction to Augustine is his definitive biography, which clearly puts his theology in context: Peter Brown's *Augustine of Hippo* (London: Faber & Faber, 1967). A wonderful read.

All in all, Augustine is worth reading, not only because he has been massively influential on subsequent Christian thought, but because he still can be. 'Take and read'!

Augustine timeline

303–5	Emperor Diocletian's 'Great Persecution' of Christianity
312	Conversion of the emperor Constantine to Christianity
354	Born in Thagaste (Souk Ahras in modern Algeria)
371	Studies in Carthage (modern Tunis, Tunisia)
372	Takes a concubine who soon bears him a son, Adeodatus; becomes a Manichee
373	Reads Cicero's exhortation to seek wisdom (*Hortensius*)
376	His unnamed Manichee friend converts to Christianity and dies
383	Moves to teach rhetoric in Rome
384	Moves to Milan, where he meets Bishop Ambrose
386	Converts to Christianity
387	Augustine's Christian mother, Monica, dies
388	Returns to Thagaste to lead a life of philosophical contemplation
391	Forcibly ordained
395	Appointed bishop of Hippo Regius (Annaba in modern Algeria)
397	Starts writing *Confessions*
399	Starts writing *On the Trinity*
410	Alaric's Goths sack Rome
413	Starts writing *City of God*
430	Dies in Hippo

5. FAITH SEEKING UNDERSTANDING

Anselm

When Augustine laying dying in Hippo in 430, Vandal hordes surrounded the city. And for the next few hundred years such Germanic tribes kept Europe so unstable and illiterate that serious theological study was well nigh impossible. Thus no truly great theological mind emerged again until the eleventh century, in Anselm.

Anselm's life

Anselm was born in 1033 in the shadow of the Matterhorn, in the northern Italian town of Aosta. Little is known of his youth, but his mother seems to have been the one who held the home together, for Anselm and his father, Gundulf, cordially disliked each other. When she died, it did not take long for things to fall apart, and, aged twenty-three, Anselm walked out. For three years he wandered Burgundy and France, perhaps looking for a life, perhaps sampling it in ways not possible back at home.

In 1059 he arrived at the Benedictine abbey of Bec in Normandy. It was not that he was interested in becoming a monk; it was that the monastery had an external school run by Lanfranc, the abbey's prior, and Lanfranc's scholarly reputation was magnetic. However, it did not take long for the appeals of the monastery to take hold, and within a year Anselm entered the abbey as a novice monk.

The all-embracing life of the cloister was perfectly suited to Anselm, who was soon known for his severe personal austerity, seriousness and precision. The lack of food and sleep also induced hallucinatory experiences that were to be part and parcel of his mystical bent. When he had arrived at Bec, Anselm had had minimal education, but his intense intellectual brilliance soon won him a name as an inspirational teacher, as exacting in his thought as he was in his lifestyle.

Anselm was no cold fish, though. Again and again contemporaries spoke of his exuberance in conversation and his winning charm. Yet his personal warmth was more than temperamental: it was an expression of his novel understanding of friendship. In the eleventh century, friendship was viewed in quite businesslike terms, as an alliance entered into to achieve some common purpose; Anselm saw friendship as a union of souls, and so a foretaste of the harmony of heaven.

As such he would write to fellow monks describing the passionate embraces and kisses they had and would share. And he would do so in language so physical it makes for embarrassing reading: 'my arms stretch out to your embraces; my lips long for your kisses'. Unsurprisingly, many have therefore wondered if Anselm was homosexual. That is quite possible, but it does not explain the rationale for the kissing and embracing. Anselm wrote of such things in open letters so that others might learn from the practice, so it is clear that Anselm was not describing forbidden yearnings and acts; moreover, he could write them to people he had never met. It was that he viewed physical embraces as the external signs of the union of souls found in friendship.

The world that Anselm had left outside the monastery was one of feudalism and strict social hierarchy, but the spiritual world he had entered was, if anything, just as tiered. At the top of the chain of being was, of course, God; just below God sat Mary, devotion to whom was gathering strength (something Anselm, who was prepared to refer to Mary as 'reconciler of the world', was instrumental in assisting); below her were the other saints, who were also used as intermediaries; they, along with the angels, existed above humans on earth, who existed above animals, plants and, finally, the inanimate.

It was also a world of deliberate, cultivated introspection as monks worked to fill themselves with the horror of self and the knowledge of God. But with no sense of spiritual security underlying the introspection, it was a theological system full of dread. The sense of sheer terror at the thought of committing any sin can be seen when, one day, Anselm ate pickled eel before remembering that eating raw flesh was against the Mosaic Law. Seeing his deep distress, his friend Eadmer consoled him, saying 'The salt has removed the rawness of the flesh,' to which Anselm responded, 'You have saved me from being tortured by the memory of sin.'[1] Almost the only hope of salvation was through the committed monastic life, and so Anselm wished that everyone would become a monk or a nun. Few would be saved, and most of those, he was sure, would be monks or nuns. Even then, the monks and nuns had to be resolute in their abandonment of the world. As he wrote to one nun:

> Let all your conversation be in the cloister, not in the world. This world is nothing to you, nothing but dung, if you wish to be a nun and spouse of God . . . Do not visit your relatives, they do not need your advice, nor you theirs. Your way of life is cut off from theirs. Let all your desire be for God.[2]

After Anselm had spent just three years in the monastery, Lanfranc moved on (ultimately to become archbishop of Canterbury), and, despite Anselm's inexperience, his aptitude for the life and his intellectual gifts meant he was elected to succeed Lanfranc

---

1. Eadmer, *The Life of St Anselm: Archbishop of Canterbury*, ed. and tr. R. W. Southern (London: T. Nelson & Sons, 1962), vol. 2, p. xiii.

2. R. W. Southern, *Saint Anselm: A Portrait in a Landscape* (Cambridge: Cambridge University Press, 1990), p. 165.

as prior. Thus the monastery's reputation grew, with Anselm (in addition to his teaching and official duties) writing such key works as his *Monologion* and *Proslogion*, and taking up his role as counsellor-by-letter to the rulers of Europe. It was not just Anselm's abilities that won him the influence and renown he soon had: during this time, William, Duke of Normandy, invaded England, giving all those in Normandy an influence far beyond what they had previously enjoyed.

His conscientiousness meant that, fifteen years after being appointed prior, when the abbot died, Anselm was elected to succeed him and so be father to the whole monastery. He could hardly have been less pleased: upon his election, he threw himself prostrate on the floor, crying to be freed from the burdens of that office. For, where Lanfranc had been an exceptionally gifted administrator and street-smart political operative, Anselm was an abysmal administrator with no understanding of finance and no political savvy. Not that Anselm himself saw any of that as a deficiency: he did not want to be wise in the ways of the world, for such things were distractions from the monastic life and he genuinely longed to be rid of them. And his fears were confirmed: after his phase of impressive theological productivity as prior, the next fifteen years saw very little theological output as administrative duties used up his time.

Worse was to come as, when visiting England in 1093, King William II, the ruthless and fiery son of the Conqueror, compelled Anselm to succeed his old master, Lanfranc, as archbishop of Canterbury. This would mean even more distractions than dealing with a few monks. Again Anselm was in tears at the prospect, so distraught that he gave himself a nosebleed as he protested to the king his inability. The king tried to force the archbishop's pastoral staff into Anselm's clenched fist, something that required the help of a number of bishops who were with him. Anselm was then lifted up, carried into the church and acclaimed archbishop.

Once again his fears became reality as he found dealing with a foreign country and a high-handed king extremely taxing. He tried to write his next major work, *Cur Deus Homo*, but hardly had any time to do so, making it a project that would drag on for years. What made things especially difficult was the king's insistence on exercising control over the church, meaning that Anselm was unable without the king's permission to reform the church as he wished to.

After a while he decided to seek the advice of the pope in Rome. The king refused to let him go, but eventually Anselm just went, to which the king responded by barring him from re-entry to the country. It was with a glimmer of hope, then, that Anselm arrived in Rome in 1098 and asked the pope to release him from the burden of his office. The pope flatly refused, instead ordering him to go to the Council of Bari in southern Italy where representatives of the Greek and Latin churches were to meet in an attempt to heal the great schism of East and West that had opened up a few decades earlier. There Anselm was instructed to defend the West's view that the Spirit eternally proceeds from the Son as well the Father. In preparation, Anselm spent a happy summer in the little hill village of Liberi above Capua, where he also completed *Cur Deus Homo* (and miraculously opened a well for the village). All in all, with time spent in Capua, Bari and Rome, it was a blissful exile from the stresses and duties of Canterbury.

Then, in 1100, King William was shot while hunting and his younger brother, now Henry I, invited Anselm to return. With a heavy tread, the archbishop made his way back to a situation that would be every bit as strained as it had been under William II. Soon Anselm was after the pope's advice again (and there was a new pope now, whom Anselm hoped might be more amenable to letting him off the hook), and history repeated itself, with Anselm leaving and King Henry refusing to allow him to return. This time, Anselm tried opening proceedings to get Henry excommunicated, but the pope went over his head to resolve the situation very awkwardly, forcing Anselm to make his way back to Canterbury.

As archbishop, Anselm did manage to write a number of other more minor works as well as *Cur Deus Homo*, though his years were increasingly distracted and troubled. His health declined, forcing him to be carried around in a litter for his last years, and then, on 21 April 1109, he died peacefully at Canterbury, surrounded by his monks.

Anselm's thought

In Anselm's day it had long been traditional for theology to be done meditatively in the monasteries; yet a phenomenon was on the rise: the new secular schools of theology, where theology would be learnt through debate. It was these schools (*schola*) that would host the scholastic style of doing theology (something we will meet properly in the next chapter).

Anselm has sometimes been called the father of scholasticism. Yet Anselm was a monk. And, while later material of his, such as *Cur Deus Homo*, is written in a dialogue form that in some faint ways can resemble scholastic debate, his whole tone and approach to theology is that of the monastery, not the schools. He never sought (as the greatest scholastic theologian, Thomas Aquinas, would) to lay out the whole sweep of his thought; instead, Anselm wrote his theology a piece at a time as monks asked him to respond to their questions. And when he wrote it, it was clearly designed to be read slowly and meditatively. This is something lost in English translations, for the elegance of Anselm's Latin, with its rhymes and rhythms, simply does not translate. But the beauty of Anselm's style was important and deliberate. Anselm believed that only beautiful words are fitting to describe God, whom he saw as Beauty itself, and he wrote his theology as an experimental exercise in the contemplation and enjoyment of that Beauty. It was the monastic style, and Anselm excelled at it.

Anselm also had his own intellectual agendum, a project he called 'faith seeking understanding', which would characterize all his theology. By it he meant that he would use unaided reason to investigate and prove the truths of the Christian faith, and would do this without ever having to fall back onto what the Bible, the church or any Christian theologian had said. God, he held, is Reason itself, and therefore Christian doctrines must be rational; furthermore, God created humans rational, and therefore those doctrines must be explicable and defensible by reason – even reason alone. Anselm thus believed that by pure reason he could prove God's existence, attributes and triune being as well as the fact that God had to send a God-man to die voluntarily in our place so that we might be saved.

Yet how, one might wonder, is this *faith* seeking understanding? By 'faith' Anselm did not mean a basic assent to the truth of Christianity, but an active love for God. It is this love of God that seeks to know God. *That* is faith seeking understanding. Moreover, this love for God is what enables us to reason purely, Anselm maintained, for without love for God we become irrational, foolish and blind.

That said, while Anselm himself found his love of God compelling him to seek a greater knowledge of God, he did not think that 'faith seeking understanding' meant that his theology was only for those who already had faith. It is not as if he saw faith as the universal prerequisite for understanding God (a belief some later scholars have mistakenly credited him with). Rather, he believed that by his reason alone he could persuade unbelievers of the truths of the Trinity, the incarnation and so on.

What exactly 'faith seeking understanding' looked like we can now see as we turn to look at the *Monologion*, the *Proslogion* and, finally, *Cur Deus Homo*.

Monologion

During his time as prior of Bec, some of the monks apparently asked Anselm to write on 'how one ought to meditate on the divine essence'. The result was the *Monologion* (Soliloquy), or, as it was originally titled, 'A Pattern for Meditation on *the Reason* of Faith' (my emphasis). One thing the monks had stipulated for this meditation was that 'absolutely nothing in it would be established by the authority of Scripture'; all would be worked out by reason alone.[3] Thus Anselm opens the *Monologion* with the following:

> If anyone does not know, either because he has not heard or because he does not believe, that there is one nature, supreme among all existing things, who alone is self-sufficient in his eternal happiness, who through his omnipotent goodness grants and brings it about that all other things exist or have any sort of well-being, and a great many other things that

---

3. *Monologion*, Prologue. All quotations of Anselm taken from Thomas Williams's translation, *Anselm: Basic Writings* (Indianapolis: Hackett, 2007).

we must believe about God or his creation, I think he could at least convince himself of most of these things by reason alone, if he is even moderately intelligent.[4]

So his aim is to persuade 'anyone [who] does not know, either because he has not heard or because he does not believe'. Or, as he put it later, he was 'adopting the role of someone who, by reasoning silently within himself, investigates things he does not know'.[5]

He starts the investigation by arguing that there must be a supremely good being, the source of all good. Being supremely good, this being must be supremely great, and being supremely great, this being 'must therefore be living, wise, powerful and all-powerful, true, just, happy, eternal, and whatever similarly it is absolutely better to be than not to be'.[6]

Having established this, Anselm finds it remarkably easy to go on to specify what this supremely great being must be like. First, it is obvious that this being cannot have been brought into being by any other being, or else that other being would be greater still, which would contradict the supreme being's supreme being. This being, then, must exist because of itself, and all other things must exist because of it. Therefore it must have created all other things out of nothing.

But as well as never having been brought into existence, this being cannot cease to exist (for 'he who assuredly is the supreme good will not perish voluntarily. But if, on the other hand, he is going to perish unwillingly, then he is not supremely powerful'[7]). This being must be omnipresent, since nothing can have any independence from him. He must exist beyond time, for 'he exists as a whole all at once in all places and times'.[8] Being supreme, it is impossible that he could ever be acted upon passively; he must, therefore, be impassible. Also, being perfect,

4. *Monologion* 1.

5. *Proslogion*, Prologue.

6. *Monologion* 15.

7. Ibid. 18.

8. Ibid. 21.

there is nothing greater for the supreme being to become (and he would never become anything less than supreme); therefore he must be immutable.

From this quite standard exploration of the divine attributes or characteristics, Anselm then moves on to an entrancing study of the Trinity as Augustine understood it (the difference being that Anselm is going to prove all by reason). The first move is made off the back of the logical conclusion that the supreme being must be the creator of all things. That is, in order to be the Creator, the supreme being must first consider or say within himself what he is going to create. But this consideration or utterance in the supreme being's mind cannot itself be a creature. It is itself the supreme being. More, since this utterance is itself the supreme being, it cannot consist of many words, for the supreme being must be a 'simple' being. (The 'simplicity' of God is important throughout Anselm's thought. It entails that God does not *have* multiple 'parts' like justice, life, wisdom etc., else he would depend on those things. Rather, he *is* those things. And since he does not have such 'parts' on which he must depend, God is a simple being as opposed to a composite being. In this case this means that God cannot 'have' words; he *is* Word.)

So far, Anselm realizes, what has been said about this utterance or Word of God could make it sound as if the Word exists only as God's preparation for creation. It is how God considers what he going to create, meaning that there would be no Word if creation did not exist. However, Anselm says, God is not ignorant (that would be an imperfection); thus he must know himself; thus he must consider or utter himself in his mind. Thus there must be a Word of God whether or not God decides to create. And because God is simple, it cannot be that God has one Word by which he utters himself, and another Word by which he utters creation. There must be one Word by which he does both.

Next, Anselm argues, because the Word of God cannot be a created being *made* by God, he must be *born* of God: not a creature, but God's own offspring and likeness. If then God has an offspring, which is more fitting: to speak of God as Father or as Mother? Surely, Anselm says, 'since the paternal cause always in some way precedes the maternal', it is more appropriate to speak of God as Father, for God is the very first, most primary being.[9] As for the Word as offspring: is it more fitting to speak of the Word as God's Son or God's Daughter? Since the Word is the very likeness of the Father, surely the Word should be called the Son, for no offspring is more like a father than a son, reasons Anselm.

How else might we speak of the Father and the Son? It is also reasonable and fitting, Anselm suggests, to call the Father 'memory', for as he knows himself he must remember himself. But how does he remember himself? By his contemplation of himself. That is, in his Word who can also then be described as the Father's 'Wisdom'. Then, out of God's self-understanding and remembrance must proceed his love for himself. Again, like the Word, this love cannot be a created thing; it must be the supreme being itself. But neither can it be construed as another Son, for it is the mutual love of the Father for the Son, breathed out by both. And how should we best refer to this love? Being 'breathed out' (*spiratur*) by both the Father and the Son, he must most fittingly be called the Spirit (*Spiritus*).

There are many questions one might ask of this whole exercise. Why, for instance, are God's Word and God's Love personalized and given such prominence, and not his justice, power, truth or goodness? Yet perhaps the answer to any such question is rather obvious: all has been deduced by reason, and the God that reason has deduced is the God of the Western, Latin church (where the Spirit proceeds from both the Father and the Son), or more specifically, the God described by Augustine (whose triune being can be compared to a person's memory, understanding and love). No surprise there.

Proslogion
Once the *Monologion* was published, Anselm began to have misgivings about it. It was not that he thought there was anything wrong with it; it just struck him as unnecessarily complex. It was,

---

9. Ibid. 42.

as he put it, 'a chaining together of many arguments'; and so he began to search for

> a single argument that needed nothing but itself alone for proof, that would by itself be enough to show that God really exists; that he is the supreme good, who depends on nothing else, but on whom all things depend for their being and for their well-being; and whatever we believe about the divine nature.[10]

It was a tall order. For this single, master argument that Anselm was after would need to prove not only the existence of God, but '*whatever* we believe about the divine nature'. Nevertheless, the search for this super-argument became an obsession with him. Anselm found himself unable to eat, sleep or concentrate in chapel. He began to conclude that the whole idea must be a temptation from the devil. Yet he found he could not let the idea go. Then, suddenly, during a middle-of-the-night service, it came to him.

Originally, he wrote the argument down under the title 'Faith seeking understanding' – it was, after all, the crown of that whole project of his – but later renamed it the *Proslogion* (Address). Where the *Monologion* took the form of a soliloquy, the *Proslogion* is an address to God. Yet the purpose of both is the same. That is, that a complete doctrine of God 'could be proved by necessary reasons, independently of the authority of Scripture'.[11] In the *Monologion* this had been done by adopting the role of an unbeliever working out the truth by reason. In the *Proslogion* it is done by a believer proving the irrationality of the fool who says in his heart, 'There is no God.'

Anselm's argument in the *Proslogion* was built on a formula of the Roman Stoic philosopher Seneca, who had described God as being 'that than which nothing greater can be thought'.[12] With

---

10. *Proslogion*, Prologue.

11. *On the Incarnation of the Word* 6.

12. Immanuel Kant referred to Anselm's argument as the 'ontological argument' (without, it seems, ever having read the *Proslogion*), and that is

this as his starting point and most basic definition of God, Anselm believed he could convince the atheist fool of his irrationality. The argument goes as follows: the fool who denies God's existence will be able to understand that basic definition of God as 'that than which nothing greater can be thought'. It is a simple concept, that God is a being so great it is simply impossible to think of a greater being. All the atheist need do at this stage is understand that definition of God.

So far, then, 'that than which nothing greater can be thought' can be seen to exist in the understanding of the atheist. However, if 'that than which nothing greater can be thought' existed *only* in his understanding, then it would be quite possible to think of a greater being, that is, a being who existed not only in the understanding but also in reality. But if it is at all possible to think of any greater being, then the atheist cannot have 'that than which nothing greater can be thought' in his understanding. And so, if he does really have 'that than which nothing greater can be thought' in his understanding, then that being must also exist in reality. For it is greater to exist in reality than merely in the understanding.

Furthermore, if we were ever able to think of 'that than which nothing greater can be thought' not existing, then, again, it would be possible to think of a greater being, a being so great that 'it cannot even be thought not to exist'.[13] In other words, 'that than which nothing greater can be thought' must be a being who could not fail to exist. Thus when the fool had said in his heart 'There is no God,' he had imagined a contradiction, that this being that cannot not exist does not exist. Thus he shows that he is stupid and a fool.

It is Anselm's argument for the existence of God (chs. 2–4 of the *Proslogion*) that has received the most attention. However, Anselm's goal in the *Proslogion* had been to prove not only the existence of God, but 'whatever we believe about the divine

---

how it is usually referred to. However, since there are today a number of variations of the ontological argument, I will speak simply of 'Anselm's argument', as his contemporaries did.

13. *Proslogion* 3.

nature'. The rest of the *Proslogion* (chs. 5–26) is therefore dedicated to establishing what we can know about God, given that God is 'that than which nothing greater can be thought'.

Anselm shows that the definition 'that than which nothing greater can be thought' has a remarkable ability to generate descriptions (or prescriptions) of what God must be like. This is for a very simple reason: if God is 'that than which nothing greater can be thought', then God must be 'whatever it is better to be than not to be'.[14] Thus, for example, God must be omnipotent, otherwise we would be able to think of a being that is greater than he. In the same way, God must be just, truthful, happy, impassible, unchanging, non-bodily and so on.

Of course, in order to establish that God is all these things, Anselm has to rely on what he believed were universally self-evident standards of what it is better or greater to be than not to be. And some of those standards seem to have troubling implications: if, for example, it is absolutely better to be non-physical and non-bodily than physical and bodily, why were we created as physical, bodily beings, and why is the Christian hope a bodily one?

The other difficulty with the attributes created by the definition of God as 'that than which nothing greater can be thought' is that they are often apparently self-contradictory. For example, it has been shown that God must be both omnipotent and just. But if God is just, then he cannot be unjust or lie, and that seems to be a limitation on his power. Anselm thus spends the bulk of the rest of the work arguing that such contradictions are not real but only apparent. To the question of whether God's inability to lie or be unjust is a limitation on his power, for example, Anselm poses the counter-question 'Or is the ability to do these things not power but weakness?'[15] Another problem is how God could be both merciful and impassible, 'For if you are impassible, you do not feel compassion.'[16] Anselm's answer is that God does not *feel* merciful even though we do receive mercy from him. And we receive mercy

---

14. Ibid. 5.
15. Ibid. 7.
16. Ibid. 8.

from him because he is just, and his justice requires that he must demonstrate his goodness in sparing some of the wicked (as well as demonstrating his justice by punishing others who are wicked).

Gaunilo's 'Reply on Behalf of the Fool'

Anselm's argument in the *Proslogion* works on most readers like a confusing optical illusion that flicks between two quite different images. The mind cannot decide if Anselm is playing word games or plumbing the depths of profundity. It is a question that keeps theologians and philosophers in work to this day.

One early critic who thought that Anselm was trapped in an unreal web of words was an otherwise unknown monk called Gaunilo, who wrote 'Reply on Behalf of the Fool', arguing that Anselm had proven nothing to the fool. In it Gaunilo satirized Anselm's argument by setting out to prove the existence of an island 'than which no greater can be thought': 'this island', he wrote, 'exists in your understanding, and since it is more excellent to exist not merely in the understanding, but also in reality, this island must also exist in reality'.[17] In other words, it is absurd to think that we can extrapolate from what we imagine in our minds to what exists in reality, for we are perfectly capable of imagining non-existent things in our minds.

Anselm was so unshaken by this answer that he wrote a casual rejoinder to Gaunilo, and stipulated that the exchange be published as an appendix to the *Proslogion*. Clearly, Anselm thought, Gaunilo's reply only showed the resilience of his original argument. It is hard to see quite where Anselm felt Gaunilo had gone wrong, but it seems to be that he thought there was a crucial difference between his being 'than which no greater can be thought' and Gaunilo's island 'than which no greater can be thought'. And that is that where an island by its very nature could fail to exist, 'that than which nothing greater can be thought' cannot not exist, for then we would be able to think of a greater being, and 'that than which nothing greater can be thought' would no longer be 'that than which nothing greater can be thought'.

---

17. Gaunilo's 'Reply on Behalf of the Fool' 6.

Whether or not Anselm was successful in answering Gaunilo, the fact is that, within a century or so, few found his argument to be persuasive any more. Perhaps that is because the whole edifice is built upon a concealed Platonic presupposition, and Plato's time as the most influential philosopher was almost over. The presupposition was that there are degrees of being, and that it is greater to have 'more' being than less. To Anselm that was self-evident, but today most people do not share that presupposition. To us, pigs do not exist 'more' than flying pigs just because flying pigs exist only in our minds. To us, flying pigs simply do not exist. And the argument would be even less compelling in a Buddhist culture where being is something that it is better to have less of.

The presuppositions of anyone using the argument clearly must affect its conclusions. How do we know what it is better or greater to be than not to be? Certainly, Anselm's idea of greatness is not everyone's. For him it was unquestionably greater to be impassible than passible, but few philosophers today would agree. But perhaps it is the very availability of the argument to be used by all that has ensured its enduring appeal. For Anselm's argument can be used alongside almost any presuppositions to prove the existence of any supreme being, whether that be the Christian God, Allah, Brahman or the Great God Om.

Cur Deus Homo

When Anselm became archbishop of Canterbury, there remained one key area of the Christian faith he had not yet 'proved': the incarnation. And the more Anselm's horizons had widened beyond the monastery at Bec, the more he saw the necessity of attending to it. Judaism, with its denial of the incarnation, was perceived to be on the rise. Certainly, there was an increasingly large and vocal Jewish community in England, and its rabbis were putting forward such intelligent arguments against the possibility of an incarnation that Christendom, having undergone centuries of cultural stagnation, felt itself to be on the intellectual back foot. There were a number of conversions to Judaism. Even one well-known bishop converted. And then, in 1095, the pope called for the first crusade. It was a time when Christendom wanted to be confident about what distinguished its faith from Islam and Judaism.

Thus Anselm began work on his apologia for the incarnation, *Cur Deus Homo* (Why God [Became] a Man). Its aim, he said, would be

> to prove by necessary reasons – leaving Christ out of the picture, as if nothing concerning him had ever taken place – that it is impossible for any human being to be saved apart from Christ . . . and that it was necessary that the purpose for which human beings were made should in fact be achieved, but only through the agency of a God-man, and that it was necessary that everything we believe about Christ should take place.[18]

Anselm would rationally defend the incarnation so that, even if we had never heard of Christ or did not believe in him, reason alone would prove that God had to become incarnate and die for us. And not only would he prove its rational necessity; he would display the beauty of God's purpose in the incarnation to answer the charge that the very thought of God becoming incarnate is an insult to the divine dignity.

The work is framed as a dialogue between Anselm and a favourite pupil of his, named Boso. Boso plays the part of a (very gentle) devil's advocate, posing the questions he thinks unbelievers would pose; Anselm answers; then Boso heartily agrees with what Anselm has said before going on to pose the next question.

Book 1

Anselm begins by demonstrating the orderly beauty of God's arrangement:

> For it was fitting that just as death entered the human race through the disobedience of a human being, so too life should be restored by the obedience of a human being. It was fitting that just as the sin that was the cause of our damnation had its origin from a woman, so too the author of our justice and salvation should be born of a woman. And it was fitting that the devil, who through the tasting of a tree defeated the

---

18. *Cur Deus Homo*, Preface.

human being whom he persuaded, should be defeated by a human being
through the suffering on a tree that he inflicted.[19]

Boso's response is that beauty itself is not persuasive to unbelievers,
who need to be shown the logical necessity of such an arrangement.
This is especially so, he says, since unbelievers (Jews are implied)
argue that if God is omnipotent he could simply have willed salvation
without having to undergo the indignity of becoming incarnate. If
he could not, then surely he is not omnipotent.

Dealing with this demand takes up most of the work, but
Anselm feels he can also respond to the underlying assumption
that the act of incarnation must be demeaning to God: 'when
we say that God was subject to lowliness or weakness, we do
not understand this according to the sublimity of his impassible
nature but according to the weakness of the human substance he
bore'.[20] In other words, and quite simply, God's divinity remains
untarnished by Jesus' lowly humanity.

Before going on to look at the logical necessity for the incarnation, Anselm wanted to remove an option that most educated
Christians in his day would have used as their answer to why God
became man. For centuries the traditional view had been that
when Adam and Eve obeyed the devil as he tempted them, they
had made themselves (and all humanity in them) his subjects. The
devil, from then on, had a just lordship over them, and assumed he
had a just lordship over their descendant, Christ. However, Christ
never followed the devil and so never was his subject. Thus when
the devil tried to exercise lordship over Christ by condemning him
to death (as he had a right to do over his own subjects), his over-
reaching abrogated his right to be lord over humanity at all, and so
humanity was freed from the devil's power by the death of Christ.
On this view, then, Christ's death was a ransom, paid to the devil
to buy off his rights over humanity.

Anselm felt that this approach was entirely wrong-headed. As
he saw it, when the devil tempted Adam and Eve, he had simply

---

19. Ibid. 1.3.
20. Ibid. 1.8.

sinned against God, the true Lord over humanity, and an act of sin could never confer rights of any sort. The devil was a mere rebel and thief, with no rights and no lordship over humanity.

Why, then, the incarnation, if not to pay off the devil? Anselm begins by explaining that humanity was created by God to be happy, but that that happiness can be achieved only through humanity's total submission of heart and life to God. Such is God the true Lord's due, and anything less is sin. Sin, then, is essentially the dishonouring of God. Yet this is precisely what humanity is guilty of, and for this reason we have forfeited the happiness for which we were created.

So far the unbeliever (Jew) is clearly expected to agree. But, says Anselm, God could not simply forgive humanity. That would deny his justice, which demands that the outrage of sin be dealt with appropriately. And that is because God's honour should not and cannot be violated. His will (and so honour) is as inescapable as the heavens above, so that if a creature 'flees from God's commanding will, he runs into God's punishing will'.[21]

God, then, cannot just forgive. Something else must happen if humanity is to enjoy the happiness for which we were created. Yet at this point Anselm inserts what to modern readers looks like a bizarre sidetrack, discussing how God created human beings to make up for the number of angels who fell. Weird and irrelevant it may appear to us, but for Anselm it is an important question concerning the reason for which humanity was created. As Anselm sees it, the spaces left in the heavenly city by the fall of the devil and his angels must be made up, and thus God creates humanity and elects a certain number of humans to fill the gaps. In fact, he will elect more humans than there are spaces to fill so that humans can have their own purpose, rather than just being substitute angels. And, Anselm adds, it is important that there be more elect humans than fallen angels, for if there were a mere one-to-one correspondence, each saved human would know that he had replaced a fallen angel, and so would sin by rejoicing over another's downfall.

---

21. Ibid. 1.15.

This rather mechanical view of the purpose and election of humans proves to be highly revealing of Anselm's view of the relationship between God and man. Here, God's plan in creation is to make humans like angels, in being subject only to himself. But that means that God's adoption of us as children, our being treated as anything other than mere servile creatures, and any idea of close fellowship with him is entirely absent from Anselm's thinking. Anselm's usual picture of the relationship between God and man is that of a feudal lord and his serfs.

With that picture in mind, Anselm resumes his main argument: humans owe all to God, but have not given him their due all. As such, they now owe God a recompense. But since we already owe God our all, there is nothing left for us to give God as a recompense. Indeed, our plight is worse even than that. Anselm asks Boso if he would sin to preserve the whole creation. Boso nobly says he would not, which Anselm takes as proof that the cost of sin is worth more than all creation. Thus something more than all creation must be given to God in recompense for sin.

However, the question then arises: If we are so completely unable to pay that recompense, surely God cannot hold us accountable for not paying it? Anselm disagrees, likening us to a servant who throws himself into a deep pit he had been warned to avoid so as to make himself incapable of doing a task his master had commanded. The servant, of course, is incapable of doing the required task, but that does not mean the master will hold him guiltless for his failure; rather, he will punish him doubly, for his failure to do the task, and for his failure to avoid the pit. His inability is his own fault.

Anselm's conclusion to Book 1 is that if Christ did not come to save us, then we would be unable ever to enjoy the happiness for which we were created. Our sin has run us into God's punishing will, and there is nothing we ourselves can do to pay the recompense we must pay to avoid it. Yet it is not as if God would leave us in that state. Some humans must attain happiness, or else God's plan in creating them would be thwarted and God would be shown to have failed, which is impossible. Thus, while God cannot simply forgive us, neither can he fail to show us mercy. The need for Christ is clear.

Boso (unsurprisingly persuaded), then says, 'Now I want you to lead me further, so that I understand on the basis of rational necessity that all the things the Catholic faith requires us to believe about Christ if we want to be saved must be true.'[22]

Book 2

Anselm has established (1) that humankind owes to God a recompense for sin worth more than all creation; (2) that we cannot pay it; and (3) that God cannot fail to complete what he began in creating a humanity not made to die but to be happy in enjoying God. Anselm's conclusion is that there must be 'someone who in payment for human sin gives God something greater than everything other than God'.[23] But what is greater than everything other than God? Only God himself. Thus only God can make the recompense. And yet it is man who owes the recompense. Man must pay it; only God can pay it.

Anselm sees that, by logical deduction, he has proved that a God-man is necessary for the salvation of humanity that God's own justice to himself requires. Only one who in his own person is perfect God and perfect man can fulfil man's obligation to God and God's obligation to himself.

But Anselm must go further than this if he is to prove 'on the basis of rational necessity that *all* the things the Catholic faith requires us to believe about Christ if we want to be saved must be true'. He starts with the conception and birth of the God-man. Anselm maintains that the God-man would have to take his humanity from a virgin, for God would only do what is best and most fitting for him to do, and to be conceived of a virgin would be 'purer and more honorable' than to be conceived in the ordinary way:

> There are four ways in which God can make a human being: from a man and a woman, as everyday experience shows; or from neither a man nor a woman, as he created Adam; or from a man without a woman, as he made Eve; or from a woman without a man, which he had never done.

22. Ibid. 1.25.
23. Ibid. 2.6.

So in order to prove that this last way was within his power and had
been held in reserve for this very deed, nothing was more fitting than for
him to assume the human being whom we are seeking from a woman
without a man.[24]

Here it becomes clear that what is most beautiful and 'fitting' is, in
Anselm's mind, the same as what is logically necessary, for God will
do only what is 'fitting'.

The God-man would then live a perfect life. For one thing, he
would have to be perfect, for imperfection would not be fitting.
For example, he could not be ignorant in any way, because that
would not be useful to his mission. Nor could he ever sin, or else
he would owe the debt of sin for himself.

And this would be the whole point of the coming of the God-
man: that only he could pay the recompense God's honour
required, but which man could not otherwise pay. God needed to
be given something that he could not already demand as an obligation. But if the God-man simply lived a perfect life, that would
be doing no more than God demands of man. To pay the necessary recompense he needed to do something more, something
God could not demand of him. Given the sinlessness of the God-
man, God could not with justice demand his death. Thus only by
giving his life and dying could the God-man make recompense to
satisfy God's honour. Moreover, being God and thus omnipotent,
his life could not be stolen from him, meaning he would have to
lay it down voluntarily.

At this point Anselm asks Boso if he would be prepared to kill
the God-man if that meant saving the whole creation. Horrified,
Boso says he would not, and Anselm takes this as proof that the
life of the God-man must be worth more than all creation. Indeed,
it would have to be, given that the debt man owes to God is worth
more 'than everything other than God'.

This is the theology of atonement that Anselm offers in place
of the idea of Christ's death as a ransom to pay off the devil. It is
not that Christ dies in our place to take any punishment we might

---

24. Ibid. 2.8.

deserve for sin; it is that Christ's death is an offering to God greater than God could justly demand. It satisfies God's honour, but it does not avert any wrath he might have.[25]

To return to the argument: once the God-man had offered to God the priceless gift of his own death, God's justice would demand that he reward the God-man. Yet the God-man is himself God, and thus would already have everything. It would be impossible to give to him anything that was not already his. So God satisfies his justice by giving the reward to those for whom the God-man died, thus cancelling their debt.

Now if the God-man died for humanity, and the reward amounts to salvation, does that mean all humanity must be saved? Anselm avoids this conclusion by reasoning that God would only offer the merits of the God-man to those who accept the pardon made possible by his death: 'And if they should happen to sin again after this pardon, they will again receive pardon through the efficacy of that same agreement, provided that they are willing to make appropriate recompense and then to amend their lives.'[26]

---

25. It is common for Anselm's atonement theory to be pitted against that of Peter Abelard (1079–1142), the controversial theologian of the next generation. However, just as Anselm is sometimes misinterpreted as holding to a penal substitutionary view of the atonement, so Abelard is routinely interpreted as teaching that, since man could not make a payment to God, and since there was no need to pay the devil, the atonement was not about payment at all, but was nothing more than a moving demonstration of God's love. This was how the enormously influential Bernard of Clairvaux, a staunch defender of the 'ransom to the devil' theory, painted Abelard in his attempt to convict him of heresy. Bernard's logic was that if Abelard did teach that, he would be guilty of Pelagianism (that we need no real reconciliation with God, only an encouragement to be more loving). However, while Abelard did think, like Anselm, that the cross moves us as a demonstration of God's love, he also held to an objective understanding of the atonement. In his commentary on Romans he is quite clear that, unlike Anselm, he held to a penal substitutionary view.

26. *Cur Deus Homo* 2.16.

Why subsequent sin could be atoned for by mere recompense and not by further deaths of the God-man is unclear. What is clear is that salvation was under conditions, and in practice those conditions were tough, requiring absolute submission to the law of God (ideally, becoming a monk).

Anselm and Boso then agree that the logical necessity of the death of the God-man has been proved, and that only through it can the salvation of humanity occur that God's justice required (though angels cannot be saved, for that would require the death of a God-angel). Boso concludes, 'everything that is contained in the Old and New Testaments has been proved . . . you would satisfy not only Jews but also pagans by reason alone'.[27]

Going on with Anselm

When theologically interested Christians consider dipping their toes in Anselm's thought, it is usually *Cur Deus Homo* they go to. Unfortunately, the experience is often rather off-putting, all the to-ing and fro-ing between Anselm and Boso taking up more time than most readers have the patience to endure (*Anselm*: 'Listen.' *Boso*: 'I'm listening.' *Anselm*: 'I will tell you what seems true to me.' *Boso*: 'That's all I can ask of you.' *Reader*: 'Get on with it!'). An easier place to begin is with the *Monologion* (which will also give a better insight into Anselm's overall thought and approach to theology). The translation to use, both for its freshness and accuracy, is Thomas Williams's superb *Anselm: Basic Writings* (Indianapolis: Hackett, 2007), which, as the title suggests, contains all Anselm's basic writings.

Beware of secondary literature on Anselm, which tends to be such that any one book will leave a rather lop-sided impression. The safest hands are probably those of the great Anselm authority, Sir Richard Southern. His incomparable biography, *Saint Anselm: A Portrait in a Landscape* (Cambridge: Cambridge University Press, 1990), gives a beautiful introduction to the man and his mind.

---

27. Ibid. 2.22.

Anselm timeline

1033	Anselm born in Aosta in Italy
1054	Schism between Eastern and Western churches
1059	Arrives at the monastery of Bec in Normandy
1063	Becomes prior of Bec
1066	Norman conquest of England
1075–6	Writes *Monologion*
1077–8	Writes *Proslogion*
1078	Elected abbot of Bec
1079	Peter Abelard born
1093	Enthroned as Archbishop of Canterbury
1095	Pope Urban II calls for the first crusade
1095–8	Writes *Cur Deus Homo*
1097	Leaves England to consult the pope
1098	Defends the Western Church's belief in the *Filioque* at the Council of Bari
1100	King William II of England dies; Henry I invites Anselm to return to England
1103	Leaves England to consult the pope; Henry I forbids his return; Anselm begins excommunication proceedings against Henry
1106	Returns to England with the dispute settled
1109	Anselm dies

6. THE DUMB OX

Thomas Aquinas

Somewhere at the forefront of the medieval mind was the idea that their generation was inferior to the last, that men of old were giants, and medieval thinkers mere pygmies. It was, then, an outlook that gave great credence to 'the authorities', those writings that had come down from grander times. So lofty were they thought to be that, as C. S. Lewis put it, the medieval mind

hardly ever decided that one of the authorities was simply right and the others wrong; never that all were wrong. To be sure, in the last resort it was taken for granted that the Christian writers must be right as against the Pagans. But it was hardly ever allowed to come to the last resort. It was apparently difficult to believe that anything in the books – so costly, fetched from so far, so old, often so lovely to the eye and hand, was just plumb wrong. No; if Seneca and St Paul disagreed with one another, and both with Cicero, and all these with Boethius, there must be some explanation which would harmonize them.

Or, as he put it more simply, the medieval mind suffered from 'an inability to say "Bosh"'.[1]

That said, particular authorities could go in and out of vogue. Augustine's esteem for Platonism had ensured Plato's pre-eminence right down to Anselm's day; yet soon after Anselm's death a number of works by Aristotle started becoming available to read in Latin for the first time. And Aristotle scratched exactly where the times were itching: where Plato had confined himself to lofty thoughts about the soul and ideas, Aristotle wrote treatises on everything from politics to meteorology to 'the parts of animals', and did so with compelling logic.

Aristotle soon divided the academic world: some seemed to swallow him whole; others saw worrying issues, such as his view that the world had always existed, and decried Christian use of the pagan Aristotle as the sin of Rachel, who smuggled her father's idols under her skirt. How to treat Aristotle became the cause célèbre. Then Thomas Aquinas proposed a system in which he sought to bring Aristotelianism into Christianity in a way that preserved the integrity of both. It would be a Christian Aristotelianism.

The result was triumphant: his masterpiece, the *Summa Theologiae*, became the standard textbook of Roman Catholic theology and was said to have been laid alongside the Scriptures on the altar at the Council of Trent, where he was given the title 'Universal Doctor of the Church'; he was hailed by popes as the 'defender of the Catholic Church and conqueror of heretics'; in 1998 Pope John Paul II issued an encyclical in which he described 'the Angelic Doctor' as 'a model of the right way to do theology'. And his influence has not been confined to Roman Catholicism: even deep in Reformed circles, Aquinas is happily regarded by many as a major influence.

---

1. C. S. Lewis, *Studies in Medieval and Renaissance Literature* (Cambridge: Cambridge University Press, 1966), p. 45.

Aquinas' life

Tommaso d'Aquino was born at some point between 1224 and
1226 in his family castle of Roccasecca, between Rome and
Naples. The castle is the giveaway that Thomas came from noble
stock. He was, however, the youngest son, and so dealt with in the
traditional manner: aged five he was handed over to be educated at
the nearby great Benedictine abbey of Monte Cassino, where he
soon became known for his repeated question 'What is God?'

After a few years, fighting in the area persuaded his family to
transfer him to the new University of Naples, and it was there that
he was introduced to two of the great future influences on his life.
The first was Aristotle, who elsewhere in Christian Europe was
quite unknown (and whose writings were actually banned in Paris).
The second was the Order of Preachers ('Dominicans'), an order
recently established by Dominic Guzman to combat heresy. Given
their intent, the Dominicans gave study an especially high priority,
which appealed to Thomas; they were also mendicant friars rather
than monks (instead of detaching themselves from the world in a
monastery, they lived by begging). Impressed, Thomas soon joined
them, and thus entered the Dominican life of study – not study so
much for the sake of monastic contemplation like Anselm, but
study for the sake of teaching, and specifically university teaching
in Thomas' case.

His family were horrified. They had hoped for some high and
respectable church office for Thomas, not that he would be on the
streets begging with some upstart bunch of radicals. So, when he
went travelling north past the family estates, they kidnapped him
and imprisoned him for a year or more while they attempted to
dissuade him from his chosen career. Dissuasion meant tactics like
slipping a scantily clad beauty into his cell to seduce him. Resilience
for Thomas meant fending her off with a burning stick (with
which he could also make encouraging signs of the cross). Unable
to be torn by such distractions from his study of Aristotle's logic
and the Bible, he was eventually released.

Thomas headed north to Paris and then Cologne, there studying under the great Aristotelian scholar Albert (who was known
even in his own lifetime as 'the Great'). Before Albert, nobody

really seemed to have noticed Thomas' intellectual potential. Thomas was physically large, tall and portly, and since such heavy features were combined with a distinct lack of personal sparkle, many assumed he was rather backward, and nicknamed him the 'Dumb Ox'. Albert saw otherwise: 'We call him the Dumb Ox,' he said, 'but the bellowing of that ox will resound throughout the whole world.'

Still today, the combination of sharp mind and slow manner make Thomas quite hard to make out. On the one hand, the hagiography has turned the mild-mannered friar into a veritable Buddha of serenity; on the other, his own theological and philosophical output reveal a ferocious intellectual energy. Then there are the anecdotes: in his prime, he would, apparently, dictate to three or four secretaries simultaneously, and would even keep dictating lucidly after he had fallen asleep. There are other stories of his phenomenal ability to concentrate. All told, they seem to suggest a quite remarkable intellectual ability, though it is very hard to know what to believe, since Aquinas' stature as a theologian has steeped his life in legend such that all sorts of miracles and mystical experiences are attributed to him, from levitating to conversing with crucifixes.

Seeing Thomas' ability, Albert arranged for him to return to Paris and study to become a 'master' (a title soon replaced by 'doctor') in theology, even though Thomas was technically too young to be eligible. And so Thomas came to spend his formative teaching years in Paris, lecturing on Peter Lombard's *Sentences* (then the standard textbook of theology), writing treatises and commentaries, and even starting to write one of his major works, his *Summa contra Gentiles*.

After a few years in Paris, he headed back to the warmer climes of his native Italy, and there spent the next decade, half with the papal court, where he became the close friend of two popes, and half in Dominican study houses. It was in one of these houses that he had set up in Rome that he began to write his magnum opus, the *Summa Theologiae*. And from then on, wherever he was (including a stint back in Paris), it was this that dominated, even though he still produced a heavy stream of other works.

He nearly finished it. He had been called back to Naples to set up another study house there, and had just finished writing on the Eucharist. Then, on Wednesday 6 December 1273, while attending Mass, he underwent some profound experience. It so affected him that he never wrote another word, explaining 'I cannot, because all that I have written seems like straw to me.'

The next February, he was travelling to the Council of Lyon, which was an attempt to reunite the Western and Eastern churches, when he hit his head on a tree branch, and had to be taken to the nearby monastery of Fossanova to recover. He never did: there, a few short miles from his birthplace, and still in his forties, he died on 7 March 1274.

Aquinas' thought

Aquinas seems to have spurted ink like a cuttlefish, producing in his short life a staggeringly daunting mountain of books. The definitive edition of his works began to be assembled in 1882, and is still not finished. Fortunately, a good deal of them lie outside the purview of this book – his strictly philosophical writings and numerous commentaries on (all the major works of) Aristotle, for instance.

Biblical commentaries

Among all the collected debates and treatises, some of the most important works are his biblical commentaries (some of which were, apparently, written with the miraculous assistance of the apostles Peter and Paul). In them he developed a highly influential method of interpretation through which he sought to check both the arbitrary manhandling of texts and naive reductionism. Scripture, he held, has two senses: the *literal* and the *spiritual*. The literal sense is about the bare bones of what happens in a passage (e.g. Eli falls off his chair). The spiritual sense is about the meaning of that event, and is a sense usually suggested by another passage of Scripture. There can, however, be three kinds of spiritual sense or meaning: the *moral* or *tropological* sense (e.g. Elijah's prayerfulness is a model for us); the *allegorical* or *typical* sense (e.g. Moses' bronze serpent is a picture of Christ on the cross); and the *anagogical* sense (about the life to come; e.g. the river Jordan represents the river of death). A passage could conceivably bear all four senses.

Summa contra Gentiles

Yet how can we grasp an overall impression of Aquinas' theology? Undoubtedly, his two greatest works are the *Summa contra Gentiles* and the *Summa Theologiae*. There is, though, a considerable deal of overlap between them, and so, rather than looking at both in minimum detail and suffering the repetition, I will briefly explain what the *Summa contra Gentiles* is, and then we will have the space for a slightly more revealing look at the *Summa Theologiae*.

Traditionally, the *Summa contra Gentiles* (Summary against the Gentiles/Unbelievers) is said to have been written to assist the arguments of missionaries working among the Muslims and Jews of Spain. That situation may well have provided the opportunity for Aquinas to write the work; however, when read, it feels more like an abstract demonstration of what theology can know in distinction to what philosophy can know.

The work divides into four sections or 'books', the first three dealing with what can be known about God from reason: Book 1 discusses what can be known about God from philosophy, especially from the study of Aristotle (who was, if anything, even more influential among Muslims and Jews); Book 2 examines the emanation of creation from God, and Book 3 the return of creation to God. Book 4 then goes on to what can be known about God from revelation (the Trinity, the incarnation, sacraments, resurrection and final judgment). The similarities with the *Summa Theologiae* should soon be obvious.

Summa Theologiae

Written over the last seven years of his life at a speed only Aquinas could manage, and still incomplete, the *Summa Theologiae* is Aquinas' crowning achievement and the mature distillation of his thought.[2] He wrote it, he said, for the instruction of beginners,

---

2. The *Summa Theologiae* (Summary of Theology) is also known as the *Summa Theologica* (Theological Summary).

though since not even friars would have had access to a copy of
the work, that probably meant that it was written as a manual for
their teachers. Certainly, it was not written for the laity: the *Summa
Theologiae* assumes that the reader is quite well versed in Scripture
and the theories and practice of scholastic theology.

The *Summa* divides into three main parts: the First Part deals
with God and creation; the Second Part deals with humanity's
advance towards God in holiness; and the Third Part deals with
Christ, the man who is our way to God. The structure can thus be
seen to tell the story of God, of how all things come from God in
creation, and finally of how all things return to God as they are
reconciled through Christ. The endpoint of it all is the resurrection and final glory. Critics have been quick to complain of how
Christ is consigned to the final, Third Part. Certainly, it was not
Aquinas' intention to relegate Christ in any way – he is treated in
the Third Part because he is the one who leads humanity home to
God. Yet Aquinas' structure does, of course, have consequences:
for one thing, Christ may be shown to be the way of salvation, but
he is not really understood as the way to know God.

Aquinas stated that his aim in writing the *Summa* was to convey
things briefly and clearly. One is tempted to laugh at his goal of
brevity, for, quite apart from the eye-watering page-count (over
three thousand in the standard five-volume English translation),
he manages to cover questions such as the following: Is there
rivalry between guardian angels as to who has the best charge? Are
demons influenced by the planets as humans are? Is the soul in
each part of the body? Is semen produced by eating too much?
Should prayer be vocal? Should Christ have been born in winter?
Into which hell did Christ descend, and did he take his body with
him? Will we be resurrected with our hair and nails? And will we
all be male? Or transparent?[3]

---

3. Fun though it would be to look at Aquinas' answers to these, we simply
   do not have the time to wander in the side streets of the *Summa* (and, in
   any case, readers can quickly find them for themselves); my aim is to give
   an inner sense of the logic and sweep of the work, picking out what is
   most characteristic of his thought.

Brief the *Summa* is not. But clear it most definitely is. Aquinas' style is so clear and clean it feels clinical, as if the theological subjects under examination have been scrubbed down, freeze-dried and then minutely dissected. A good part of this 'feel' comes from the way Aquinas structures things. He divides his material into topics, which he calls 'questions'; these topics are then subdivided into articles. So far that merely feels precise; it is how he then deals with each article that tends to strike the modern reader as rather obsessive-compulsive.

Aquinas writes almost as if each article was a transcript of a medieval scholastic debate. The idea of these university debates was that, as theologians argued with each other, they would gradually chip away each other's misunderstandings, enabling them together slowly to focus in on the truth of the matter at hand. Thus, as in a scholastic debate, Aquinas opens each article with the thesis or question to be discussed, objections to it are offered, and then counter-objections are put forward (introduced by 'On the contrary').[4] At this point in a scholastic debate the master would step in with a final response; just so, Aquinas steps in here with his final assessment of the subject, introducing it with 'I answer', usually tending to agree with the main thesis, and then dealing with any outstanding objections. It is the final response that forms the meat and body of the article.[5]

---

4. Special care is needed when reading the 'On the contrary' section: to our eyes today it looks like this is the part where Aquinas' own position is laid out. Sometimes it is. But not always. It is the next section ('I answer') that should be looked to for Aquinas' final opinion.

5. Given this complex structure, the *Summa* has its own decidedly intimidating reference system. Basically, the first number in any reference refers to the Part (First, Second or Third); the second number refers to the question; the third to the article. So *ST* 3.22.6 refers to the sixth article in the twenty-second question of the Third Part of the *Summa Theologiae*. The only complication here is that the Second Part actually divides into two, which are imaginatively named 'First Part of the Second Part' and 'Second Part of the Second Part'. These are referenced as 1-2 and 2-2, making *ST* 2-2.4.5 the fifth article of the fourth question of the Second

First Part

On theology and philosophy The first question Aquinas deals with is highly revealing. He asks if philosophical reasoning is able to yield enough knowledge of God to make any other form of knowledge superfluous. Essentially, his answer is that reason and philosophy have their place, but can only go so far, and that 'it was necessary for the salvation of man that certain truths which exceed human reason should be made known to him by divine revelation'.[6] It is an answer that will provide the framework for all his theology. Aquinas holds that reason and natural knowledge provide a foundation on which any supernaturally revealed knowledge received by faith must build.

Aristotle (whom Aquinas refers to as 'the Philosopher') is clearly at the forefront of his mind; and Aristotle, he is suggesting, can *generally* be relied upon in what he said. However, Aristotle knew only the natural order of things, which philosophy investigates; lacking divine revelation, he was ignorant of the supernatural order, which theology must investigate. Nevertheless, Aristotle was able to provide reliable philosophical foundations upon which theology could build. More, despite Aristotle's own ignorance of the supernatural, his logic was so reliable that it could be extended to analyse the supernatural realm he had never known.

This model would not simply inform Aquinas' view of how we know things; it lay at the heart of his notion of reality. There are two realms, he believed: the *natural* and the *supernatural*, but the two never conflicted; rather, the supernatural (including faith) always built upon and perfected the natural (including reason).

Part of the Second Part. I will make my referencing no more complicated than that(!); however, other books on Aquinas do use variations: instead of *ST* 1-2.3.4, one can find *ST* I-II.3.4, *ST* 1ᵃ–2ᵃᵉ.3.4, *ST* Iᵃ–IIᵃᵉ.3.4 and more. To add to the merriment, some like to specify which part of an article they are referencing. *ST* 1.6.3c, for example: the c is for the corpus or body of the article, Aquinas' final assessment. *ST* 3.5.3 *ad* 3: *ad* 3 stands for the reply to the third objection. *ST* 1-2.6.4 *sed contra*: *sed contra* refers to the counter objection.

6. *ST* 1.1.1.

On the One God What, then, can reason by itself know of God?
A good deal, it will turn out:

> The existence of God and other like truths about God, which can be
> known by natural reason, are not articles of faith, but are preambles to
> the articles; for faith presupposes natural knowledge, even as grace
> presupposes nature, and perfection supposes something that can be
> perfected.[7]

But how is it that reason can know of God's existence? Aquinas
does not agree with Anselm, that God's existence is hard-wired into
our very logic so that if we are logical we have to acknowledge the
existence of God. However, he does think that by looking at the
world around us we can see God's effects, and that by working up
from there we can deduce God's existence. This, in contrast to
Anselm's Platonic presuppositions, is itself a very Aristotelian way
of proceeding: to start with what can be observed by the senses.

In particular, Aquinas suggests that there are five ways of
proving the existence of God from what we know of the world
about us. The first (and, Aquinas suggests, the clearest) way works
from the fact that we see motion or change in the world. Now
everything that moves or changes must be moved or changed *by*
something. And, like a series of dominoes, there cannot be an
endless chain of movers; otherwise, there would be no first
mover and thus no motion or change at all. There must, therefore,
be a first unmoved mover, 'and this everyone understands to be
God'.[8]

The second way argues quite similarly that there must be a first
uncaused cause.

The third way works from the fact that we see things that are
capable of not existing. Yet it cannot be the case that everything is
capable of not existing, for then at one time nothing would have
existed, and nothing can come from nothing. There must, therefore, be a necessary being.

---

7. I.2.2.
8. I.2.3.

The fourth way argues that we see 'more' and 'less' all around; there must, therefore, be something which is hottest, something which is highest, something which is 'uttermost being', 'and this we call God'.

The fifth way is effectively an argument from design, that we see even inanimate things working in ways that seem designed, and so ways that suggest a designer.

These proofs completely lack Anselm's grand ambition of building a complete doctrine of God on an argument. All Aquinas has sought to do with them is establish the existence of a first cause, a mover, a necessary and most perfect being, a designer. In fact, even though he believes we can deduce that God exists, Aquinas is adamant that we cannot know what God is. For Aquinas, we know things by sensing them, but God is not a being we have seen with our eyes, whom we have looked at and our hands have touched; therefore we cannot know God.

This is the point where Aquinas most clearly reveals his reliance on the fifth/sixth-century apophatic theologian, Pseudo-Dionysius (who, in Aquinas' day, was still thought to be the Dionysius of Acts 17, and whose writings were consequently revered as next to canonical). Pseudo-Dionysius had taught – and Aquinas now agrees – that God is such that it is easier to speak of what he is not than of what he is. For example, God is not changeable, for that would imply imperfection (that he had something better to become); God is not bodily, for that would imply that he is somehow spread out in such a way that he can be divided, which is impossible; God is not dependent on anything, even existence.

And yet, if God is so unknown, how can we say anything true about him, wonders Aquinas? Ultimately, then, merely saying negative things about God strikes Aquinas as deficient, especially since he has already 'proved' five positive things about God (that he is a first cause, etc.). Aquinas therefore wonders if, somewhat like Anselm, he should seek to derive an understanding of God from what little we do know of him – that he is the first cause. One could, for example, call God good since he causes good things. But then, he realizes, one could equally call God a nostril or a flea, for he causes nostrils and fleas to exist as well. And, on that track we would remain just as ignorant of what God was eternally like, for was he wise *before* he caused any wisdom to be created?

Yet, because God has caused all things to exist, all things, Aquinas maintains, must resemble him, however weakly. Thus in the end, Aquinas wants to affirm that we can speak truly, if inadequately, about God. We can speak of God, he says, by analogy. That works something like this: if I were to say at one time 'John is an idiot,' and at another 'Rob is an idiot,' I could mean that one of them is merely rather inept while the other is intensely stupid; yet, whatever exactly it was that I meant, you would still have a reasonable grasp of my gist. Just so, when I say 'God is good,' I am not using the word 'good' in exactly the same way as when, for example, I say 'bacon is good'; nevertheless, my basic meaning is clear, for I am using the word in similar, recognizable (analogical) ways.

So we can speak truly of God. What, then, can our reason say, according to Aquinas? Obviously, God is perfect. He is also good – but by this Aquinas is not talking about moral goodness; rather, to be good is to have being. 'Goodness and being are really the same.'[9] This will be an important concept for Aquinas. First, it will mean that nothing can be essentially evil, since being is good; badness is only a lack of being, an incompleteness (thus a bad umbrella, full of holes, lacks the complete being we expect of an umbrella). Second, since Aquinas holds that the essence of goodness is desirability, God, as the supreme being and therefore the supreme good, must be the most desirable being.

What else can reason say? That God is infinite (since everywhere depends on God, he must be everywhere). That God is unchanging (else there would have to be some being prior to him who changed him, making God no longer God). That there is no 'before' and 'after' with God (since time involves change and God does not change). That God is simple, not composed of 'parts' on which he depends.

The next thing about God deduced by reason is especially important for Aquinas: God's knowledge. Aquinas argues that the less material something is, the more free it is to know.

---

9. 1.5.1.

things; being completely immaterial, then, God's knowledge must be infinite (which, Aquinas says, is fitting, since intelligence is the highest perfection). Yet Aquinas wants to ask more closely what exactly God knows. Aristotle held that God's infinite knowledge was only of his infinite self – nothing else would be worthy of his consideration. And essentially, Aquinas sounds very similar:

> Since therefore God is outside the whole order of creation, and all creatures are ordered to Him, and not conversely, it is manifest that creatures are really related to God Himself; whereas in God there is no real relation to creatures, but a relation only in idea, inasmuch as creatures are referred to Him.[10]

However, by knowing himself, Aquinas argues, God must know himself as creator, and through that knowledge must have a knowledge of his creation. In fact, creation exists only because God knows it (rather than vice versa). So while God has 'no real relation to creatures', he does have a relation 'in idea'.

The way that works out is that God, who knows and wills what is good (i.e. himself), wills to have beings who reflect his goodness, and he destines them for good (for himself). It is in this way that God loves his creatures. Now at this point it looks like Aquinas is being inconsistent: if God loves his creatures, surely he has a real relation to them? However, by 'love' Aquinas does not mean that God feels affection for his creatures. Far from it; if God could be affected by anything, that thing would have a power over God that Aquinas would consider blasphemously improper. It is, rather, that in all this, God is being true and doing justice to himself. But as he does justice to himself, so he is just to his creatures. The thing is, they do not deserve any goodness or justice from him, and so as he is simply just to himself, so his ways with his creatures can be seen to be merciful.

On the Trinity 'Having considered what belongs to the unity of the divine essence, it remains to treat of what belongs to the

10. 1.13.7.

Trinity.'[11] Reason has taken Aquinas so far in his knowledge of God; now he needs revelation to fill in the picture (reason, though, has clearly given Aquinas most of what he wanted to say about God; he is content to be quite brief here). And yet one feels no lurch of a gear being changed here. Aquinas ended his section 'On the One God' by speaking of how God enjoys himself, and this opens the way to a discussion of the Trinity. And, though Aquinas has averred that reason is incapable of discovering the Trinity by itself, reason is quite capable of discussing it, he feels.

Thus the new section flows on smoothly from the previous discussion of God's knowledge: 'whenever we understand', he writes, 'by the very fact of understanding there proceeds something within us, which is a conception of the object understood'.[12] Anyone who has read Anselm's *Monologion* must feel here a certain sense of déjà vu, for this concept now becomes the starting point of a very similar argument. That is, God knows himself, and his concept of himself can be described as a word in his mind, a word that is in God, and yet distinct from God. Next, God loves this concept of himself with a love that is also somehow distinct from himself. And thus there are three in God.

Then, on to each of the three: the Father is described essentially as the principle of the Son and the Spirit; the Son as the Father's concept; the Spirit as the love between them. Their relations distinguish them from each other, and it is for this reason, he holds, that the Spirit must proceed from the Father *and* the Son: if he came from the Father alone, like the Son, then the Spirit would be a second Son.

Aquinas has already explained that God knows himself in his Word, his idea or concept. And 'in idea' he knows his creation. Similarly, the Spirit is God's love for himself, and it is in that love for himself as creator (in the Spirit) that he loves creation.

On creation Having considered God, Aquinas begins to move his story on to consider the creation (of the universe as a whole, of angels, and of man). Medieval theologians are, of course,

---

11. 1.27.Introduction.

12. 1.27.1.

famed for the question 'How many angels can dance on the head of a pin?' There is no evidence that that particular question was ever debated, and yet angels do feature prominently in medieval theology, and first-time readers of the *Summa* are often struck by how much angels figure (more space is given to angels than to the Trinity, for instance). There is a reason, though: angels were perfect subjects for thought-experiments, especially when a theologian was trying to grasp what is true of spiritual beings. He could ask questions about angels that would get him into hot water (literally) if he made God the subject of his enquiry.

Probably the most important section of Aquinas' doctrine of creation is his doctrine of humanity, and this is dominated by his discussion of the soul's relation to the body. Aquinas is emphatically opposed to any sort of dualism whereby the soul and body are construed as two self-contained parts, thrown together. Rather, the soul (*anima*) is the principle of life that animates. I am alive by having a soul. Thus it is not as if I *am* my soul, and that my body is a disposable possession that I could lose without losing myself. Yet nor am I reducible to my bodily functions: I have a life beyond the body. For, Aquinas argues, I think, and that is an activity of the soul.

Now since the soul is capable of acting on its own, the soul must be capable of some sort of independent existence, even after the death of the body. However, it is not so simple as then to say that it is my *soul* that actually understands and thinks. *I* am the one who does that, not my soul. Thus the soul that survives after the death of the body is somehow incomplete and unnatural. That is, Dan's soul, if I part it from his body, is not Dan. And being so incomplete, the soul after death has 'an aptitude and a natural inclination to be united to the body' – by its very nature it awaits re-embodiment and resurrection.[13]

It is with a look at God's providential government of creation that Aquinas ends the First Part, and in it he provides a framework within which much of the rest of the *Summa* will operate. There is, he maintains, no competition between God's

---

13. 1.76.1.

ordering of creation and human free will. Quite the opposite: it is because God wills things that we freely choose them. 'God works in things in such a manner that things have their proper operation.'[14] God is the ground of their being, and so they can only be and do as he allows, but it is not that his will excludes theirs; instead, it enables it. Aquinas' God is a God who enables free will.

First Part of the Second Part

The Second Part of the *Summa* is Aquinas' most original contribution to theology. Having looked at God in his freedom, Aquinas turns here to look at man, the image of God, as in his own freedom he moves towards God. Because Aquinas is dealing here with the 'natural' as opposed to the 'supernatural' realm, he feels able to depend on Aristotle with little alteration (and reveals no sense that Aristotle's God might generate a different world with different ethics to the God of the Bible). The Second Part has thus been described as Aquinas' commentary on Aristotle's *Nicomachean Ethics*; certainly, the argument follows Aristotle's order, though Aquinas knows he must extend Aristotle's logic to examine man's growth in the 'supernatural' realm, something of which Aristotle was ignorant. At points this produces something that just looks rather dated (such as his use of Aristotle's idea that 'the female is a misbegotten male'[15]); overall, though, the result became the definitive Roman Catholic ethic.

He starts with a look at the goal of human life, which, he says, is happiness. All men seek their own happiness where they will. But 'perfect happiness can consist in nothing else than the vision of the Divine Essence'.[16] And how might we attain that? Aristotle had taught that like is known by and drawn to like. Which means that to know God we must be like God; and since God is holy, we must be holy.

On habits Aristotle had averred – and Aquinas agreed – that the

---

14. 1.105.5.

15. 1.92.1.

16. 1-2.3.8.

deep change we need is a matter not so much of our individual actions, but of our habits. Those habits are the tendencies we all have to certain forms of behaviour (whether good or bad), tendencies that are so much a part of who we are that they are hard to break (or form). Such dispositions or aptitudes run much deeper than single actions. For example, one could say 'Reeves is wonderfully athletic': that does not necessarily mean that, right now, Reeves is *doing* something athletic, like running a marathon. Reeves might be sitting at his desk, slurping tea. What it does mean is that whatever Reeves is currently doing, he has a real disposition to long jumps, hurdling and so on.

When Aquinas talks about 'habits', then, he is speaking of something like ethical 'muscle memory', whereby certain behaviour comes more naturally to the person with a certain habit. A good habit is a 'virtue'; a bad habit a 'vice'. To be virtuous – to be the sort of holy person who can know God – one must have virtue, according to Aquinas. But that is a deep thing: one act of virtue will not make a person virtuous, just as one act of vice will not make a person vicious (though repetition of an act will start ingraining a habit). The grain of a person's being runs deeper than single acts, and it is that very fibre of the soul that Aquinas sees must be made virtuous if ever we are to know God.

On law But how, then, can we acquire the virtues we need? According to Aquinas, God gives us two basic forms of help. The first is law, which seems here to be God's fundamental mode of operation. The essential principle of law is that 'good is to be done and pursued, and evil is to be avoided' (note that 'the good' is not about a relationship with God).[17] This principle is built into nature so as to guide our natural aptitude to virtue. On top of this natural law is God's revealed law, both the old and the new. The old law (of Moses) had three parts: the moral, which basically spelt out the natural law; and the ceremonial and judicial, which proclaimed Christ's future work, and thus were annulled when he performed it. The new law (the gospel) has the same purpose as all law, to

---

17. 1-2.94.2.

subject us to God, but with the difference that it is 'instilled into man, not only by indicating to him what he should do, but also by helping him to accomplish it'.[18]

On grace The second way God helps us to acquire the virtues is grace. That is, God pours his love into our hearts, making our hearts lovely and Godlike. This grace is absolutely essential for salvation, for it is not as if I can simply do good things and expect salvation; without grace, nothing I do can be meritorious before God.

Yet when Aquinas came to discuss grace, he found himself forced to disagree with Peter Lombard (c. 1100–1160), author of the *Sentences*, the standard textbook of medieval theology. Lombard had argued that the love of God poured into our hearts is actually the Spirit himself. Aquinas saw this view as hugely problematic, for if that were the case, then not only would our human free will have been violated, but also, it would not really be *us* loving God, but only the Spirit loving God *in* us. But for Aquinas, the whole point of grace is that it is something that changes *us*, that makes *us* virtuous, that enables *us* to merit eternal life. And it is given in such a way that it does not violate human freedom by forcing us to act in a particular way; rather, it is only by co-operation with grace that our dispositions change.

Second Part of the Second Part

Aquinas now proceeds to devote the largest section of the *Summa* to a discussion of the virtues themselves. And here he feels he must go beyond Aristotle, extending Aristotle's scheme into the supernatural realm the philosopher never knew. Aristotle, he holds, knew about the sort of natural virtue that produces a natural human happiness, but since there is also a supernatural happiness of which Aristotle was ignorant, there must be such things as supernatural virtues as well. Once again, Aquinas is showing what little disjunction he sees between the realms of nature and grace. It is as if sin has hardly affected nature at all; grace can simply take nature as it is, extend and perfect it. Certainly, the sense in this Part of the *Summa* is that our problem is not so much sin as lack of grace.

---

18. 1-2.106.1.

On the theological virtues Aquinas, then, starts with the three 'theological' virtues – those virtues that transcend our natural capacities and that can be received only by grace. The first of these is *faith*, which makes the 'intellect assent to what is non-apparent'.[19] Faith, in other words, is that act of the intellect whereby we choose to believe the truths of the church's creeds. Faith, for Aquinas, did not involve anything like personal trust (in fact, none of the virtues is oriented towards personal relationship with God).

The second theological virtue is *hope*, which is the longing for the vision of the divine essence. Hope, according to Aquinas, should not be confused with presumption: only those who persevere in good works can have true hope, and in any case, true hope always involves fear of the loss of what we hope for.

The third theological virtue is *charity*, for which Aquinas takes Augustine's definition: 'By charity I mean the movement of the soul towards the enjoyment of God for His own sake.'[20] There is a sense, however, in which Aquinas understands charity in a vitally different way to Augustine. For Augustine, charity was a heartfelt delight in God; for Aquinas, charity is a quality in the will. This was important for Aquinas, for he saw that if charity is something in the affections, then something must have affected the soul and caused charity to be there. But if that was the case, then charity could not truly be a meritorious product of the soul itself, but must be a response that God could never reward.

Charity, Aquinas believed, is the most important of the virtues, and the root of all merit before God. Without it, faith is nothing but a bare assent that, understandably, could never save. Furthermore, it is charity that makes all the other virtues truly virtuous. 'Charity is said to be the end of other virtues, because it directs all other virtues to its own end.'[21]

---

19. 2-2.4.1.

20. 2-2.23.2, citing Augustine, *On Christian Doctrine*, 3.10. It should not be thought that by 'charity' Aquinas means anything like giving money to the poor, which he would call 'alms-giving'.

21. 2-2.23.8.

On the cardinal virtues As well as the three 'theological' virtues of the supernatural realm, Aquinas taught that the natural realm has its own, entirely valid, virtues. These virtues could be attained by anyone, Christian or pagan, through their own efforts (though on their own they would not be sufficient to save). Chief among them are the four 'cardinal' virtues (from the Latin word *cardo*, meaning 'hinge'): prudence, justice, fortitude and temperance.

Prudence is the virtue without which there can be no virtue, for goodness, according to Aquinas, consists in choosing well. Prudence, then, is the virtue of reasoning what the good is, and then governing the will to act towards it.

Prudence on its own, however, would be impotent, for a whole host of factors always conspires to conflict with what our reason has chosen in prudence. The first, Aquinas says, is that while my will always seeks what is good, naturally it will only seek what is good for me. Yet, somehow, what is good for me is not always what is good for society as a whole. Thus I need the virtue of *justice*, which orients the will towards choosing the common good.

But it is not just the existence of other people that can conflict with my prudence. My own body has appetites that can war against my reasonable choices, and I need other virtues to assist prudence and bring those appetites under the government of my reason. One such appetite is my instinctive desire for self-preservation: naturally, I run from danger, difficulty and death. It is in such situations that the virtue of *fortitude* tells me when to stand up to and endure those things. Another such appetite is my desire for ever more food, drink and sex. Here the virtue of *temperance* enables my reason to govern how much of those things are actually good for me.

While these 'cardinal' virtues belong to the natural realm, and can be acquired by non-Christians, they can also be infused directly into the Christian's soul by God. In this way God can perfect my natural capacities. However, as always in Aquinas, supernatural things only ever build upon natural foundations, and thus, even were God to infuse the virtue of temperance into my soul, if I did not cultivate temperance through natural means, I would remain as vicious, lecherous and gluttonous as ever.

Third Part

Aquinas' aim in the third part was to consider (1) the person and work of Christ; (2) the sacraments by which his work is extended and applied; (3) the final resurrection and last things that his work accomplished.

On the incarnation Aquinas starts with the question of whether Christ had to become incarnate. It was a question he had unique struggles with, struggles highly illuminative of the driving forces in his thinking. Unsurprisingly, he sets out from his understanding of the nature of God, which

> is goodness, as is clear from Dionysius (Div. Nom. i). Hence, what belongs to the essence of goodness befits God. But it belongs to the essence of goodness to communicate itself to others, as is plain from Dionysius (Div. Nom. iv) . . . Hence it is manifest that it was fitting that God should become incarnate.[22]

So far, then, Aquinas seems to be saying that God would by virtue of his nature become incarnate – whether or not sin existed.

That said, he feels distinctly uncomfortable with the thought that he might then be constraining God's absolute omnipotence. For, if God is unrestrictedly omnipotent, then the cross cannot have been the way God had to save; if it was, then God's hand would be forced by it. The Almighty must have been free to choose to save the world in another way. In fact, God must have been free to have the Father or the Spirit become incarnate, rather than the Son, or for all three persons to become incarnate in one (presumably rather confused) man; it is even possible, Aquinas feels, that the Son could at some point assume another human nature.

In the end, though, Aquinas feels we simply do not know enough about whether God should have become incarnate, and thus, while our reason suggests that Christ would have become incarnate even had Adam not sinned, the reason he did become incarnate seems to have been that Adam did sin.

From there on, Aquinas' main intention is to show Christ the

---

22. 3.1.1, referring to Pseudo-Dionysius, *On the Divine Names.*

man as the one who exemplifies the standards of virtue laid out in the Second Part. The only virtues Christ did not have were faith (he had knowledge, and so did not need faith) and hope (he already had the union with God that hope desires). And, just as we win merit before God through grace, so, supremely, Christ the man won merit by virtue of the fact that he was actually united to God, the source of all grace. Then, as the exemplary, grace-filled man, he is shown to be the head of the church.[23]

It then remains for Aquinas to look at the actual act of incarnation itself: how Christ took flesh, lived, died, descended to hell, rose and ascended to heaven. This includes a relatively substantial discussion of the role of Mary, who was not immaculately conceived, Aquinas argues, but was sanctified in her mother's womb so that she never committed any sin (making it proper for her to give birth painlessly, live ever after as a virgin, and then be bodily assumed into heaven rather than seeing death). It leaves one of Aquinas' more interesting circular arguments, that through his life and death, Jesus sanctified Mary so that he might live and die.

Aquinas' understanding of the cross is especially significant and illuminative. Like Anselm, he essentially thought of Christ's death as making satisfaction for sin (though, of course, where Anselm saw such satisfaction as necessary, Aquinas did not). Aquinas saw more going on, though: by his death, Christ *acquired merits for us* (as well as freeing us from sin, the power of the devil and the debt of punishment, demonstrating God's love to us and giving us an example of obedience). Thus the cross is made part of Aquinas' overall scheme of salvation by the acquisition of merits.

---

23. Readers of the *Summa* are often struck by the fact that Aquinas does not dedicate any real space to a theology of the church (nobody did until the Reformation). However, Aquinas weaves a quite detailed understanding of the church into his discussion of Christ and the sacraments, and has a large, even cosmic, vision. The church, he explains, includes the Old Testament believers, who 'were borne to Christ by the same faith and love whereby we also are borne to Him' (3.8.3); it also includes angels. We will see more of his ecclesiology as we proceed, though it does remain largely under the surface of the *Summa*.

On the sacraments Aquinas has one, fundamental, governing thought concerning the sacraments: it is that the salvation of the Word-made-*flesh* is given to us through *physical* things. Christ is, as it were, the primary sacrament. He was not just a sign of some invisible grace outside himself. He was and is God acting graciously towards humankind. Thus grace was and is to be found in his very flesh. That, indeed, was the very reason he took flesh: so that through it we might receive grace. Just so, then, the sacraments of the church are not mere signs of some invisible grace outside and somehow separate from themselves; they really contain God's grace within themselves. The sacraments are thus, in a sense, extensions of the incarnation.

It is not, though, as if the incarnation somehow changed things in how God works. God, according to Aquinas, is a God who has and always would work through these sacraments:

> Now, though our faith in Christ is the same as that of the fathers of old; yet, since they came before Christ, whereas we come after Him, the same faith is expressed in different words, by us and by them. For by them was it said: 'Behold a virgin shall conceive and bear a son,' where the verbs are in the future tense: whereas we express the same by means of verbs in the past tense, and say that she 'conceived and bore.' In like manner the ceremonies of the Old Law betokened Christ as having yet to be born and to suffer: whereas our sacraments signify Him as already born and having suffered.[24]

And even in the Old Testament, the sacraments, he argues, were effective: 'circumcision bestowed grace, inasmuch as it was a sign of faith in Christ's future Passion'.[25] And all this is because Aquinas' God is a God who always builds the supernatural (grace) upon natural foundations (bread, wine, water etc.), making it impossible for Aquinas to conceive God ever giving grace other than through physical things.

There are now, he says, seven sacraments. The first is *baptism*,

---

24. 1/2.103.4.
25. 3.70.4.

which washes away our sins and begins the work of transformation in us. Given what it does, baptism is the most necessary
sacrament (though it is just possible to be saved without it – if, for
example, one undergoes the martyr's 'baptism of blood', or if one
desires baptism but cannot have it for some reason). The second
sacrament (dealt with in a blink) is *confirmation*.

The third is the *Eucharist*, and Aquinas' seminal treatment of it
has made him *the* Roman Catholic authority on the subject. To
explain what happens in the Eucharist, Aquinas took Aristotle's
view that each thing has its own 'substance' (inner reality) as well
as 'accidents' (appearance). Then, at the moment of consecration
by the priest, 'the whole substance of the bread is changed into the
whole substance of Christ's body, and the whole substance of the
wine into the whole substance of Christ's blood'. Only the appearance ('accidents') of the bread and wine remain. This miraculous
transformation, he said, 'can be called "transubstantiation"'.[26]
Aquinas meant all this entirely literally: 'By the power of the sacrament there is contained under it, as to the species of the bread, not
only the flesh, but the entire body of Christ, that is, the bones, the
nerves, and the like.'[27] For this reason, he believed, the Eucharistic
elements can and should be reverenced as Christ himself, for they
truly are Christ himself. For all their appearance, they are no longer
bread and wine, but Christ.

As such, Aquinas sees the Eucharist as the crowning sacrament,
for in it God shares himself through the very flesh of Christ. By
so perfectly extending the incarnation, it uniquely encapsulates
what a sacrament is. And, like the incarnation, it is about drawing a
body (of people) together into unity with God. Thus, in many
ways, Aquinas' entire understanding of the church is able to be
fitted into his explanation of the Eucharist, for the Eucharist
enfolds the meaning and reality of the church within itself.

It is, however, a strange irony that, at this very pinnacle of
Aquinas' theology, the scheme we have seen throughout, of the
supernatural building upon and perfecting the natural, has been

26. 3.75.4.

27. 3.76.1.

undone. For here the natural creation is annihilated and entirely replaced by another, supernatural substance. Only the husks of the appearance of the original remain. It is enough to make one tremble at the thought of being saved.

Supplement

It was at this point, having just completed his section on the Eucharist, and as he started work on the sacrament of penance, that Aquinas underwent the experience that made him determine never to write again. As a result, he never finished the *Summa*. However, knowing that his intention had been to examine the remaining sacraments (*penance*, *last rites*, *ordination* and *marriage*) and then the last things, after his death his students cut and pasted material from his earlier works to fill in what they assumed he would have said.

Going on with Aquinas

Aquinas' style is so dry that he is extremely hard to digest if one bravely tries to read through the *Summa Theologiae*, one article after another; he is, however, so neat and methodical that it is a very easy work to dip into. And he is so lucid that he still makes himself perfectly understood without the need for any great mental effort by the reader (no mean feat after the best part of a millenium). In other words, the *Summa* – which is, quite obviously, the place to get to know Aquinas – is genuinely open to the public.

The best version to use, both for reliability and ease, is the translation by the Fathers of the English Dominican Province. It is freely available online at <http://www.ccel.org/ccel/aquinas/ summa> or in print in five volumes under the title *Summa Theologica* (Westminster, Md.: Christian Classics, 1981). There are abridgements available, but the *Summa* is so easy to navigate that they are hardly necessary.

While it is now a little dated, James Weisheipl has written what is still perhaps the most useful single-volume introduction to the man and his thought, *Thomas D'Aquino: His Life, Thought and Work* (Washington D. C.: Catholic University of America

Press, 1974). Two more detailed – and quite brilliant – examinations of Aquinas' theology are Brian Davies' *The Thought of Thomas Aquinas* (Oxford: Clarendon, 1992) and Eleonore Stump's *Aquinas* (London: Routledge, 2003).

Thomas Aquinas timeline

1215	Dominic Guzman founds the Order of Preachers ('Dominicans')
1221	Dominic dies
1224–6	Aquinas born
1226	Francis of Assisi dies
1239	Enters University of Naples
1244	Kidnapped by family en route to Paris
1245	Arrives in Paris
1248	Goes to Cologne with Albert the Great
1252	Returns to Paris to complete studies and begin teaching
1259–64	Writes *Summa contra Gentiles*
1259	Leaves Paris for Naples
1261–5	With the papal court in Orvieto
1265	Opens study house in Rome
1266	Begins writing *Summa Theologiae*
1267	Goes to Viterbo
1268	Returns to teach in Paris
1272	Returns to teach in Naples
1273	An experience leads him to refuse to write any more
1274	Aquinas dies

INTERMEZZO

When Thomas Aquinas died at Fossanova in 1274, the monks there cut off his head and various other body parts to keep as relics. Some years later, they also exhumed his corpse so as to boil off the flesh and keep the bones in a more convenient place for veneration.

Nearly two hundred and fifty years would pass. Then another monk – this time from northern Germany – would set out to oppose the veneration of Aquinas' head. For this monk would like neither relics nor so much of the content of that skull. Directly challenging the now 'Saint' Thomas Aquinas and his use of Aristotle's logic and ethics, he would write:

> Virtually the entire *Ethics* of Aristotle is the worst enemy of grace . . . It is an error to say that no man can become a theologian without Aristotle . . . Indeed, no one can become a theologian unless he becomes one without Aristotle . . . Briefly, the whole Aristotle is to theology as darkness is to light.

This monk would not pull punches! There was about to be a revolution in theology.

7. THE WORD DID EVERYTHING

Martin Luther

Five hundred years after his extraordinary life, Martin Luther remains perhaps the most controversial theologian of all time. His piercing thought, uncompromising directness and often lavatorial offensiveness have made him as vilified by some as he is venerated by others. Yet the strength of his grasp on the sheer graciousness of God towards sinners, coupled with the originality and vigour of his expression, make him incomparably stimulating for anyone to read. Actually, 'stimulating' is hardly the word; reading Luther is like being slapped in the face. It hardly ever fails to leave one gasping.

The difficulty with Luther is that he never wrote a systematic presentation of his thought; he devoted his efforts instead to biblical commentaries, sermons and small treatises. The advantage is the easy accessibility of the short works; the disadvantage is that, because there are so many of them, it can be hard to grasp the overall shape of his theology. In order to get a toehold on him, we will focus on the crucial turns in his theological development, looking especially at his Heidelberg Disputation, and then leaf through the essential points of his mature thought as seen in his main Reformation treatises.

Luther's life

On 10 November 1483 Luther (or Luder as he then was) was born in Eisleben in central Germany. Like most people in Eisleben, his father was in the mining industry, but he had aspirations for his son, and so, when he could, he sent him off to study law. Young Martin, however, suffered more than most from a classic fear of the age: that of sudden death. The worry was that, without the chance to confess all your latest sins to a priest, you would fail to die in a state of grace. Imagine, then, his terror when a summer lightning bolt knocked him to the ground as he walked from his parents' house to his university. 'Saint Anne, help me! I shall become a monk!' he cried to his patron saint. A monk he thus became, and yet that only served to intensify his spiritual anxiety (or *Anfechtung* as called it, meaning 'conflict', 'assault' or 'temptation'). Conducting his first mass, for instance, he was terrified by the thought of the holy majesty of God. He spent more and more time obsessively confessing his sins to a superior, paranoid that he would forget some and so fail to be completely absolved. It forced him to start seeing sin as something deeper than a matter of particular lapses, as a total sickness. Through extreme asceticism he sought to earn merit before God. On a visit to Rome this included climbing the Scala Sancta on his knees, repeating the Lord's Prayer for each step, and kissing it.[1] Yet at the top he began to doubt whether it had been of any avail.

On his return to Germany he was transferred to the Augustinian monastery in Wittenberg. His superior, Johann von Staupitz, had suggested that he become a doctor of theology and lecture on the Bible at the university there. At least in that way Luther might find some consolation in the Scriptures. Wittenberg was a fitting place for Luther to think about repentance and forgiveness, for its overlord, Frederick 'the Wise', Elector of Saxony, had amassed there one of the largest collections of saints' relics.

---

1. The Scala Sancta was the staircase that Jesus had supposedly climbed to appear before Pilate, and that had subsequently been brought to Rome by the emperor Constantine's relic-obsessive mother.

It was believed that the saints, through their exceptional holiness, had earned a surplus of merit that the pope could confer on souls, both living and dead, to alleviate the time they must spend in purgatory, the place where they must be purged and fitted for heaven. And, since the necessary merit came from the saints, it seemed appropriate to offer it to those who venerated their relics.

One of these papal 'indulgences' or gifts of merit was to be offered in the Castle Church of Wittenberg on 1 November (All Saints' Day) 1517 in return for a fee that would be used to build the new basilica of St Peter in Rome. Such offers were commonplace, but the issue of indulgences had recently been given special prominence by the antics of a travelling indulgence-monger, Johann Tetzel. Using crude emotional blackmail, he advertised the indulgences with such jingles as 'As soon as the coin in the coffer rings, / the soul from purgatory springs,' and 'Place your penny on the drum, / the pearly gates open and in strolls mum.'

In a pre-emptive strike, on 31 October, All Saints' Eve, Luther posted on the church door a summons to an academic disputation on the issue, consisting of ninety-five theses for debate. In it he asked questions such as why the pope did not release all souls from purgatory out of love, instead of charging for it. But at the heart of his criticism was the fact that the practice of indulgences effectively replaced the need for true repentance of the heart with a mere external transaction. Supporting this argument, he soon found that the proof-text used to validate the sacrament of penance from the Latin Vulgate was a mistranslation of the original Greek. In the Vulgate, Matthew 4:17 reads *penitentiam agite* (do penance), whereas the Greek meant 'change your mind', something internal and not merely external.

He could never have predicted the consequences of his action, but popular local grievance at German money being taken to Italy fuelled support for his critique. Meanwhile, his subsequent debates with church officials soon made it clear that the real issue was one of authority. Which had the final say: Bible or pope? In all this, though, Luther had not yet formulated his mature doctrine of justification by faith alone. That would come only in his 1519 'tower experience' (so named because he had his study in the monastery tower).[2] Then, studying Romans 1:17,

> I began to understand that the righteousness of God is that by which the righteous lives by a gift of God, namely by faith. And this is the meaning: the righteousness of God is revealed by the gospel, namely, the passive righteousness with which the merciful God justifies us by faith, as it is written, 'He who through faith is righteous shall live.' Here I felt that I was altogether born again and had entered paradise itself through open gates.[3]

With this, Luther's confidence in his stand against Rome grew dramatically. In late 1519 he declared that the pope was antichrist, and events began to move swiftly. In 1520 Pope Leo X issued a bull excommunicating Luther. Luther then publicly burned the bull along with the papal constitutions and books of scholastic theology, writing a counter-blast entitled *Against the Execrable Bull of Antichrist*. That same year he also wrote his key Reformation tracts *Treatise on Good Works*, *To the Christian Nobility of the German Nation*, *The Babylonian Captivity of the Church* and *The Freedom of a Christian*.

Luther now had the Holy Roman Emperor (Charles V), the pope, a number of high-ranking churchmen and seemingly a thousand years of church history against him. The following year he was summoned to a session (or 'diet') of the imperial court

---

2. There is a debate among Luther scholars as to precisely when Luther had his 'tower experience' and discovered the true meaning of the righteousness of God. Because he does talk about justification by faith early on, some believe his experience happened as soon as 1513, thus making the ninety-five theses a product of his new theology. Others hold that it was not until 1519, meaning that the ninety-five theses and his other early lectures pre-date his mature understanding of justification by faith. Luther himself clearly placed it in 1519, and I have followed his dating here.

3. 'Preface to the Complete Edition of Luther's Latin Writings', *Luther's Works*, ed. J. Pelikan (vols. 1–30, St. Louis: Concordia; vols. 31–55, Philadelphia: Fortress, 1955–76), vol. 34, pp. 336–337.

in Worms, where most assumed he would soon be burned for
heresy. When he arrived he was initially so intimidated by the
questioning in the presence of all the princes that he could hardly
speak. The papal nuncio took Luther to be too stupid to have
written all that he had, and wanted to know who really was behind
the Reformation tracts. Then, after an order to recant, came
Luther's final answer:

> I am bound by the Scriptures I have quoted and my conscience is
> captive to the Word of God. I cannot and I will not retract anything,
> since it is neither safe nor right to go against conscience. I cannot do
> otherwise, here I stand, may God help me, Amen.[4]

Luther was condemned to death as a heretic. But he had already
disappeared.

What had happened was that his prince, Frederick 'the Wise'
of Saxony, had decided to hide him. He arranged for armed
horsemen to kidnap Luther and take him to the Wartburg Castle
where he remained, in disguise, for nearly a year. In that time he
translated the entire New Testament from its original Greek into
German. For the first time in a millennium the people would be
able to read a reliable version of the Scriptures for themselves.
Thus Luther repaid Rome in kind, sounding the death-knell to all
its power.

Unfortunately, during his time in hiding, trouble was brewing in
Wittenberg. Church practice was being reformed at a rate that the
people were unable to cope with. Also, three men from Zwickau
arrived, claiming to be prophets who had no need of the Bible
since the Lord spoke to them directly; they repudiated infant
baptism and advocated the speeding of the kingdom of God
through the slaughter of the ungodly. Wittenberg was spiralling
into chaos, and Luther found himself facing a new opposition: the
'fanatics' of the radical Reformation.

Luther returned with a call for more careful reform:

---

4. 'Luther at the Diet of Worms', ibid. vol. 32, p. 112.

> I will constrain no man by force, for faith must come freely without
> compulsion. Take myself as an example. I opposed indulgences and all
> the papists, but never with force. I simply taught, preached, and wrote
> God's Word; otherwise I did nothing. And while I slept, or drank
> Wittenberg beer with my friends Philip and Amsdorf, the Word so
> greatly weakened the papacy that no prince or emperor ever inflicted
> such losses upon it. I did nothing; the Word did everything.[5]

He also reacted strongly to the radicals, who, he believed, had
mistaken the point of the Reformation: where he was revolting
against the spiritual pretensions of sinners, they were tilting at the
external things of the faith, such as the Bible and the sacraments.
He saw in their theology a new anti-external legalism.

In 1525 the ex-monk married an escaped nun, Katharina von
Bora, and proceeded to have five children with her. Together they
converted Luther's old Augustinian cloister into a family home
that became something of a model for the Protestant minister's
household. There Luther would dole out thoughts on anything to
eager students at the dinner-table (much of it recorded as his *Table
Talk*); there he wrote his hundreds of letters of pastoral advice.
Like his theology, his advice is consistently startling:

> Whenever the devil pesters you with these thoughts, at once seek out
> the company of men, drink more, joke and jest, or engage in some other
> form of merriment. Sometimes it is necessary to drink a little more, play,
> jest, or even commit some sin in defiance and contempt of the devil in
> order not to give him an opportunity to make us scrupulous about trifles.
> We shall be overcome if we worry too much about falling into some sin.
>
> Accordingly if the devil should say, 'Do not drink,' you should reply
> to him, 'On this very account, because you forbid it, I shall drink, and
> what is more, I shall drink a generous amount.' Thus one must always
> do the opposite of that which Satan prohibits. What do you think is
> my reason for drinking wine undiluted, talking freely, and eating more
> often if it is not to torment and vex the devil who made up his mind to

---

5. 'Second Sermon, 10 March 1522, Monday after Invocavit', *Luther's Works*,
vol. 51, p. 77.

torment and vex me? Would that I could commit some token sin simply for the sake of mocking the devil, so that he might understand that I acknowledge no sin and am conscious of no sin. When the devil attacks and torments us, we must completely set aside the whole Decalogue. When the devil throws our sins up to us and declares that we deserve death and hell, we ought to speak thus: 'I admit that I deserve death and hell. What of it? Does this mean that I shall be sentenced to eternal damnation? By no means. For I know One who suffered and made satisfaction in my behalf. His name is Jesus Christ, the Son of God. Where he is, there I shall be also.'[6]

Luther knew that, for all the political support he might receive, the Reformation would be a superficial thing if it did not win hearts and minds. The first need, then, was for a translation of the entire Bible that everyone could read in their own German. This he provided, richly illustrated, in 1534. For Luther, the Bible is our supreme authority. While even prophets and apostles could and have erred, the Bible as God's Word never does. It authenticates and interprets itself, never needing anything external for its validation, nor surrendering its authority to any other source of information. He was adamant that the Bible is clear and self-evidently intelligible. Without it, God cannot be truly known. For this reason, the vast majority of Luther's theology is biblical commentary (and most of that on the Old Testament).

Luther was no bibliolater, though. His attitude to the Bible was governed by his view that its sole content and message, from Genesis to Revelation, is Christ. So strongly did he maintain this that he made the test of a book's canonicity whether it teaches Christ, not who wrote it. It was because he felt that the apostle James's letter was not sufficiently clear in its proclamation of Christ that he wrote, 'I almost feel like throwing Jimmy into the stove'![7]

---

6. To Jerome Weller, July 1530, in *Luther: Letters of Spiritual Counsel*, Library of Christian Classics, ed. T. G. Tappert (Vancouver: Regent College, 2003), pp. 86–87.

7. 'The Licentiate Examination of Heinrich Schmedenstede', *Luther's Works*, vol. 34, p. 317; cf. pp. 362, 396.

Even the Old Testament section of his translation was filled with woodcut illustrations of Christ, for he believed that Christ was actually present with the Old Testament believers, whom he called 'Christians'. Their faith was in no way pre-Christian; rather, they had faith in Christ and wrote their prophecies about him.

It was this belief that undergirded Luther's most notorious writings against the Jews. In 1523 he had written a tract that condemned the persecution of Jews, advocating instead that Christians use the Old Testament to prove to them Jesus' messiahship. Yet by 1542 he had come to see a devilish stubbornness in the Jewish refusal to acknowledge that their own Scriptures spoke so clearly of Christ. He therefore wrote *On the Jews and Their Lies*, advocating the application of blasphemy laws to Jews. This would entail the destruction of synagogues and the expulsion of the Jews. Unsurprisingly, the Nazis sought to justify their anti-Semitism with this (Luther having become a national hero for his stand against the foreign power of Rome and his Bible translation's shaping of the German language). One could wish Luther had never written the work. It is, without doubt, the most unpleasant product of a pen that could pour forth obscene scatological vulgarity at his opponents. However, for all that, twentieth-century anti-Semitism is too often read back into Luther incorrectly. Nazism developed its racism out of nineteenth-century Darwinism and Romanticism, not Lutheranism.[8] Luther's intolerance of the Jews was not racial but spiritual, based on what he saw as their refusal to acknowledge the clear Christian meaning of the Old Testament. Thus, while he became entirely intolerant of Jews who rejected Christ, he could aid and befriend those who converted.

For Luther, the written word should not exist without becoming a spoken word, a word talked about and understood by the people.

---

8. 'Luther's antagonism to the Jews was poles apart from the Nazi doctrine of "Race" . . . I suppose Hitler never once read a page by Luther. The fact that he and other Nazis claimed Luther on their side proves no more than the fact that they also numbered Almighty God among their supporters' (Gordon Rupp, *Martin Luther: Hitler's Cause or Cure?* [London: Lutterworth, 1945], pp. 75, 84).

He thus corrected abuses in the liturgy and rewrote it to make it a Bible teacher. He also wrote two catechisms, the Large Catechism for adults and the Small Catechism for children, introducing the Ten Commandments (law) to illuminate sin; the Apostles' Creed (gospel) to apply forgiveness; the Lord's Prayer as our prayerful response; and the two sacraments as means of grace to sustain the believer. Then, applying his belief in the priesthood of all believers, he introduced congregational singing (where previously the congregation had been mere spectators). Everyone would now sing of God's truth. And it would be important for Luther that they were singing it: Luther believed music to be of next importance after theology. Like the word and the sacraments, he viewed music as an external thing that affects the heart; like them it chases away the devil, dispersing the spiritual anxieties he attacks us with. Luther even wrote a number of hymns, the most famous being that battle-hymn of the Reformation, 'A Mighty Fortress is our God'.

Spearheading the Reformation under a death sentence, and with repeated attacks on his theology and life, it is no wonder that his health cracked. For ten years or so it declined until, in the cold winter of 1546, it gave out and Luther died, excommunicated from the church he had hoped to reform. His last written words were 'We are beggars. That is true.' They sum up so much of his thought: we are nothing but spiritual beggars who contribute nothing to our salvation or understanding of God; but there is, outside ourselves, God's word of truth. On that we depend.

Luther's thought

To feel the bite of Luther's theological revolution, we need to track the development of his thought in those crucial early years. Only then does it become clear that his was a truly theological revolution, and not merely a protest at abuses. Only then is the staggering and disturbing radicality of his proposal made clear.

Perhaps more than anything else, the years leading up to the 'tower experience' of 1519 see the development of his theology of the cross. In his lectures of 1515–16 on Romans, his theology of the cross was that God's blessing comes to us only through his condemnation of us. Our problem is that, full of self-love, we naturally attempt to use God in order to get and enjoy heaven for ourselves. The only remedy for such self-love is self-accusation, for it is only when we resign ourselves to hell in submission to God's condemnation of us that we can say that we are loving God for his own sake, and not for the gifts or the heaven he can give us. Freely handing ourselves over to damnation, we are submitting to God, and are clearly no longer just using God for his gifts. This, then, was a form of justification by faith alone, but the faith is in his condemnation of us, not his gospel-word of free salvation. What distinguishes it from Luther's mature doctrine of justification is that it does not have the passive quality he would later give it. Where later it would involve simple belief in God's declaration of forgiveness, here it looked more like an exercise in humility: we are justified by condemning ourselves. Thus he can talk still of striving to be made righteous, and of becoming more and more righteous – language he would later renounce.

In 1518 Luther was invited to explain his theology to the German congregation of his Augustinian order in Heidelberg. Although the Heidelberg Disputation caused less of a stir than his ninety-five theses, it was in the end far more influential theologic-ally. Six future Reformers were present to hear Luther. There he expounded a substantially developed theology of the cross that was to underlie all his mature thought (despite the fact that still he had not understood justification as he later would). His theological argument consisted of four steps:[9]

Theses 1–12: The problem of good works

Luther begins with a refusal to allow that any human works have intrinsic merit before God. Instead he argues that, naturally, our best works are nothing but damnable sins. To explain this he brings in a sharp distinction between law and gospel that he would always maintain. For Luther, law is not limited to Sinai or the Old Testament; it is all that accuses us of sin. We cannot be saved by

---

9. For this structure I am indebted to the analysis of Gerhard O. Forde, *On Being a Theologian of the Cross: Reflections on Luther's Heidelberg Disputation, 1518* (Grand Rapids: Eerdmans, 1997).

doing the good works demanded by the law. Instead, 'law brings the wrath of God, kills, reviles, accuses, judges, and condemns everything that is not in Christ'.[10] To think that any work of ours might advance our righteousness before God is to confuse law with gospel. The gospel, in contrast, is a proclamation that the law's demands have been met in Christ, and, similarly, is not limited to the New Testament. Yet the gospel's message of salvation can be understood only by first hearing the law's pronouncement of the judgment we need saving from. Christians then find themselves living in a tension between law and gospel: as sinners we feel the law's accusation, yet through faith in Christ we fulfil the law.

Theses 13–18: The problem of the will

Having ruled out any merit in our works, Luther delves to the real problem: the corrupt human will, which can produce only corrupt human works. Ever since the Fall we have sought a freedom for our wills that is entirely unbounded, even by God. This is sin. So, with our works condemned and our very wills incapable of pleasing God, what can we do? Luther says, 'fall down and pray for grace'.[11] Thus he reveals that he had not yet attained his mature understanding. Here grace still comes by something we do (by prayer). In his mature understanding, grace comes through accepting God's promise; we remain entirely passive.

Theses 19–24: The way of glory versus the way of the cross

Luther then outlines the essential difference between his theology and the one he is opposing. The theology of glory is the theology of the natural man, who believes that works are good, suffering is bad and that we need no more than some encouragement to raise ourselves up to God. In shattering contrast, the theology of the cross attacks all those things that we believe to be the best in religion, showing that we cannot raise ourselves up, that the cross is our desert, and that only through suffering death can glory be reached. Thus we are reduced to utter dependence on Christ and his way of the cross.

---

10. 'Heidelberg Disputation, Thesis 23', *Luther's Works*, vol. 31, p. 54.
11. 'Heidelberg Disputation, Thesis 16', ibid. p. 50.

Theses 25–28: God creates us out of nothing

All that said, the theology of the cross presupposes resurrection. This is its goal: the sinner must be reduced to nothing – he must die – before he can receive new life. God only creates life out of nothing; he never looks to build on our foundations. 'The love of God does not find, but creates, that which is pleasing to it.'[12]

This theology of the cross was to provide the dynamics of all his thinking to come.[13] The point is that God clothes himself to come to us (whether in the incarnation, the Bible or the sacraments), yet his appearance is the complete opposite of what we would expect. We expect him to be pleased with us and our works; we expect him to be like us. Yet the truth is hidden in an alien disguise, and thus, to the blinded sinner, God appears to be the devil, and the devil appears to be the lord of the world. Even what we receive from God (the cross, death, suffering, the world's hatred etc.) is the opposite of what we would expect from him. This being the case, Luther would always exploit the paradoxes and contrasts of the gospel as far as he could.

The life of faith is thus one of constant *Anfechtung* (conflict or temptation) as we believe in opposition to our hearts, minds and consciences. 'To believe means to live in constant contradiction of empirical reality and to trust one's self to that which is hidden.'[14] Our hearts believe that our works can please God. Faith says otherwise. Our consciences condemn us, since we are sinners. Faith turns to the gospel, for only there can we know the truth about ourselves. Faith trusts Christ instead of the heart or the conscience.

Finally, for Luther, faith contradicts reason, and this requires some more detailed examination. Luther was not attacking the proper use of the mind, but the presumption of the mind to think

---

12. 'Heidelberg Disputation, Thesis 28', ibid. p. 57.

13. As he put it, *CRUX sola est nostra theologia* (the cross alone is our theology); indeed, *crux probat omnia* (the cross tests all) (*Luther's Commentary on the First Twenty-Two Psalms*, tr. J. N. Lenker [Sunbury, Pa.: Lutherans in All Lands, 1903], vol. 1, pp. 289, 294–295).

14. P. Althaus, *The Theology of Martin Luther*, tr. R. C. Schultz (Philadelphia: Fortress, 1966), p. 33.

that it could know God and his ways unaided by revelation. He described scholastic and natural theology as enemies of the cross in just the same sense as moralism.[15] They are all, he believed, forms of Pelagianism. Without revelation, the human mind does not even know what its own sin is, because it does not know the God that sin offends. The only God it can imagine is the devil. The true God is a God who is revealed. He is revealed only in

---

15. J. I. Packer pulls together a number of Luther's concerns as he explains, 'It was in her capacity as the prompter and agent of "natural" theology that Mistress Reason was in Luther's eyes the Devil's whore; for natural theology is, he held, blasphemous in principle, and bankrupt in practice. It is blasphemous in principle, because it seeks to snatch from God a knowledge of Himself which is not His gift, but man's achievement – a triumph of human brain-power; thus it would feed man's pride, and exalt him above his Creator, as one who could know God at pleasure, whether or not God willed to be known by him. Thus natural theology appears as one more attempt on man's part to implement the programme which he espoused in his original sin – to deny his creaturehood, and deify himself, and deal with God henceforth on an independent footing. But natural theology is bankrupt in practice; for it never brings its devotees to God; instead it leaves them stranded in a quaking morass of insubstantial speculation. Natural theology leads men away from the Divine Christ, and from Scripture, the cradle in which He lies, and from the *theologia crucis*, the gospel doctrine which sets Christ forth. But it is only through Christ that God wills to be known, and gives saving knowledge of Himself. He who would know God, therefore, must seek Him through the Biblical gospel ... Man is by nature as completely unable to know God as to please God; let him face the fact and admit it! Let God be God! let man be man! let ruined sinners cease pretending to be something other than ruined sinners! let them realise that they lie helpless in the hand of an angry Creator; let them seek Christ, and cry for mercy. This is the point of Luther's polemic against reason. It takes its place as a part of his all-embracing prophetic onslaught against the proud vainglory of helpless sinners who deny their own helplessness' (J. I. Packer and O. R. Johnston, 'Historical and Theological Introduction' to *Martin Luther on The Bondage of the Will* [Cambridge: James Clarke, 1957], pp. 46–47).

Christ, the God on the cross, made known in the Old and New Testaments, which preach him. Even then, we sinners can only know him when we are reduced to nothing and die with him on the cross. Thus, he can write, there is 'only one article and one rule of theology, and this is true faith or trust in Christ'.[16]

In some ways Luther's serious spiritual anxiety really began with the sacraments, when he conducted that first mass; in 1519 it was the sacraments that helped him solve his crisis. In a sermon on penance (which he still viewed as the third sacrament), he argued against the official view that said it was a presumption to assume one had definitely received grace through the sacrament. Luther retorted that God promised grace through the sacraments, and that therefore it was a sin to deny what God had promised. Ironically, Luther was, in a sense, defending a higher view of the sacraments than Rome! Yet this formed the structure of his gospel-discovery. He saw in the sacraments something external, outside himself, that promised God's grace. This, he saw, was the nature of the gospel: we do not look to ourselves; we look to something external, the promise of God, and by receiving that, receive his grace. When next he turned to Romans 1:17, he could understand the righteousness of God to be something passively received in a way he never had before.

The year after that final piece fell into place, 1520, was a year of extraordinary productivity for Luther. He produced a number of popularly accessible tracts to promote and explain the theology of the new Reformation: *Treatise on Good Works*, *To the Christian Nobility of the German Nation*, *The Babylonian Captivity of the Church* and *The Freedom of a Christian*.

Treatise on Good Works

Luther needed to establish that his theology was not about devaluing good works, and so in this first treatise set out his own analysis of the Ten Commandments. Underpinning it all is Luther's distinction between the mere outward appearance of obedience to

---

16. *Table Talk*, no. 1583: 'The Tempted and Afflicted Understand the Gospel', Between 20 and 27 May 1532, *Luther's Works*, vol. 54, p. 157.

the commandments, through works, and real obedience through faith. What matters is our trust in Christ. Only born out of that trust can any of our works be good, for only then do we honour God's name and not ours. This is because faith acknowledges who God is and what he is like. In other words, faith is true worship. And that being the case, holiness can be cultivated only through the preaching of the gospel:

> In fact, when we see it properly, love comes first, or at any rate it comes at the same time as faith. For I could not have faith in God if I did not think he wanted to be favorable and kind to me. This in turn makes me feel kindly disposed toward him, and I am moved to trust him with all my heart and to look to him for all good things . . . Look here! This is how you must cultivate Christ in yourself, and see how in him God holds before you his mercy and offers it to you without any prior merits of your own. It is from such a view of his grace that you must draw faith and confidence in the forgiveness of all your sins. Faith, therefore, does not originate in works; neither do works create faith, but faith must spring up and flow from the blood and wounds and death of Christ. If you see in these that God is so kindly disposed toward you that he even gives his own Son for you, then your heart in turn must grow sweet and disposed toward God . . . We never read that the Holy Spirit was given to anybody because he had performed some works, but always when men have heard the gospel of Christ and the mercy of God.[17]

All that being the case, there can no longer be any hierarchy of works. Whether staying at home, fasting or going to church, what matters is the state of the heart towards God. Has the work been done out of a heartfelt love for God, sprung from a knowledge of his love for me?

To the Christian Nobility of the German Nation

Luther believed that, in order to safeguard her power, Rome had built three defensive theological walls around herself: she asserted first that all earthly rulers had to bow to the pope as the supreme

---

17. 'Treatise on Good Works', *Luther's Works*, vol. 44, pp. 30, 38–39.

temporal power; secondly, that only the pope might interpret the Scriptures; thirdly, that no one but the pope could summon a council and thus reform the church. These Luther now sought to bring down with a blast of his pen.

His essential move was to destroy the distinction between clergy and laity. This stripped away any rationale for the pope's being the supreme temporal power. It also allowed every Christian the right to interpret Scripture and to call a council to reform the church. For this last point Luther enjoyed playing a trump card: Nicea, the most important council in church history, had been called by a layman, the emperor Constantine.

This being the case, Luther could call on the ruling classes of Germany to protect the spiritual, as well as temporal, welfare of their people against the ravages of Rome. In practice, Luther got what he sought: the Reformation in Germany could never have thrived as it did without the protection of the princes, many of whom became its patrons. Nine years after the Diet of Worms, a number of the German princes who had watched Luther's defence before Charles V presented the Augsburg Confession of Lutheran faith to the same emperor for his approval. There were consequences, however, that Luther did not intend. Having effectively set up the German princes as emergency bishops, unwittingly he had steered subsequent Lutheranism on to a course in which churches would exist subservient to governments.

What Luther proposed was a theology of government derived from Augustine's idea of the two cities (of God and man). In keeping with the other dualities in his thought (gospel and law, inner faith and outer works, the way of glory and the way of the cross etc.), Luther developed a distinction between the kingdom of God and the kingdom of the world. The kingdom of God is the church, God's instrument of mercy. In that kingdom, God rules hearts persuasively by his word. If everyone were to obey that word, there would be no need for the other kingdom. As it is, God provides the state as the kingdom of the world, his instrument of wrath against the disobedient. In that kingdom, God rules outward behaviour coercively by the sword. Through the kingdom of the world God restrains evil and exercises his providential care for all.

Rome, he argued, had confused the two kingdoms by making

the pope the lord of both. Yet Luther would never stand with the radicals, who separated themselves from everything to do with the state. Christians, he held, are citizens of both kingdoms, and are to be active in both. The two kingdoms are to support each other: as the prince protects the church, so the pastor urges the people to obey the prince (so long as he is no tyrannical opponent of the church). Then, he maintained, the gospel can flourish.

The Babylonian Captivity of the Church

Luther's new understanding of the gospel required a complete break from Rome's sacramental system. The freedom of the Christian could never be preserved when the church herself was in captivity to it. Rome's spiritual power depended on the idea that grace was administered automatically through the clergy's performance of the sacraments. Luther's insistence on the need for personal faith had already robbed the clergy of that control. In *The Babylonian Captivity of the Church* he set about dismantling their control further, by proposing a new theology of the sacraments.

Luther defined a sacrament as a word of promise from Christ, accompanied by a sign. Sacraments, then, are words from God, to be received by faith. He never ceased to value the sacraments as powerful demonstrations of the external objectivity of God's Word, as well as the fact that, as the sacraments are given to me, personally, so God's promise is given to me, personally. (He would go further, to say that as the sacraments are given to our bodies, so the grace promised in them is meant also for our bodies.)

With this definition of a sacrament in place, Luther reduced their number from seven to two. Marriage, he argued, is a gift to all humanity, not a promise for believers only. Confirmation, while acceptable, entails no promise from God, and therefore cannot be classified as a sacrament. Extreme unction was instituted by the apostle James, not Christ himself. The sacrament of ordination he rejected for having no basis in Scripture (he accepted that some believers should be authorized by God's people to teach God's Word, but denied that that set them apart as an intermediary priesthood). Instead, he argued, all believers are priests, charged with the duty to teach and spread God's Word. This left three sacraments: penance, baptism and the Lord's Supper. Giving a sense of how fast his theology was moving, at the beginning of the work Luther treats penance as a valid third sacrament, but by the end excludes it on the grounds that it has no external sign. This left baptism and the Lord's Supper.

Baptism, he maintained, is a promise of new life in Christ, signified by water. Having received the promise, we are called to respond to it in faith. This distinguished his position from Rome's, but it would also lead him into conflict with the new radicals and 'Anabaptists' (literally 'rebaptizers'). Many of the radicals rejected all sacraments because of their externality (thus, Luther wrote, rejecting how God himself has willed to deal with us). The Anabaptists rejected infant baptism (and thus would seek to baptize adults who had already been baptized as infants). Luther's response to the Anabaptists was a clear example of his overall theology in action. He believed that their rejection of infant baptism compromised the gospel, for it made one's own confession of faith, rather than God's Word, the essential thing. For Luther, it looked like a return to dependence on something internal, so letting faith become a work. It was pastorally vital for him that God's promise in baptism was in no way dependent on anything within a person: when troubled in conscience it was Luther's habit to write on his desk in chalk *baptizatus sum* (I am baptized). His consolation was always external; he would never trust even his own faith, but only direct that faith at God's objective Word.

Luther believed that the other sacrament, of bread and wine, had been taken captive by Rome in a number of ways: Rome forbade the laity from receiving the wine out of fear that it might be spilt; she taught that the mass is a new sacrifice or good work before God; and she taught the doctrine of transubstantiation. Justification by faith alone and the resultant priesthood of all believers dealt with the first two errors. His objection to transubstantiation was that it was an Aristotelian, as opposed to biblical, doctrine whereby the earthly (bread and wine) is entirely replaced by the heavenly (body and blood). It also propagated an individualism among those who individually received its benefits, whereas the true sacrament of the Lord's Supper creates communion.

The disagreement with Rome over the Lord's Supper was not to be Luther's last word on the subject. In fact, after justification, the

Lord's Supper was the doctrine Luther gave most time to. This was largely because of his disagreement with other Reformers, especially Zwingli of Zurich. Zwingli argued that Christ's body is not literally present in the sacrament, but is instead symbolized by the bread. The Lord's Supper, he believed, was a mere symbol to help us commemorate Christ's sacrifice and signify our membership of his body. This was entirely unacceptable to Luther, who believed that Zwingli had hardened his heart against the clear words of Christ: 'This is my body.' The result, thought Luther, was that Zwingli fell into the same error as the Anabaptists, of replacing grace with works and converting the sacrament into an opportunity for us to do something (i.e. remember Christ and signify something about us). Such a view simply could not be reconciled with Luther's understanding. Luther maintained that Christ's body and blood are really present and given to all in the bread and wine, to the harm of those who refuse to trust him, but to the blessing of those who receive him by faith.

The Freedom of a Christian

Perhaps even more remarkable than his output in 1520 was the fact that, only two weeks after the appearance of his incendiary *Against the Execrable Bull of Antichrist* he produced one of the most beautiful and positive statements of evangelical theology – and addressed it to the pope! 'I have never thought ill of you personally,' he wrote, for 'I have no quarrels with any man concerning his morals but only concerning the word of truth.' This, despite the fact that he could still tell the pope that

> the Roman church, once the holiest of all, has become the most licentious den of thieves [Matt. 21:13], the most shameless of all brothels, the kingdom of sin, death, and hell. It is so bad that even Antichrist himself, if he should come, could think of nothing to add to its wickedness.[18]

Luther was seeking to rescue the pope himself from Rome!

---

18. 'The Freedom of a Christian', ibid. vol. 31, pp. 335–336.

The Freedom of a Christian is organized around two propositions: 'A Christian is a perfectly free lord of all, subject to none.
A Christian is a perfectly dutiful servant of all, subject to all.'[19]

Inward freedom

The work depends heavily on the story of the lover and his beloved
in Song of Songs (especially 2:16, 'My lover is mine and I am his'),
understood as an allegory of Christ and his church. Luther likens
the gospel to the story of a prostitute who marries a king.

First, the marriage is effected by the wedding vow. Just so, Christ
gives himself to us through his own promise. This was at the heart
of Luther's departure from Augustine (or at least the earlier and
more Catholic side of Augustine). Augustine had held that God
gives grace to those who pray for it. Luther held that grace is given,
not on the basis of what we say, but what God says. We receive grace
by believing God's promise. When we accept the word, we receive all
that belongs to the word. It might be more helpful to describe this
as 'justification by God's word' instead of 'justification by faith',
because it is God's word that justifies here, not our faith as such.
Pastorally this was revolutionary, for in contrast to the introspective
piety he had grown up with, Luther would always point doubters
outwards to God's sure word, not inwards to their own fickle faith.

Secondly, upon the declaration of the wedding vow, the prostitute finds that she has been made a queen. It is not that she has in
any way made her behaviour or character more queenly; it is that
now she has been given a new status. Just so with the believer:
because of an external word she receives a righteous status that is
also external to her, and unrelated to her character and behaviour.
Or, as Luther put it, her righteousness is both alien (external) and
passive (unearned). And so, as the prostitute remains wayward in
heart but a queen by status, so the believer is simultaneously righteous and a sinner (*simul justus et peccator*), and will always remain so
(*semper justus et peccator*).

The prostitute did not marry the king for his crown or wealth, and
yet when she accepts him she also receives them. So the believer,

---

19. Ibid. p. 344.

when she accepts Christ, receives all that is his, just as he takes all that is hers (her sin). Then she can confidently display 'her sins in the face of death and hell and say, "If I have sinned, yet my Christ, in whom I believe, has not sinned, and all his is mine and all mine is his."'[20] Yet the believer has received Christ himself, and not merely his status. He, then, sets about the transformation of the heart of the believer such that she becomes increasingly righteous herself. Thus by faith she receives the Christ who both justifies and sanctifies.[21]

Luther's argument entailed a different understanding of faith from that of the Roman Catholicism of the day. In Catholicism, faith was essentially an assent that meant attending mass. For Luther it became personal trust in Christ; and, because he had demonstrated the idolatry of any good works done without faith, he had come to see faith as the only worship that pleases God.

This gave Luther an infinitely more powerful definition of sin. Sin, he saw, is essentially unbelief. 'The worst sin is not to accept the Word.'[22] This is the ultimate sin against the first commandment, for it refuses to take God seriously for who he is:

> what greater contempt of God is there than not believing his promise? For what is this but to make God a liar or to doubt that he is truthful? – that is, to ascribe truthfulness to one's self but lying and vanity to God? Does not a man who does this deny God and set himself up as an idol in his heart?'[23]

---

20. Ibid. p. 352.

21. It is necessary to note that Christ himself is received into the believer's heart as well as the believer's being clothed externally with Christ's righteousness. A historical overemphasis on the latter has led to a fascinating and hotly debated reappraisal of the subject by some Finnish Luther scholars who reject the idea that Luther had a forensic understanding of justification (see C. E. Braaten and R. W. Jenson [eds.], *Union with Christ: The New Finnish Interpretation of Luther* [Grand Rapids: Eerdmans, 1998]).

22. 'Lectures on Isaiah, Chapters 40–66', *Luther's Works*, vol. 17, p. 383.

23. 'The Freedom of a Christian', ibid. vol. 31, p. 350.

No good works could avail one who had committed this sin of sins. Such works could only compound the idolatry by the implicit suggestion that they could create righteousness and life. Given this, it is small wonder that the believer should experience *Anfechtung* when she looks away from Christ to her own self and achievements, thus for a while failing to trust Christ. To look to one's self and one's work is not to have faith.

Luther believed that the failure to grasp this lay behind all the rotten structure of Rome. Like the Pharisee who had built his own idolatrous self-confidence on the failures of the tax collector, Rome's moralism only served to foster competition between individuals and thus hierarchy. Yet when faith becomes the only worship, all are levelled. Only then is there genuine community.

Outward subjection

If the first proposition ('A Christian is a perfectly free lord of all, subject to none') was concerned with faith, the second proposition ('A Christian is a perfectly dutiful servant of all, subject to all') looks at the true role of good works. For all the strength of his polemic against the misuse of works, Luther is no advocate for licence. Put simply, Luther sees good works as the natural result of justification, but never its cause. The prostitute/queen, though only queen because of her husband, now becomes queenly and begins to represent her husband to all; just so, since we now know and love Christ, we become Christs to our neighbours, serving them as Christ serves us, and thus representing him. The Christian, therefore, 'lives in Christ through faith, in his neighbor through love. By faith he is caught up beyond himself into God. By love he descends beneath himself into his neighbor.'[24]

The Bondage of the Will

In the very earliest days of Luther's protest against Rome, there seemed to be an alliance between the Reformer and a number of

---

24. Ibid. p. 371.

Renaissance scholars, such as Erasmus. Luther had used Erasmus' printing of the New Testament for his translation into German, and Erasmus initially welcomed Luther as a much-needed new broom who could clean up the corruption of Rome. The alliance, however, was entirely superficial, for while Erasmus attacked Rome's moral and practical abuses, Luther was attacking Rome's doctrine. Erasmus had little interest in theology, but he was soon disturbed by what he saw flowing from Luther's prolific pen.

Eventually, in 1524, he wrote *The Freedom of the Will*, arguing in effect that Luther had gone too far, that the sinner is merely weak-willed, and does have some ability to perform actions that are genuinely pleasing to God. If man had no freedom of choice, how could he ever have any merit before God? Why would God ever command anything of us? Erasmus had not exactly intended it, but what Luther saw was that *The Freedom of the Will* was a direct attack on *The Freedom of the Christian* – on the heart of the Reformation, in fact:

> you alone have attacked the real issue, the essence of the matter
> in dispute, and have not wearied me with irrelevancies about the
> papacy, purgatory, indulgences, and such like trifles (for trifles
> they are rather than basic issues), with which almost everyone
> hitherto has gone hunting for me without success. You and
> you alone have seen the question on which everything hinges,
> and have aimed at the vital spot; for which I sincerely thank
> you.[25]

To protect *The Freedom of a Christian*, Luther thus wrote *The Bondage of the Will*.

Luther saw that, if the sinner has in fact some basic ability to produce for himself a righteousness before God, then our salvation cannot be from God's grace alone, meaning that salvation is not received by faith alone. Erasmus, of course, had brought in our own contribution to our salvation with extreme subtlety; but

25. 'The Bondage of the Will', *Luther's Works*, vol. 33, p. 294.

in Luther's eyes that only made it more dangerous. It was a concealed trapdoor of Pelagianism.[26]

Luther thus set out to prove the absolute impossibility of the idea that naturally we might ever even desire to love and please God. He was not suggesting that we are unable to adhere to social norms and codes of morality, only that that is something quite different from having any true desire to love God. This inability of ours, he argued, comes from the fact that our wills are simply not free in that way. Here people are commonly confused. Luther never meant that somehow we are pushed into sin: 'when a man is without the Spirit of God he does not do evil against his will, as if he were taken by the scruff of the neck and forced to it'.[27] Quite the opposite: we freely choose to do the things we do. We do what we want. The trouble is, we never naturally want God, and our choices are entirely tied to that. We freely choose to do the things we love, but we are unable to choose *what* to love, and since we do not love God, we cannot choose for him. The only solution is for God in his grace to change our hearts and their desires; only then, finding that we love him, will we choose him.

All this simply expressed what Luther had found for himself. When, as a monk, he had thought of God as one who merely judges and demands perfection. Luther said, 'I did not love, yes, I hated the righteous God who punishes sinners, and secretly, if not blasphemously, certainly murmuring greatly, I was angry with God.'[28] All his zeal to serve God and win heaven only drove him to hate God more. But, through the gospel of God's loving and free grace, his heart was changed, and only then did he find he could love God and choose him. As he put it soon after, 'When this faith is rightly present the heart must be made glad by the testament. The heart must grow warm and melt in the love

---

26. Pelagianism, which is essentially the belief that we can (and must) save ourselves by our own efforts, is discussed in the chapter on Augustine, pp. 98–102.
27. 'The Bondage of the Will', *Luther's Works*, vol. 33, p. 64.
28. 'Preface to the Complete Edition of Luther's Latin Writings', ibid. vol. 34, pp. 336–337.

of God. Then praise and thanksgiving will follow with a pure heart.'[29]

Going on with Luther

Luther is effortless to read: he is stimulating, amusing and clear. Thus it could not be easier to deal with the man himself. Timothy Lull's anthology *Martin Luther's Basic Theological Writings* (Minneapolis: Fortress, 1989) contains an excellent collection of the most important works. *The Freedom of a Christian* is probably the place to start (also available on www.great-theologians.org). One slight shame is that space did not allow Lull to include the full text of *The Bondage of the Will*; this can be found, along with an outstanding introductory essay by J. I. Packer, in *Martin Luther on The Bondage of the Will*, ed. J. I. Packer and O. R. Johnston (Cambridge: James Clarke, 1957). Luther's *Letters of Spiritual Counsel* (Vancouver: Regent College, 2003) and *Table Talk*, both easily available, add some of the best vignettes of insight into the humanity of the man himself.

There are two books of essential readings in the secondary literature. The first is Roland Bainton's classic biography of Luther, *Here I Stand: A Life of Martin Luther* (Nashville: Abingdon, 1950). Though published in 1950, it is still an addictive read, and also attractively illustrated with contemporary woodcut illustrations. The other is Paul Althaus's *The Theology of Martin Luther*, tr. R. C. Schultz (Philadelphia: Fortress, 1966). It remains the best single-volume overview of Luther's theology, but is worth reading just for the material on sin and justification, irrespective of relevance to Luther himself!

---

29. 'Treatise on Good Works', ibid. vol. 44, p. 56.

Martin Luther timeline

1483   Luther born in Eisleben

1505   Thunderstorm; joins Augustinian monastery in Erfurt

1511   Moves to Wittenberg

1517   Posts the ninety-five theses on the door of the Castle Church in Wittenberg

1518   Heidelberg disputation

1519   'Tower experience'

1520   Writes *Treatise on Good Works*, *To the Christian Nobility of the German Nation*, *The Babylonian Captivity of the Church*, *Against the Execrable Bull of Antichrist*, *The Freedom of the Christian*; burns the papal bull excommunicating him

1521   Diet of Worms; taken into protective custody in the Wartburg Castle, Eisenach, where he translates the New Testament into German

1522   Returns to Wittenberg

1524   Peasants' War begins; Erasmus writes *On the Freedom of the Will*

1525   Writes *On the Bondage of the Will*; marries Katharina von Bora

1529   Luther and Zwingli fail to agree on the Lord's Supper at the Marburg Colloquy

1530   Lutheran princes present the *Augsburg Confession* of Lutheran belief to the emperor at the Diet of Augsburg

1534   First complete edition of Luther's translation of the Bible

1546   Luther dies visiting his home town of Eisleben

8. KNOWING A LOVING GOD

John Calvin

Geneva: today it is an international symbol of peace and stability, but even to mention the city in the sixteenth century was to invite argument. For some it was a shining beacon of gospel hope; for others it was a hotbed of revolution, a nest of heresy. All this because of one man: John Calvin. Today we tend to know more about Calvinism than Calvin himself. Yet still the man manages to polarize opinion. On the one hand there are those who see him in stained glass; on the other are those for whom he was Geneva's cantankerous and cruel dictator, a man whose belief in a terrifying God inspired a reign of religious terror. 'Better with Beza in hell than with Calvin in heaven!' as his enemies used to say. Of course, neither picture is accurate. In fact, the real problem with Calvin is how enigmatic he was. He was extraordinarily reticent about speaking of himself, and, lacking Luther's white-hot charisma, his personality has become much harder to make out down through the centuries.

What we can know more easily is his theology. And when the caricatures are left to one side, Calvin can be appreciated as a theologian who has much to offer both those who call themselves Calvinist and those who do not. Karl Barth put it like this:

Calvin is a cataract, a primeval forest, a demonic power, something
directly down from Himalaya, absolutely Chinese, strange, mythological;
I lack completely the means, the suction cups, even to assimilate this
phenomenon, not to speak of presenting it adequately. What I receive
is only a thin little stream and what I can then give out again is only a
yet thinner extract of this little stream. I could gladly and profitably set
myself down and spend all the rest of my life just with Calvin.[1]

Calvin's life

Jean Cauvin, as he was known before he Latinized his name, was
born on 10 July 1509 in Noyon, some 60 miles north of Paris.
Intended by his father for the priesthood, at the age of eleven or
twelve he was sent to the University of Paris to study theology.
About five years later his father changed his mind and withdrew
Jean from Paris, sending him instead to Orléans to study law.
There he was introduced to a new world of humanism, and
made friends with a group sympathetic to the ideas of renaissance
and church reform.[2] Some of these, such as Melchior Wolmar and
Calvin's cousin Pierre Robert, were actually committed to the
Reformation.

At this time Wolmar taught Calvin Greek, which was highly
significant. Greek was a language intimately associated with the
Reformation, Greek being used to challenge the church's Latin
Vulgate translation and thus challenge the authority of the church
itself. As T. H. L. Parker puts it, 'Greek spelt the beginning of the

1. Karl Barth to Eduard Thurneysen, 8 June 1922. Barth uses the
   term 'demonic' in its original sense here, meaning that Calvin was
   a supernatural force. No connotation of evil is implied!
2. Sixteenth-century humanism has nothing to do with twentieth-century
   secular humanism. Humanism then was a movement dedicated to the
   rediscovery of classical Greek and Latin culture. Its motto, *Ad fontes!*
   (To the Sources!) showed its aim: humanism sought to drink directly
   from the clear intellectual waters of antiquity rather than from what it
   saw as the stagnant pond of constipated medieval scholasticism.

end for the Latin church, at least in its then form.'[3] At any rate, it was around this time that, as Calvin later wrote, 'God by a sudden conversion subdued and brought my mind to a teachable frame.'[4] Surprisingly, we know no more than that about the conversion of the great Reformer. We can only say that it is highly likely that it was brought about through his reading of Luther's 1520 Reformation treatises.

There was one other telling event during those years: Calvin wrote a commentary on the Roman philosopher Seneca's call for the emperor Nero to exercise clemency (*De clementia*). More than anything it was an attempt by Calvin to make his mark as a humanist scholar. Yet it was to provide the foundation for all the biblical commentaries to come. Calvin would use all the critical and linguistic tools of humanism to develop a method of exegesis that is recognizably modern.

The time for enjoying such humanist study was soon to be over for Calvin, though. While he was back for a short time in Paris, the new rector of the university, Nicholas Cop, delivered an address that was considered heretically Lutheran. Before Cop could be arrested, he fled to Basel in Switzerland (a free city in favour of the Reformation, where Erasmus, Heinrich Bullinger, Guillaume Farel and Pierre Robert were already living). The authorities quickly came looking for Calvin, who was perhaps suspected of being Cop's ghostwriter. Apparently, Calvin only just escaped, lowered from the window on a rope of bed sheets.

It was not an easy time to be on the run in France; and with friends and co-Reformers being burned, the situation was getting more difficult by the day. Thus he made his way to join Cop in Basel. While there he helped Pierre Robert with his new French translation of the Bible and, incredibly, having been a Christian for no more than five years, completed the first edition of his *Institutes of the Christian Religion*.

If anything could be more momentous, it was to follow. After

---

3. T. H. L. Parker, *John Calvin: A Biography* (Oxford: Lion, 2006), p. 9.
4. Calvin's preface to his commentary on the Psalms (Edinburgh: Calvin Translation Society, 1844–56; repr. Grand Rapids: Baker, 1993), 1.40.

about a year he began travelling again with friends. Having made his way back to Paris, he intended to go on to Strasbourg, one of the major centres of the Reformation in Europe. However, the armies of Francis I and Charles V lay in the way, forcing him to take a long detour to the south. Calvin intended therefore to stop overnight in Geneva, a city which had recently become evangelical by constitution, but which was far from being settled in its evangelicalism. Unfortunately for Calvin, he was waylaid by the fiery Guillaume Farel, who begged him to help build up the church in Geneva. When Calvin replied that he wanted instead to devote himself to private study, Farel

> proceeded to utter an imprecation that God would curse my retirement, and the tranquillity of the studies which I sought, if I should withdraw and refuse to give assistance, when the necessity was so urgent. By this imprecation I was so stricken with terror, that I desisted from the journey which I had undertaken.[5]

So Calvin settled in Geneva (!), at first as an academic, but soon as a full-time pastor. Thus, like his hero Augustine, Calvin found himself dragged from the comfort of the study to the rigours of the pulpit.

However uncomfortable the shift might have felt, Calvin showed no signs of heel-dragging. With unnerving speed he and Farel set about the reformation of the church in Geneva. Unsurprisingly, this raised hackles, and the popular mood began to turn against them. They were accused of being French spies, and finally, when in 1538 they refused to obey the city council's order to use unleavened bread in the Easter Communion, they were banned from preaching and then expelled from Geneva.

Calvin believed that he had effectively ruined the church in Geneva and so had been removed from pastoral ministry by God. Yet this, of course, meant that he could resume the quiet life of scholarship from which Farel had dragged him two years earlier. And the perfect place for such a life was Strasbourg, his original destination. Geneva had been a mere interlude.

---

5. Ibid. 1.43.

One can only feel sorry for Calvin, for there in Strasbourg he was accosted by Martin Bucer, who followed Farel's example and called Calvin a Jonah for fleeing from his calling, urging him instead to the work of pastoring the many French refugees in the city. This Calvin did, and in the process learned more about the pastorate than he had from anyone else. The lessons learned in Strasbourg would profoundly shape Calvin's understanding of what a church should look like. Also during his time in Strasbourg, Calvin was invited to some of the great Protestant–Catholic dialogues, such as at Regensburg in 1541. There he was disappointed, not only by the concessions some Lutherans were prepared to make to Rome, but also by their lack of discipline and over-dependence on the state. In the years to come they would serve as a warning in his mind as he sought to shape the church in Geneva.

Calvin's theological work hardly suffered from his pastoral demands. When the eminent Cardinal Sadoleto wrote a letter to Geneva inviting her to return to the Roman fold, the city council, despite having exiled Calvin, saddled him with the task of responding. In reply Calvin produced a tour de force of Reformation theology, vindicating it biblically and historically and exposing the weakness of Sadoleto's thought. He also produced his first major commentary (on Romans) and produced a substantially revised edition of his *Institutes*.

In Strasbourg his friends also sought to get him married. Calvin was hardly a natural romantic. He once wrote, 'I know not if I shall ever marry. If I did so, it would be in order to devote my time to the Lord, by being the more relieved from the worries of daily life.'[6] Yet in 1540 he came to marry Idelette de Bure, a sickly widow who brought with her two children from her former Anabaptist husband, and Calvin evidently loved her dearly. In 1542 they had a son, Jacques, who died after two weeks. The consolation Calvin received at this time from his strong doctrine of divine sovereignty is movingly evident from what he wrote to a

6. F. Wendel, *Calvin: The Origins and Development of his Religious Thought* (London: Collins, 1963), p. 65.

friend soon afterwards: 'The Lord has certainly inflicted a severe and bitter wound in the death of our baby son. But He is Himself a Father and knows best what is good for his children.'[7] In 1549 Idelette herself died, leaving Calvin to care for her two children.

Calvin was only to remain in Strasbourg for three years, for in that time the politics changed in Geneva, and then they wanted him back. He was extremely reluctant to return, but was again persuaded. And so, in 1541, Calvin returned to Geneva for good. As soon as he was back in the pulpit he simply resumed his sermon series at the verse where he had left off three years earlier. (Here was a preacher dedicated to sequential exposition!) Yet even before that, on the very day of his return, he submitted to the city council his Ecclesiastical Ordinances for the comprehensive reformation of the church in Geneva.

In them he proposed details such as that every family in Geneva had to receive a pastoral visit once a year and be catechized, only those who passed being admissible to communion. Perhaps the most important proposal, though, was for the establishment of a consistory, an ecclesiastical disciplinary committee. If Geneva was not to end up like the ill-disciplined Lutheran churches, if she was not to be associated with the city of Münster, he believed Geneva must be disciplined.[8] The proposals were largely accepted, and so a consistory was established. Essentially, its business consisted of giving practical instruction to individuals. For example, one recalcitrant family was directed 'to frequent the sermons and the catechism and to buy a Bible in their house and have it read'.[9]

---

7. Letter 90, to Viret, *The Letters of John Calvin*, tr. Jules Bonnet (New York: Franklin, 1972), vol. 4, p. 332.

8. In 1534 radical Anabaptists had seized control of the German city of Münster, turning it into a cultish and polygamous commune that had horrified all Europe. After a bloody siege the city was retaken, but for more than a century Münster cast a long shadow of suspicion over the idea of reforming cities.

9. *Registers of the Consistory of Geneva in the Time of Calvin*, vol. 1, 1542–4, ed. Robert M. Kingdon, Thomas A. Lambert and Isabella M. Watt, tr. M. Wallace McDonald (Grand Rapids: Eerdmans, 1996), p. 134.

Much of Calvin's bad reputation stems from the fact that the consistory could be overzealous: we read of disciplinary action taken against individuals for merely stating that the pope was a good man, for making a noise during a sermon, or for singing a rude song about Calvin, and so on. Certainly, it created a city very unlike Luther's Wittenberg: for a while inns in Geneva were forbidden for citizens, and in their place five 'abbeys' were provided in which guests were given a French Bible and placed under supervision.

Such moral policing exasperated many in Geneva, who often then reacted against Calvin personally. But did Calvin deserve his reputation as the moralizing despot? The fact is that he was never capable of being such a figure. Calvin was a mere resident alien in Geneva, not a citizen, and thus had no right to vote or hold any secular office. He could be dismissed or expelled at the whim of the city council. Despotic power was simply beyond his grasp, and his scholarly temperament makes the thought that he would ever have wanted it incredible.

The crucible for Calvin's reputation has always been the burning of Michael Servetus for heresy in 1553. Servetus' denial of the Trinity and consequent reconstruction of the doctrine of salvation was acknowledged by Catholic and Protestant alike to be spiritually homicidal heresy. Thus, after he escaped arrest for his views in Catholic France, it was hardly surprising when he was arrested upon arrival in Geneva. All Europe was watching, for the question was, would Geneva be more tolerant than Rome and countenance arch-heresy? Geneva itself was accused of being heretical; if she tolerated Servetus, it would prove the point. Thus the city council put Servetus on trial, calling on Calvin to act as their prosecutor. However, we should not imagine Calvin to be the puppet-master behind it all; at the time the council were so hostile to Calvin that Servetus thought he could get Calvin banished instead of himself. The council consulted with other Protestant cities in Switzerland and Germany: all agreed that Servetus should be sentenced to death. When the sentence was pronounced, Calvin asked that Servetus be given the more lenient sentence of death by beheading rather than being burned. He was refused, and Servetus was burned at the stake on 27 October 1553. From all this it seems absurd that Calvin should be held personally responsible. He was complicit in Servetus' execution, it is true, but why should Calvin's reputation be so tarnished when the execution of Protestants and radicals by Catholics and vice versa was a commonplace of the sixteenth century? All Europe was agreed on Augustine's principle that heresy should ultimately be dealt with by the secular sword. Unease with capital punishment was simply not a feature of the times. Thus, if there was a fault, it can be seen only as a fault of the age, not the man.

Two years after the Servetus affair, in 1555, the tide began to turn for Calvin in Geneva. The council now began to be dominated by his supporters, leaving him freer not only to reform Geneva, but to turn it into an international centre for the propagation of the gospel, especially in his native France. Calvin had already become the inspiration and leader-in-exile of French Protestantism, writing letters of support to churches as well as providing them with his works of theology. Now, however, he could seriously set about the evangelization of France. A secret programme was established to infiltrate agents of the Reformation into France, using an underground network, with safe houses and hiding places, so that pastors, once trained in Geneva, could be slipped across the border to plant covert new churches. Its success was astounding: the Reformed faith exploded in numbers and influence in France. More than 10% of the entire population became Reformed, as well as something like a third of the nobility. The complete reformation of France looked possible (that is, until 1572, after Calvin's death, when the St Bartholomew's Day massacres of Protestants ended all such hopes). But it was not only France: John Knox returned to Scotland full of the vision of Geneva; English Protestants, who had fled from Queen Mary's persecution, returned to bring the principles of Geneva to Canterbury; missionaries were dispatched from Geneva to Poland, Hungary, the Netherlands, Italy, even South America. Geneva had become a nerve centre for world evangelization.

In 1559, to underpin all this mission and ministry, Calvin opened a college and academy in Geneva, appointing Thèodore de Bèze (or Beza) as rector. This was to provide a general education, starting with classes in secondary studies, with theology as the queen of the sciences. For the ripple effect it was to have on the world, especially through the pastors trained there, the academy was probably Calvin's crowning achievement.

On top of all this, Calvin preached and lectured almost daily and produced a steady stream of tracts, commentaries and revised editions of the *Institutes*. His contemporary Colladon wrote:

> Calvin for his part did not spare himself at all, working far beyond what his powers and regard for his health could stand. He preached commonly every day for one week in two. Every week he lectured three times in theology . . . He was at the *Consistoire* on the appointed day and made all the remonstrances. Every Friday at the Bible Study . . . what he added after the leader had made his *declaration* was almost a lecture. He never failed in visiting the sick, in private warning and counsel, and the rest of the numberless matters arising out of the ordinary exercise of his ministry. But besides these ordinary tasks, he had great care for believers in France, both in teaching them and exhorting and counselling them and consoling them by letters when they were being persecuted, and also in interceding for them, or getting another to intercede when he thought he saw an opening. Yet all that did not prevent him from going on working at his special study and composing many splendid and very useful books.[10]

All this was clearly to the detriment of his health, which declined to such an extent that he spent the last ten years of his life often in excruciating pain.[11] Yet he appears never to have taken a day off. He

---

10. T. H. L. Parker, *Calvin's Preaching* (Louisville, Ky.: Westminster John Knox, 1992), pp. 62–63.

11. A few months before his death he wrote, 'at that time I was not attacked by arthritic pains, knew nothing of the stone or the gravel – I was not tormented with the gripings of the cholic, nor afflicted with hemorrhoids, nor threatened with expectoration of blood. At present all these ailments as it were in troops assail me. As soon as I recovered from a quartan ague, I was seized with severe and acute pains in the calves of my legs, which after being partially relieved returned a second and a third time. At last they degenerated into a disease in my articulations, which spread from my feet to my knees. An ulcer in the hemorrhoid veins long caused me excruciating sufferings, and intestinal ascarides subjected me to painful titillations, though I am now relieved from this vermicular disease, but

died on 27 May 1564 and, according to his request, was buried in an unmarked grave so that in death he might not become a relic and so deny the Reformation he had lived for.

Calvin's thought

Calvin's theology was not original. Rather, it was 'fundamentally so old-fashioned that it seemed a novelty'.[12] Its brilliance lay instead in its clarity of exposition, its consistent rigour and orderly arrangement. Yet, because of its lack of originality, to understand Calvin best it is worth having a working knowledge of those theologies

---

immediately after in the course of last summer I had an attack of nephritis. As I could not endure the jolting motion of horseback, I was conveyed into the country in a litter. On my return I wished to accomplish a part of the journey on foot. I had scarcely proceeded a mile when I was obliged to repose myself, in consequence of lassitude in the reins. And then to my surprise I discovered that I discharged blood instead of urine. As soon as I got home I took to bed. The nephritis gave me exquisite pain, from which I only obtained a partial relief by the application of remedies. At length not without the most painful strainings I ejected a calculus which in some degree mitigated my sufferings, but such was its size, that it lacerated the urinary canal and a copious discharge of blood followed. This hemorrhage could only be arrested by an injection of milk through a syringe. After that I ejected several others, and the oppressive numbness of the reins is a sufficient symptom that there still exist there some remains of uric calculus. It is a fortunate thing, however, that minute or at least moderately sized particles still continue to be emitted. My sedentary way of life to which I am condemned by the gout in my feet precludes all hopes of a cure. I am also prevented from taking exercise on horseback by my hemorrhoids. Add to my other complaints that whatever nourishment I take imperfectly digested turns into phlegm, which by its density sticks like paste to my stomach' (Letter to the physicians of Montpellier, February 1564, *The Letters of John Calvin*, tr. Jules Bonnet [New York: Franklin, 1972], vol. 4, pp. 371–372).

12. Parker, *John Calvin*, p. 9.

that influenced him most. Above all, two figures come to mind: Luther and Augustine. Luther's influence is more immediately obvious; but it is Augustine's name that appears more frequently than any other in Calvin's writings. In fact, it can hardly be said too strongly: to understand Calvin one must know Augustine.

That said, how might we best try to assimilate this phenomenon that is Calvin? In his 1541 Ecclesiastical Ordinances, four permanent church offices are mentioned: pastors, teachers or doctors, elders and deacons. Doctors are provided to teach the universal church (especially its pastors) and protect its doctrine; pastors teach a particular congregation, applying Scripture to them and administering the sacraments; elders are responsible for order and discipline; deacons provide for the social welfare of the people. Understanding these four offices not only serves to outline Calvin's view of how churches should operate; it also reveals how Calvin viewed the different aspects of his own ministry. Calvin believed that he had been given two offices: that of pastor and that of doctor/teacher. As a teacher he sought to teach the church, and especially its pastors, doctrine (which he did in the *Institutes*). This was done so as to understand Scripture (which he did in his commentaries and lectures). Thus he would equip pastors (including himself) who would then in turn teach the people doctrine (through the catechism) in order that they might understand Scripture better (which would happen primarily in sermons).[13] The *Institutes*, the commentaries, the catechism and the sermons thus serve as the four wheels of his ministry, and we can best acquaint ourselves with Calvin's thought by looking at each in turn.

The Institutes of the Christian Religion

It is his *Institutes*, however, that should take most of our time, for it is there that the distilled spirit of Calvin can be sampled. As such,

---

13. For a thorough unpacking of the relationship between these modules in his school of Christ, see Randall C. Zachman, *John Calvin as Teacher, Pastor and Theologian: The Shape of His Writings and Thought* (Grand Rapids: Baker, 2006).

it is an immensely rich and multifaceted work, and we must resist the popular temptation to reduce it to a single theme (the idea that Calvin was a theologian of one subject is usually attributed to him by those who would give him their own theme). What sort of work is the *Institutes*, then?

Calvin wrote the first, 1536, edition in refuge from the persecution of evangelicals in his native France. He dedicated it to Francis I, the king of France, arguing in the preface that accusations of heresy against them were unjustifiable, for they were following the true Christian religion that the king claimed to uphold as the legal religion of France. Such an apologia for the evangelical faith was vital not only for the authorities to read, but also for the evangelicals themselves, and thus was published as a physically small book, making it easy to be carried around (and hidden in a coat pocket when the time came for it to be banned).

It was much more than an apologia, however. The full title he gave the work was *Institutes of the Christian Religion Embracing Almost the Whole Sum of Piety, and whatever Is Necessary to Know of the Doctrine of Salvation: A Work Most Worthy to Be Read by All Persons Zealous for Piety, and Recently Published*. In Latin *Institutio* means 'instruction', and this was to be Calvin's chief aim. The work was thus structured on the framework of a traditional catechism as follows:

- Chapter 1: On the law (with an exposition of the Ten Commandments)
- Chapter 2: On faith (with an exposition of the Apostles' Creed)
- Chapter 3: On prayer (with an exposition of the Lord's Prayer)
- Chapter 4: On the sacraments

Two final chapters then deal polemically with issues of the day:

- Chapter 5: On the five 'false sacraments' of Roman Catholicism (confirmation, penance, extreme unction, ordination, marriage)
- Chapter 6: On the liberty of the Christian, ecclesiastical and civil government

He never understood this instruction in a merely cerebral way, however: his purpose, he wrote 'was solely to transmit certain rudiments by which those who are touched with any zeal for religion might be shaped to true godliness'.[14] It is this aim that falsifies the accusation that Calvin, being a theologian of the word and concerned with the knowledge of God, intellectualized faith. The *Institutes* is not a cold work to read. For true knowledge of God, as Calvin will make clear, is not something limited to the brain. 'How then is it possible for you to know God and yet be touched by no feeling?' he once asked.[15] Rather, Calvin wanted readers to feel the force of the truths under discussion so that their hearts might be won for Christ. He would speak repeatedly of God ravishing us with his love, wooing and inflaming our hearts with the knowledge of himself. This, he believed, was the point of doctrine: properly arranged and rightly taught, it is the most powerful force for real change deep in the hearts of real people.

Three years later, in the 1539 edition, Calvin substantially revised his creation. Rearranged, bulked up to seventeen chapters, at three times the size of the previous edition, the *Institutes* now had a more specific agenda: 'to prepare and train aspirants after sacred theology in reading the Divine Word'.[16] No longer just a catechism; here was a guide to Scripture. By this move the *Institutes* and Calvin's biblical commentaries could begin to work in tandem: with doctrine explained here, the commentaries could be dedicated to pure exegesis and kept from becoming overly long or cluttered by theological digressions. Two of his great concerns are thus revealed: first, he wanted his theology to be brief and simple, for he was interested in communicating theology rather than restricting it to specialists; secondly, he wanted the Bible to be read and understood by all so that the Christ of the Bible might be known by all. Both were in stark contrast to the withholding of the Bible from the people in medieval Roman Catholicism, and all of his efforts flowed from those concerns.

---

14. Epistle Dedicatory to Francis I, *Institutes of the Christian Religion, 1536 edition*, tr. F. L. Battles (Grand Rapids: Meeter Center & Eerdmans, 1975), p. 1.

15. Commentary on 1 John 2:3.

16. *Calvini Opera Selecta*, ed. P. Barth and W. Niesel (Munich: Kaiser, 1936), p. 255.

Calvin produced expanded and updated editions of the *Institutes* in 1543, 1545 and 1550. In 1559, however, he made his final and most radical revision. Now at about five times the size of the original, the material was arranged into four books. Not only does the new structure show how profoundly trinitarian Calvin's theology is; it also expresses his ongoing desire to show that the evangelical faith is simply creedal orthodoxy.

- Book 1: *The Knowledge of God the Creator* (corresponding to the first section of the Apostles' Creed, 'I believe in God the Father almighty')
- Book 2: *The Knowledge of God the Redeemer in Christ* (corresponding to the second section of the Apostles' Creed, 'I believe in Jesus Christ his only Son our Lord')
- Book 3: *The Way in which we Receive the Grace of Christ* (corresponding to the third section of the Apostles' Creed, 'I believe in the Holy Spirit'[17])
- Book 4: *The External Means or Aids by which God Invites us into the Society of Christ and Holds us therein* (corresponding to the section of the Apostles' Creed on 'the holy catholic Church')

Instead of making up a compendium of doctrines, the four books present a flowing argument that follows the proper development of a knowledge of God. In Book 1 we see that, while we have an innate awareness of divinity, we need enlightening by Scripture so as to distinguish the true God from all pretenders to true divinity. Then, in Book 2, we find that through knowing him we are made aware of our slavery to sin, and so are led to seek righteousness and wholeness in Christ. In Book 3, having been justified, we repent of our sinful ways, express our trust in God through prayer, and look with confidence to both our past (God's election of us) and future (the resurrection). Finally, in Book 4, we live out our

---

17. Though the person of the Spirit is not specifically dealt with, Calvin explains in the title of the first chapter of Book 3 that the things already spoken of concerning Christ (in Book 2) 'Profit Us by the Secret Working of the Spirit'.

faith in the world, enabled by the institutions of the church and the
sacraments.

Such is the elegant structure of the 1559 edition. Now to some
of the details that fill it.

Book 1: The Knowledge of God the Creator

'Nearly all the wisdom we possess, that is to say, true and sound
wisdom, consists of two parts: the knowledge of God and of ourselves.' So Calvin begins and, in many ways, encapsulates the
argument of the *Institutes*. The knowledge of God and ourselves are
intertwined, he argues: man cannot know God until he knows himself as a sinner against God, his Creator. However, despite the fact
that God's being is indelibly etched on all his creation, man ungrate-
fully and culpably refuses to acknowledge him, and so remains a fool
incapable of true wisdom. Thus 'whatever by ourselves we think
concerning him [God] is foolish, and whatever we speak, absurd'.[18]
It is as though by nature we were blind men in a theatre, unable to
see or understand everything being communicated. Yet God graciously gives us the Scriptures to serve as spectacles, so that through
them we might clearly perceive God, ourselves and all reality.

At this point Calvin needs to establish how these spectacles of
Scripture have any authority. How can we trust them as being
God's true revelation of reality? Calvin strongly denies that anyone
or anything other than God (whether it be the church or our own
reason) can authenticate God's Word to us. Thus 'they who strive
to build up firm faith in Scripture through disputation are doing
things backwards'.[19] Only God can do this, and he does so by his
Spirit in Scripture itself:

> Scripture indeed is self-authenticated; hence, it is not right to subject it to
> proof and reasoning. And the certainty it deserves with us, it attains by the
> testimony of the Spirit. For even if it wins reverence for itself by its own

---

18. *Institutes of the Christian Religion*, tr. F. L. Battles (Philadelphia: Westminster,
    1960), 1.13.3. References to the *Institutes* consist of three numbers,
    identifying the book, chapter and section, respectively.
19. Ibid. 1.7.4.

majesty, it seriously affects us only when it is sealed upon our hearts through the Spirit. Therefore, illumined by his power, we believe neither by our own nor by anyone else's judgment that Scripture is from God; but above human judgment we affirm with utter certainty (just as if we were gazing upon the majesty of God himself) that it has flowed to us from the very mouth of God by the ministry of men. We seek no proofs, no marks of genuineness upon which our judgment may lean; but we subject our judgment and wit to it as to a thing far beyond any guesswork![20]

This was to be essential to all Calvin's thought (and, indeed, all the Reformation). His theology was to have God's Word as its very deepest foundation, and he refused to smuggle in some other foundation or support for that, for then the entire edifice of his theology would be built upon the sand of human reason or tradition, rather than upon the solid rock of God's Word. That said, in the next chapter Calvin demonstrates that the belief we have come to in Scripture as God's Word is not misplaced, for there are reasonable evidences of its divine origin. This is not to contradict what he has already argued: these evidences could never foster belief; they are for the assurance of those who *already* believe.

Scripture, then, according to Calvin, is both indispensable and absolutely foundational for true godliness. However, exactly how he viewed the Bible is a hotly debated subject. What commentators are agreed on is that Calvin drew a very sharp distinction between God and man. God is infinite and spiritual; we are finite and material. As such, God must as it were use baby-talk when he speaks to us. 'Thus such forms of speaking do not so much express clearly what God is like as accommodate the knowledge of him to our slight capacity.'[21] The question that divides commentators is this: does this distinction between God-as-he-is and God-as-he-reveals-himself mean that there might be something misleading in his self-revelation? Or, to put it another way, might the sharpness of distinction between God and man mean that, for all the infallibility of God, a human author of Scripture might make a mistake?

---

20. Ibid. 1.7.5.
21. Ibid. 1.13.1.

Many – perhaps most – Calvin scholars today are happy to allow that Calvin thought so. Commonly cited are his comments on Acts 7:14, 16 (also Matt. 27:9), where he did say that there were errors in the text that ought to be amended. However, he seems to attribute them to later copyists. He does not ascribe error to Luke, but believed that the process of textual transmission could allow for minute and circumstantial error to creep in (more than that he could not allow, for he believed in the providential preservation of the Scriptures[22]). Such comments also need to be read within the context of his view that the Spirit, being concerned for all details great and small, literally dictated words to the human authors of Scripture 'as though he had said, "Let not a syllable be omitted, but let that which I once proclaimed by thy mouth, remain unchanged."'[23] The result for Calvin was the belief that in the Bible we hear 'the living words of God' as if 'having sprung from heaven'.[24] It is hard to imagine a much stronger affirmation of the complete inerrancy of Scripture.

To return to the argument, so far Calvin has shown that through Scripture we are taught the knowledge of the true God in distinction to all idols. He therefore spends the next chapters dealing with various forms of idolatry. The true God, he then argues, is most clearly distinguished from all idols by the fact that when we encounter the one living God, we encounter three persons. Indeed, unless when we consider the one God we think of the three persons, 'only the bare and empty name of God flits about in our brains, to the exclusion of the true God'.[25] Here Calvin feels the need to depart from Augustine, since he is critical of Augustine's use of analogies for understanding the Trinity (though, out of affection, he desists from naming and shaming his hero).[26] Calvin prefers instead to look to the Old and New

---

22. Ibid. 1.6.3; 1.8.9–10.
23. Commentary on Jeremiah 36:28; cf. comments on Jer.36:4–8; 2 Tim. 3:16; *Institutes* 1.18.3; 3.25.8; 4.8.6, 9.
24. *Institutes* 1.7.1.
25. Ibid. 1.13.2.
26. Ibid. 1.13.18.

Testaments to understand the relationships that exist between the Father, Son and Spirit. He then uses Scripture to deal with various trinitarian heresies that were problematic at the time.

From chapter 14 Calvin moves on to the work of the triune Creator, his providential rule and relation to humans and angels. However, the chapters on God's providence that most readers have been anticipating from Calvin show none of the cold tone commonly expected. He states instead that God's work as Creator is not understood unless it includes an understanding of God's all-encompassing fatherly guidance of his creation. This providence is nothing like fate or chance; it is God's personal, ongoing kindness that brings the believer an otherwise unattainable comfort in this world of dangers. This is especially true of God's guidance in what appears to be accidental or out of control evil:

> When dense clouds darken the sky, and a violent tempest arises, because a gloomy mist is cast over our eyes, thunder strikes our ears and all our senses are benumbed with fright, everything seems to us to be confused and mixed up; but all the while a constant quiet and serenity ever remain in heaven. So must we infer that, while the disturbances in the world deprive us of judgment, God out of the pure light of his justice and wisdom tempers and directs these very movements in the best-conceived order to a right end.[27]

Does this make God the author of evil? Calvin takes the example of Judas and the answer of Augustine: when Judas sinned in handing over Jesus, why was the Father not considered equally guilty for handing over his Son? Because by it Judas meant evil and the Father good.[28]

Book 2: The Knowledge of God the Redeemer in Christ

Having shown how the knowledge of God is revealed in the Scriptures, Calvin now explains what we learn there about ourselves. That is, Adam became a sinner by refusing to trust God's

---

27. Ibid. 1.17.1.
28. Ibid. 1.18.4.

word; he then propagated from himself a race of sinners born
with his guilty status and sinful nature. As such, we find that we are
all sinners, not by imitation, but by birth; and not merely empty of
good, but full of evil. Our wills are instinctively bent towards evil
faithlessness so that we always choose evil and find ourselves
incapable of doing anything good. This, Calvin argues forcefully, is
the testimony of both Scripture and the church fathers, that we are
by nature helplessly enslaved to sin. Thus we see our desperate
need for redemption.

That redemption is found in Christ alone, as it always has been
from the beginning of the world, for 'apart from the Mediator,
God never showed favor toward the ancient people, nor ever gave
hope of grace to them . . . [so that] the hope of all the godly has
ever reposed in Christ alone'.[29] Thus, he argues, true faith always
has been and always will be faith in Christ. This was why the law
of Moses was given, full of visual aids proclaiming Christ's work,
so that, being made aware of their sin, the people might seek the
Redeemer. The law would then sustain them in the obedience of
faith, restraining them from evil and from becoming careless
about righteousness, and giving them instruction about the Lord's
will and pleasure.

This leads Calvin into an examination of the relationship
between the Old and New Testaments. His view is simple: they are
exactly the same in their substance, and differ only in administra-
tion. To help the reader understand this, he provides three
principles for correctly understanding the Old Testament: first, the
Jews were given not merely earthly blessings but everlasting hopes;
secondly, the covenant was one of mercy, not works; thirdly, 'they
had and knew Christ as Mediator, through whom they were joined
to God and were to share in his promises'.[30]

After this essential excursion we see how Christ redeems.
He begins with the incarnation, how Christ assumed our flesh
without sin so as to take what was ours (guilt and death) and give
what was his (righteousness and life). So far this sounds

---

29. Ibid. 2.6.2–3; cf. 4.8.5.
30. Ibid. 2.10.2.

historically conventional; however, Calvin's next point quickly became perhaps the most fundamental point of disagreement between Lutherans and Calvinists.[31] Calvin argues that while the Word truly became flesh, the Word was not limited to the man, Jesus. When Jesus was in Mary's womb, the Word also remained outside Jesus in heaven. Lutherans objected that this 'Calvinist extra' was a denial of Colossians 2:9, and made Christ a separate being behind and outside Jesus. Yet for Calvin this was not a point to be conceded lightly: it entailed a complete understanding of what God is like and how he reveals himself. Just as God cannot reveal himself to us entirely when he speaks, but must accommodate his revelation to our weak capacity, so the Word cannot give himself entirely to us. Just as there is a distinction between God-as-he-is and God-as-he-reveals-himself, so there must be a distinction between the Word as he is and the man, Jesus.

Next Calvin explains how Christ is prophet, priest and king. He was anointed to these three offices by the Holy Spirit for the sake of his body, the church, so that not only might we enjoy his prophetic revelation, his priestly mediation and his kingly rule, but also, filled with the Spirit of his anointing, we might be prophets, priests interceding and offering sacrifices of prayer and praise, and kings ruling over sin, death and the devil. Not only remarkably comprehensive for its brevity, it also remains one of the most powerful arguments for the replacement of the Roman sacerdotal priesthood with the priesthood of all believers.

Finally, he turns to see how we who are dead can find life through the death, resurrection and ascension of Christ. Our problem, he emphasizes, is God's wrath at sin. Yet (and here he quotes Augustine) 'in a marvelous and divine way he loved us even

---

31. The differences, in fact, were not at all new: Lutheranism was in many ways the child of the ancient school of theology in Alexandria (which emphasized the unity of God and man in Christ), while Calvinism was much more closely aligned with the theological school of Antioch (which emphasized the distinction between divinity and humanity).

when he hated us'.[32] So, through the obedience of Christ, this became our acquittal:

> the guilt that held us liable for punishment has been transferred to the head of the Son of God. We must, above all, remember this substitution, lest we tremble and remain anxious throughout life – as if God's righteous vengeance, which the Son of God has taken upon himself, still hung over us.[33]

Having defeated hell on the cross, Christ was then raised up to give us life before entering heaven 'in our name'.[34] That he will return in judgment Calvin shows is a comfort for believers who know and love the Judge. Christ's person and work having then been presented, Calvin finishes the book by exhorting readers to seek their every blessing in Christ.

Book 3: The Way in which we Receive the Grace of Christ

The way in which Calvin now moves the argument on is explained in the title of chapter 1: 'The Things which Have Been Said about Christ Profit us by the Secret Activity of the Spirit.' That is, by the Spirit we are united to Christ so as to enjoy all he has done for us.

The Spirit's first work, he says, is to create in us faith, which Calvin then defines. True faith is not an opinion or a mere assent that the gospel is true, nor is it belief in 'God' in general. Rather, as argued before, true faith always has been and always will be specifically faith in Christ. In fact, true faith can only be defined in a trinitarian way, as 'a firm and certain knowledge of God's benevolence toward us, founded upon the truth of the freely given promise in Christ, both revealed to our minds and sealed upon our hearts through the Holy Spirit'.[35] As such, true faith is unwavering. This is not to suggest that the true believer has no doubts, but that 'at heart believers are on the side of their faith and its object in

---

32. *Institutes* 2.16.4.
33. Ibid. 2.16.5.
34. Ibid. 2.16.16.
35. Ibid. 3.2.7.

opposition to their doubts and temptations'.[36] In faith we 'prick up the ears [to God's Word] and close the eyes [to the doubt-causing lies of the world, the flesh and the devil]'.[37]

True faith is, fundamentally, something of the heart, not merely an act of the brain acknowledging truth. For this reason true faith is inseparable from love to God. Calvin therefore moves to speak of the repentance (or 'regeneration', as he puts it) that flows from faith. Repentance must originate in faith, for it is impossible to be truly conscious of sin without faith; it then reaches its goal in such a self-denying, total submission to God's good pleasure that one is never miserable with one's lot. A happy definition of repentance indeed!

Only after covering the life of repentance and sanctification does Calvin return to look at justification by faith alone. He seems to have proceeded in this unusual order to pre-empt the Roman Catholic criticism that justification by faith alone leaves a Christianity devoid of Christian living (it is not that Calvin is weak on justification – this section, chs. 11–19, is one of the longest in the *Institutes*). At heart, justification, he explains, consists of Christ's righteousness being imputed to the sinner. He uses an illustration of Ambrose's to explain: in order to receive a blessing from his father, Jacob approached him while wearing the clothes of his firstborn brother, Esau. Just so, to be blessed by God the Father, sinners approach him, not on the basis of any righteousness in their own lives, but by clothing themselves with the righteousness of the firstborn, Christ.[38]

This justification is understood properly only if it entails a real belief in the Christian's freedom, which he explains next. One quotation from this chapter should suffice to break the image of Calvin the pernickety moralist:

> when consciences once ensnare themselves, they enter a long and inextricable maze, not easy to get out of. If a man begins to doubt

---

36. T. H. L. Parker, *Calvin: An Introduction to His Thought* (Louisville, Ky.: Westminster John Knox, 1995), p. 82.

37. *Institutes* 3.13.14.

38. Ibid. 3.11.23.

whether he may use linen for sheets, shirts, handkerchiefs, and napkins, he will afterward be uncertain also about hemp; finally, doubt will even arise over tow. For he will turn over in his mind whether he can sup without napkins, or go without a handkerchief. If any man should consider daintier food unlawful, in the end he will not be at peace before God, when he eats either black bread or common victuals, while it occurs to him that he could sustain his body on even coarser foods. If he boggles at sweet wine, he will not with clear conscience drink even flat wine, and finally he will not dare touch water if sweeter and cleaner than other water.[39]

He comes next to prayer, the 'chief exercise of faith'. Faith is that wise recognition of our own lack and of Christ's fullness of grace. Prayer puts that recognition into action. Furthermore, prayer not only recognizes Christ's riches; it must know him as mediator: the thought of God's majesty naturally makes us shrink from prayer, and we are capable of approaching the living God with boldness only when we remember and depend upon Christ. Pastorally concerned as ever, Calvin proceeds to give practical advice and encouragement in this chief exercise.

It is only now (on p. 920 of the standard F. L. Battles edition of the *Institutes*!), and briefly, that Calvin comes to deal with the doctrine for which he is most famous: election. As an integral part of his overall pastoral argument, Calvin presents election not as a doctrine of fear but as one of comfort in that it proclaims God's absolute and free mercy. That is, God, in his free pleasure, rather than on the basis of anything in individuals, chooses to predestine some to salvation and others to damnation. Yet, Calvin argues, election is not primarily an individualistic thing: it is about being destined by God to be engrafted into Christ. Thus all grounds for confidence and salvation are found in him, not in ourselves. In Christ the elect are eternally secure and cannot fall away. As for God's rejection of sinners, Calvin strongly maintains that this is entirely just (God could not act otherwise). Sinners deserve to be rejected, and God has chosen not to be merciful to some so as to magnify his own glory.

---

39. Ibid. 3.19.7.

From the eternity past of God's election Calvin next takes us to the end of all things: the universal bodily resurrection. Christ's bodily resurrection is shared by his body, the church, and all things over which he is Head, thus accounting for the resurrection of unbelievers to judgment.

Book 4: The External Means or Aids by which God Invites us into the Society of Christ and Holds us therein

Following the Reformation break with Rome, the credible survival of Protestantism depended on the ability of the Reformers to produce a robust ecclesiology. If Rome really was the one true church, then Protestants were just schismatics. It was Calvin above all who rose to the challenge, by dedicating the final quarter of his *Institutes* to providing the most comprehensive and definitive ecclesiology of the Reformation.

Instead of shying away from a high view of the church, Calvin agreed with Rome's Augustinian principle that the church is the necessary mother of all believers. He disagreed with the separatist dream that the church in this age could ever be perfect. Instead, he believed, the true church could be recognized, not by its allegiance to the pope, nor by its perfect separation from the world, but by two marks: 'Wherever we see the Word of God purely preached and heard, and the sacraments administered according to Christ's institution, there, it is not to be doubted, a church of God exists.'[40] That is, Christ governs his body through his Word in both proclamation and sign; in contrast, in the false church of the pope, there Christ does not rule through his Word, meaning that there the church has lost connection with its Head and is like a man with his throat cut. Thus, while Rome accused the Reformers of schism, Calvin, by his definition of the church, turned the tables to accuse Rome of schism.

Calvin then moves with telling speed to speak of the ministers

---

40. Ibid. 4.1.9. Reformed theology after Calvin tended to make discipline a third mark of the church. Calvin did not do so, though that is not to say he would have disagreed: he certainly spoke strongly of the necessity of church discipline (*Institutes* 4.12.1) and sought to enforce it in Geneva.

of God's Word in his church. They are the vital sinews that hold the body together, for through them the word that constitutes the church is ministered. He held that Ephesians 4:11 taught that there are five sorts of ministers: apostles, prophets, evangelists, pastors, teachers. The first three he saw as temporary offices that had generally ceased (though he believed that God still uses them in extraordinary circumstances, Luther having been just such an extraordinary apostle). The offices of pastor and teacher have been explained above. In case any misunderstand Calvin to be sending the church back to Roman Catholic structuralism, by simply replacing bishops with preachers, he then (after a largely historical analysis of the claims of Rome) examines the question of authority in the Church. Authority, he argues, resides not with the ministers per se, but only in God's Word, which they are to minister.

What then of the sacraments? They too are about the preaching of the gospel in that they confirm and present it by external signs.[41] In contrast to Zwingli, Calvin did not believe that sacraments are essentially oaths of our allegiance to Christ. Primarily, they are from God to us: they truly present and offer us the blessings of the gospel. Yet that is not to agree with Rome's sacramentalism: sacraments have no inherent power to bestow grace, but are efficacious only in so far as they are used by the Spirit.

While many different sacraments were given in the Old Testament to lead people to Christ, now just two flow from him to us: the water and the blood. Baptism, corresponding to circumcision, presents initiation into Christ with all its benefits. Calvin is quite relaxed about questions of immersion and sprinkling; he is, however, prepared to argue at some length that infant baptism accords best with the nature of the sacrament. The Lord's Supper is the next sacrament, for the nourishment of those who have been baptized into Christ. In it we are invited to feed on the body and blood of Christ crucified.[42]

---

41. Ibid. 4.14.1.

42. Unfortunately, there is simply not the space here to examine the important question of how Calvin distinguished his understanding of the Lord's Supper from that of Zwingli, Luther and Rome. For a brief but

Calvin's great work then ends on what might seem like an anti-climax: a chapter on civil government. Yet it is a quite proper end point for him, since true knowledge of God, once received, must then be lived out in the world. Calvin carefully maps out his position in contrast to the many political views of the magisterial and radical Reformations: he refuses to follow the Zwinglian confusion of church and state; he avoids the Lutheran submission of church to state; Anabaptist separatism, he holds, forgets that we still live in these bodies in this age; radical revolution confuses Christian liberty with the removal of political hierarchy. Instead, political powers exist to protect and prosper the work of the Word through the church. Yet even when they do not, and they become unjust, Christians are enjoined to civil obedience. Calvin has one qualification, on which he appropriately, if somewhat abruptly, ends: that our first and overriding obedience is always to God.

Commentaries

Through the *Institutes* Calvin provided a guide to Scripture; the other half of his doctoral office involved the plain exposition of the Scriptures. In this way he sought to avoid both the imposition of doctrine onto texts and the study of doctrines in abstraction from their place in the story of Scripture.

Calvin managed to expound almost every book of the Bible. Yet most of what we think of as Calvin's commentaries are in fact transcripts of expository lectures given to Genevan schoolboys and ministers. They were delivered in Latin, with Greek and Hebrew being used and analysed. To the relief of the students, Calvin's breathing difficulties meant that all this happened extremely slowly!

In his exegesis, as elsewhere, Calvin was concerned to remain within the orthodox tradition; however, it is here that Calvin's

extremely helpful introduction to this, see F. Wendel, *Calvin: The Origins and Development of his Religious Thought* (London: Collins, 1963), ch. 5, pt. 4, pp. 329–355.

humanist training shows through most clearly, making him a true pioneer. He did not share Luther's paramount determination to see how each page of Scripture proclaims Christ; his overriding concern was to find each passage's original, simple, grammatical meaning, and then to convey it equally simply. For this, he believed, context was essential, context being not only a passage's place in the overall text, but also its linguistic context (how matters are expressed in the language in which the passage was written) and historical context (for which he was keen to use as much extra-biblical material as possible). The result is that Calvin's commentaries look distinctly modern.

Catechism

For Calvin, doctrine is too useful to be restricted to books: it must be put into the hands, hearts and minds of every Christian. Thus, in 1538, shifting from his doctoral to his pastoral role, he boiled down the first edition of his *Institutes* to make a catechism for the people, especially the children. In 1545 he revised this to create the Geneva Catechism, which was to have an important role in the spread of the Reformed faith, and became the basis for the Heidelberg Catechism, the primary Reformed catechism. The catechism consists of five sections: on faith, then law (significantly reversing Luther's order), prayer, the Word, the sacraments. Through this, children in Geneva – unlike those in Rome – were encouraged to investigate their faith. They were compelled to consider what they believed and why, to know the benefits of their belief, and to have ready arguments against, for example, Rome's denial of justification by faith alone or the Anabaptist denial of infant baptism. The result was that the Reformed faith was to have resilient grassroots.

Sermons

Calvin is rarely thought of as a preacher, yet, when standing in his pulpit, his leading biographer, Émile Doumergue, exclaimed,

'That is the Calvin who seems to me to be the real and authentic Calvin, the one who explains all the others: Calvin the preacher of Geneva.'[43] Certainly, he spent much of his time in Geneva preaching: twice on Sundays (New Testament) and, on alternate weeks, every weekday as well (Old Testament), each time for about an hour.

His sermons were transcribed for us to read, but he had no manuscript himself; instead, he would study his text for a day, walk straight from his study to the pulpit and preach directly from the Hebrew or Greek (without any anecdotes or 'display'). His lack of notes gave his sermons a much more popular feel than his lectures, a feel he deliberately cultivated as he removed all specialist language and technical material. He did not cite any Greek, Hebrew or Latin, but spoke a plain, everyday French (though with a little less ease than Luther spoke the earthy German of the people). Yet he treated his listeners as real students of the Bible, and assumed they had also been reading it for themselves. And undoubtedly their biblical literacy would have been high as, week by week and verse by verse, he worked through entire books of the Bible with them.

This surely is the authentic Calvin who explains all the others, for his entire life's work was to open and convey the Word of God so that the people might be won, heart and mind, to true knowledge of God.

Going on with Calvin

Calvin usually surprises first-time readers with his warmth and accessibility. Nobody who has survived this introduction will have any trouble reading and enjoying the *Institutes*, and that should be where to go from here. The Ford Lewis Battles two-volume translation of the 1559 edition (Philadelphia: Westminster Press, 1960) is undoubtedly the standard and best: quite apart from the quality

---

43. Quoted by L. Nixon, *John Calvin, Expository Preacher* (Grand Rapids: Eerdmans, 1950), p. 38.

of translation, it has excellent footnotes and indices that make it markedly superior to the old nineteenth-century Beveridge translation. John Dillenberger's anthology *John Calvin: Selections from His Writings* (New York: Anchor, 1971) provides a good collection of some of Calvin's other works.

Readers need to be more careful with biographies and secondary literature on Calvin: many are highly opinionated and biased. François Wendel's *Calvin: The Origins and Development of his Religious Thought* (London: Collins, 1963) is the classic single-volume introduction to the man and his thought. After that, try anything by T. H. L. Parker, who has written first-rate books on the man, the *Institutes*, his commentaries and his preaching.

If you start the journey, you should soon find that, like Karl Barth, you could gladly and profitably set yourself down and spend at least some of your life just with Calvin.

John Calvin timeline[44]

1509	Calvin born in Noyon, France
1520–21?	Theological studies at the University of Paris
1525–6?	Moved to study law at the University of Orléans
1529–30?	Studies at the University of Bourges; converted
1534?	Flees Paris
1535?	Arrives in Basel
1536	First edition of the *Institutes* is published; he arrives in Geneva
1537	Submits *Articles on the Organization of the Church and its Worship at Geneva* to council
1538	Expelled from Geneva; he settles in Strasbourg with Bucer
1539	Second edition of the *Institutes*
1540	Marries Idelette de Bure
1541	Returns to Geneva; submits Ecclesiastical Ordinances to council
1543, 1545	New editions of the *Institutes*
1549	Idelette dies
1550	Fifth edition of the *Institutes*
1553	Michael Servetus arrested and burned
1559	Final edition of the *Institutes*; college and academy opened
1564	Calvin dies

---

44. Some of the early dates of Calvin's life, especially those of his studies and conversion, are uncertain. The date of his conversion is especially disputed, being placed anywhere between 1527 and 1534. I have followed the revisionist chronology of T. H. L. Parker, who has been most rigorous in sifting the documentary evidence ('Arguments for Re-dating', in *John Calvin: A Biography* [Oxford: Lion, 2006], pp. 192–198).

9. LET US SEEK HEAVEN

John Owen

For some reason, Britain has never been a great breeding ground for theologians. Perhaps it is the pragmatism of the national spirit that stifles things; perhaps the curse of the Welshman, Pelagius, lies on the land. In any case, after him one struggles to think of many theologians who are both pre-eminent and British. The prize of being Britain's greatest-ever theologian may, then, be relatively uncontested, but one of the hottest candidates is probably John Owen. Once dubbed 'the Calvin of England', he was elephantine in almost every way.

Owen's life

In 1616, the year William Shakespeare died, John Owen was born into a Puritan parsonage and a country seething with religious and political tension. Of course, growing up in the little village of Stadham (now Stadhampton), outside Oxford, it would be a few years before he really felt that tension for himself.

At twelve years of age he entered Queen's College, Oxford. To start student life so young is what surprises us, but what was actually exceptional for the time was the manic intensity with which he drove himself to work. Allowing himself just four hours' sleep a night, he wracked his health so that he might learn faster. He sought to refresh himself especially through flute-playing, javelin-flinging and long-jumping, but his relentless timetable would take its toll in the years to come.

Aged nineteen he received his MA and was ordained, but in the 1630s 'high church' Oxford was no place for a young pastor with Owen's Puritan convictions. He decided to take some household chaplaincy jobs: there in private homes he could minister and study unmolested by a church hierarchy increasingly intolerant of his views.

All this time he was sinking ever deeper into depression and self-isolation. Having spent his whole life in Puritan circles, he was acutely conscious of his sin, but knew nothing of the assurance of salvation that some preached. Then, in 1642, he moved to London and went to hear a renowned preacher, Edmund Calamy, in St Mary's Church, Aldermanbury. As it turned out, however, Calamy was not there that day, and an unknown preacher was in the pulpit instead. He took Matthew 8:26 as his text, 'Why are ye fearful, O ye of little faith?' (Authorized Version). And with that message Owen felt an immediate assurance that he had been born again of the Spirit and was a child of God.

Even before that great personal turning point, Owen had started on his first book, a work entitled *A Display of Arminianism*. There was nothing particularly special about it – it was really the polemic of a young man seeking to make his mark – but it laid out a basic theological position Owen would always hold. Owen believed passionately in the 'five points of Calvinism',[1] and Arminianism,

---

1. The 'five points of Calvinism', agreed at the Synod of Dordt in 1618–19, affirm (1) *Total Depravity* (meaning, not that we are as sinful as we possibly could be, but that sin has so comprehensively affected us that we have no ability to do anything towards our own salvation); (2) *Unconditional Election* (meaning that God unconditionally chooses some people for salvation and others for damnation, and does not base that decision on anything

which denied those five points, he viewed as a disturbing heresy
that opened the door to the worst denials of the gospel. In the
years to come he would pen lengthy defences of limited atonement
(*The Death of Death in the Death of Christ*) and the perseverance of the
saints (*The Doctrine of the Saints' Perseverance Explained and Confirmed*).
For now, *A Display of Arminianism* focused on total depravity, pre-
destination and the irresistibility of God's grace.

It might seem strange that Owen, who, not long before, had left
Oxford because of his views, should now consider such polemical
theology to be career advancing. But by this time civil war had
broken out between the largely 'high church' party of King Charles
I and the predominantly Puritan forces of Parliament. And to the
Parliamentarians *A Display of Arminianism* was, indeed, welcome.
They made him vicar of Fordham, a village just outside Colchester.

Fordham gave Owen plenty to do. The previous incumbent
had been an ardent high churchman, and so the parishioners had
received no evangelical teaching. Thus, on top of his ordinary
duties, Owen composed a catechism for adults and a catechism for
children and went about the village instructing them. What with
the time he still had for his own writing, the Fordham years seem
to have been some of Owen's very happiest. And it was there that
he met and married Mary Rooke. That surely added to the happiness in Fordham. But the next thirty years of their marriage would
be scarred by pain: Mary bore John eleven children, all of whom
died before him, only one even surviving to adulthood.

After three short years, circumstances forced him to move to
minister in nearby Coggeshall. It was becoming quite obvious now
that Owen was a rising star (in 1646 he was asked to preach before
the House of Commons in Westminster) and the people of
Coggeshall, who had become gourmands of evangelical preaching,

---

within those people, whether good or bad); (3) *Limited Atonement* (meaning
that, on the cross, Christ paid for the sins of the elect only, not for the sins
of all humanity); (4) *Irresistible Grace* (meaning that, when God intends to
save a person, that person will be unable to resist and refuse to be born
again); and (5) the *Perseverance of the Saints* (meaning that God preserves
true Christians to the end, never letting them 'fall away' from salvation).

were eager to have Owen in their pulpit. Every Sunday some two thousand people now crowded into the church to hear him.

Then, on 30 January 1649, King Charles was executed, along with the hopes of the 'high church' party. It is testimony to Owen's newly acquired national stature that he was the one asked to preach to Parliament the next day. And what he said was highly revealing. Clearly, he was excited at what he saw happening in England. He believed it had all been prophesied as God's plan for the last days: with the execution of the king and the defeat of his tyranny, the reign of the antichrist was coming to an end, and with his destruction a triumphant millennial age for the church was being ushered in. Now the gospel could be proclaimed without hindrance, the church could be reformed and Christ would fill the world with light and love. It was an optimistic, millenarian vision that more and more were flocking to.

Owen's message certainly sat well with Parliament. He was invited to preach to them again, and this time was heard by Oliver Cromwell, the general of the Parliamentarian army and a man deeply interested in prophecy and how the cause of Parliament was the prophesied cause of God. Cromwell was just preparing to leave for Ireland to subdue a Catholic uprising there and asked Owen to come along as his chaplain.

The next couple of years thus saw Owen as Cromwell's chaplain, first in Ireland (where he hoped to turn Trinity College, Dublin, into a seminary of gospel preachers), and then in Scotland, where Cromwell's army turned next. But that role was really just a stepping stone to the big opportunity won for him by Cromwell's victories: in 1651 he was appointed Dean of Christ Church, Oxford, and, a year later, Vice-Chancellor of Oxford University.

The fact that Owen could be appointed Vice-Chancellor shows how much England had changed since he had left Oxford fifteen years earlier. And Oxford itself had changed: many of the 'high church' old guard had been replaced by Puritans from Cambridge. There was much still to be done, but Owen was positive that Oxford and Cambridge could be turned into the seedbeds of England's gospel renewal. What was needed was for a generation of young scholars and preachers to be educated in the gospel; they would then go out to educate the nation. As a result, Owen saw his principle duties as Vice-Chancellor being preaching and teaching. In addition to his lectures and occasional sermons around Oxford, he made sure that he preached at the University Church of St Mary's every second Sunday (one series becoming perhaps his most popular devotional work, *On the Mortification of Sin*).

In many ways they were golden years in Oxford: the university was transformed and Owen enjoyed the work. Of course, it helped that he earned something like ten times the average pastor's wage. But then it was for just such reasons that he began to be criticized by fellow Puritans. The money he spent in his preference for fine clothes and Spanish leather boots rather than academic garb attracted much vitriol. One censor (from Cambridge) complained that Oxford's Vice-Chancellor had 'as much powder in his hair as would discharge eight cannons'. Others complained that he was abandoning the local church.

In 1657 Owen felt it right to hand on the office of Vice-Chancellor, and from that moment he drifted out of the national spotlight. His great patron, Oliver Cromwell, died the next year, and the balance of political power fell, once again, into the hands of his antagonists. For more than ten years Owen had been a Congregationalist in his view of the church (i.e. he believed that each local church should be independent), and Cromwell's agreement with Owen gave protection to what was otherwise a minority position. But with Cromwell's death, the Presbyterians (who believed that local churches should be governed in groups by 'presbyteries' or meetings of assembled elders) gained the upper hand and Congregationalists like Owen started to be sidelined. The Congregationalists quickly arranged a conference to be held at the Savoy Palace in London, and produced a *Declaration of Faith and Order* 'to clear ourselves of that scandal which not only some persons at home but of foreign parts have affixed on us, viz. That Independentism [Congregationalism] is the sink of all heresies and schisms'.[2] But the tide was irreversible and Owen was left to a quiet retirement back in Stadham.

---

2. *The Savoy Declaration of Faith and Order*, ed. A. G. Matthews (London: Independent, 1959), p. 12.

At least it gave him time to write. Tucked away in rural Oxford-shire he managed to produce his monumental Latin treatise *Theologoumena Pantodapa* (Theological Statements of All Sorts), a grand history of theology from the time of Adam, including a look at the growth of idolatry in the nations, true theology in Israel, right on down to the practice of theology in his day.[3]

Those easy days were not to last, though, for in 1660 the be-headed king's son returned from exile and was crowned Charles II. Prospects were not good for a former chaplain to Cromwell, and life over the years that followed was made increasingly difficult for those, like Owen, now outside the Church of England. Before long, his house was raided by the militia and he was caught and prosecuted for preaching to some thirty people (religious assem-blies of more than five people outside the parish church having been made illegal).

He considered emigrating (and there were universities and churches in Holland and New England that were eager to have him). Eventually, though, he decided to stay, to keep preaching and to campaign for toleration to be shown to non-Anglicans like himself. Given his status as a leading Congregationalist theologian, it was important for English Nonconformism that he did stay: where he went, others would follow. And he had connections that could help them, as his Congregationalist friend John Bunyan found out. Owen could not keep him out of prison for his preach-ing, but he could find him a publisher for his new book, *Pilgrim's Progress*.

For Owen in these later, more harassed years, the nature of the church became a major concern in his writings. He wanted more than toleration; he wanted to show that the Congregational way is the biblical way. But these writings reveal something more funda-mental than Owen's view of how the church should operate: they

---

3. While it was originally included in Goold's nineteenth-century collection of Owen's works, Banner of Truth cut all Owen's Latin writings from their edition. However, *Theologoumena Pantodapa* has now been translated and published under the title *Biblical Theology*, tr. Stephen P. Westcott (Morgan, Pa.: Soli Deo Gloria, 1994).

express his very understanding of reformation. For Owen, reformation was essentially about separation from the ungodly. 'Come
out from among them' was the sort of phrase heard much in his
sermons.

Owen moved to London to pastor a church there while continuing to produce major works of theology. The London years
saw such mature pieces as his massive commentary on Hebrews,
Pneumatologia, *The Doctrine of Justification by Faith* and *Christologia*. If
one knew no more, Owen would sound like just another harmless
theologian. There was, however, a secret side to Owen's life.
Behind closed doors he dabbled in radical politics: he seems to
have been in on a plot to assassinate Charles II and place the
Protestant Duke of Monmouth on the throne; government spies
monitored his activity, considering him a threat; and once, when
his house was searched, six or seven cases of pistols were discovered. Not the sort of thing found in the homes of respectable
academic theologians!

In 1675 Mary, his wife for a little over thirty years, died. Not
having his personal journals, we can only imagine how he reacted.
But within eighteen months he was married again, this time to
Dorothy D'Oyley. Owen was now sixty years old, and there were
no children from this second marriage. Six years later, the one
daughter (from the first marriage) who had made it to adulthood
died. A year after that, Owen himself fell terminally ill, and
on 24 August 1683 died in the quiet village of Ealing, outside
London. Had he survived another six years he would have lived to
see the religious liberty he had fought for granted in the Toleration
Act of 1689.

Owen's thought

Death seemed unable to take Owen quickly, something ascribed by
his doctor to 'the strength of his brain'. Whatever exactly that
meant to a seventeenth-century physician, Owen's brain was
strong. He did not have the piercing brilliance of an Athanasius or
a Luther. Owen was much more ponderous. However, there was a
breadth to his intellect that invited grand projects, meshing

linguistic skill and doctrinal sensibility, biblical exegesis and historical theology.

As such, he was more than a theologian of one theme. He
had a particular concern for high Calvinist and Congregationalist
theology, but his interests ranged much more widely, as his personal reading, as much as his writing, attests: his library contained
books on almost everything from classical literature and language
to music, magic and home-brewing.

However, while he did not have one pet theme, he did bring to
the theology of the day his own particular flavour. Even putting it
so mildly could be misleading, for perhaps more than anything else
that flavour is trinitarianism, and it would be absurd to call that
Owen's own. And yet Owen's thought was so entirely moulded
by the Trinity that trinitarianism became a (possibly *the*) driving
characteristic of his theology. He believed that knowledge of
God's triune being should shape all Christian belief and practice.
Of course, all Christians nod along in agreement, but for Owen
this actually made a profound difference. Owen's theology has
been divided up and arranged in various ways, but he himself
believed that God's triune being places all studies of his ways
under one of two governing 'heads': Christology, which deals
with God's giving of his Son; and pneumatology, which deals with
God's giving of his Spirit.

Owen never wrote a systematic theology, and so probably the
best way to get under his theological skin is to focus on those
works where he deals with the doctrines he believed shape all true
theology: *Communion with God*, *Christologia* and *Pneumatologia*.

Communion with God

*Communion with God the Father, Son and Holy Ghost, Each Person
Distinctly, in Love, Grace, and Consolation*(!) was published shortly
after Owen stepped down as Vice-Chancellor of Oxford University, but probably grew out of sermons he had given back in
Coggeshall. Perhaps more than any other work, it captures Owen's
heartbeat for theology to be both resolutely trinitarian and thoroughly applied. Essentially, it is a summons for Christians to be
trinitarian in practice.

Owen was emphatic that it is quite impossible for anyone ever to have anything to do with 'God', simply put. There is no undifferentiated Godhead for any to deal with:

> And those who in their worship or invocation do attempt an approach
> unto the divine nature as absolutely considered, without respect unto
> the dispensation of God in the distinct persons of the holy Trinity, do
> reject the mystery of the Gospel, and all the benefit of it. So is it with
> many.[4]

Rather, Christians worship each person distinctly. That is not to say we imagine one person is separable from the others (we can only, for example, worship the Son as the Son of the Father, meaning that when we worship the Son aright, we worship the Father who begets him and the Spirit who unites us to him). But the Father, Son and Spirit are distinct persons, and Owen wants to show how we have distinct communion with each.

Communion with the Father

The essence of the Father's communion with us is, Owen says, *love*. Perhaps there is a little deliberate provocation there, for Owen was acutely aware that we tend not to think of the Father as a lover, but instead shy away from him in our belief that he is stern and thunderous in his transcendental distance from us:

> At the best, many think there is no sweetness at all in him towards us,
> but what is purchased at the high price of the blood of Jesus. It is true,
> that alone is the way of communication; but the free fountain and spring
> of all is in the bosom of the Father.[5]

---

4. John Owen, *The Works of John Owen*, ed. William H. Goold, 24 vols.
   (Johnstone & Hunter, 1850–55; republished Edinburgh: Banner of
   Truth, 1965–91), vol. 1, p. 112. All quotations here are from this, most
   accessible, edition. I have, however, removed all instances of italics found
   in this edition, not only since it is very unclear which are original, but also
   because they tend to be confusingly haphazard.
5. *Works of John Owen*, vol. 2, p. 32.

Owen observes what Jesus says in John 16:26–27, 'I am not saying that I will ask the Father on your behalf. No, *the Father himself* loves you . . .' (my emphasis). In fact, the Father is the very origin and fountain of love: 'Jesus Christ, in respect of the love of the Father, is but the beam, the stream; wherein though actually all our light, our refreshment lies, yet by him we are led to the fountain, the sun of eternal love itself.'[6] All the Father's love is given to us only in Christ (he compares the grace of God in the Spirit to the oil poured out on Aaron the High Priest's head: it is all poured on the head, just as all the Father's love is poured on Christ, but then it runs down onto his body, the church). The source of love, however, is the Father. 'Sit down a little at the fountain, and you will quickly have a farther discovery of the sweetness of the streams. You who have run from him, will not be able, after a while, to keep at a distance for a moment.'[7]

Communion with the Son

The next (and by far the longest) section of the work is dedicated to the Son's communion with us, the essence of which is *grace*. Here Owen suffuses the pages with the language and imagery of Song of Songs. Understanding it to be a parable of the love between Christ and his bride, the church, he keeps returning to it so as to make readers feel the sweetness of communion with the Son.

Owen starts by looking at some of 'the personal excellencies of the Lord Christ', for it is by appreciating them that 'the hearts of his saints are indeed endeared unto him'.[8] Christ is shown to the reader to be so irresistibly attractive ('a fit object for your choicest affections'[9]) that our hearts are allured. More, he is not only beautiful and desirable in himself; he delights in his beloved believers and gives himself over entirely to love for them. Thus he causes them to delight in him and give themselves over in love for him.

In all this, the Son is actually revealing the Father. It is no

---

6. Ibid. p. 23.

7. Ibid. p. 36.

8. Ibid. p. 59.

9. Ibid. p. 53.

wonder that what he reveals is utterly surprising, for without the Son, we would have no knowledge of the Father; we would be helplessly mired, in idolatry, worshipping a god that was not at all the true and living God. The Son, then, is the revealer and mediator, through whom we have communion with the Father.

Next Owen moves on to look at what the Son has done for us. And what undergirds his argument here (and so much of his theology elsewhere) is his 'covenant theology'. Essentially, what Owen envisages is this: Adam was created to exist in a 'covenant of works' with God. That meant that only if Adam obeyed God would he live. Of course, he disobeyed. God, however, continued to relate to humanity by this covenant of works: if humans obeyed, they would live. None did. But in eternity the Father had entered into another covenant with the Son (the 'covenant of redemption') to save the elect; as a result, Christ came and fulfilled the covenant of works by obeying God. With a relationship with God thus earned, in Christ the elect are as righteous as Adam would have been had he obeyed, and are able to relate to God by way of a 'covenant of grace'.

How Christ is a mediator between God and us is thus dealt with through the specific lenses of this covenant theology (something vital for Owen); but Owen's basic point is just that, that Christ, in his life, death, resurrection and ascension is a mediator 'to bring us to an enjoyment of God'.[10]

Communion with the Spirit

Lastly, the Spirit's communion with us, the essence of which is *comfort*. The Spirit, he argues, is essentially a Spirit of sanctification. That means that, first, he sets people apart by giving them new birth; and secondly, he comforts those who have been set apart. By 'comfort' Owen is referring to the comfort of Christ, which is the only comfort the Spirit brings. That is, the Spirit makes communion with the Son and the Father both real and delightful, spreading their love and confirming the truth in our hearts. Where Satan comes to rob confidence and comfort, the Spirit brings assurance

---

10. Ibid. p. 78.

and enjoyment of the truth. And only the Spirit can do that: when on earth, Owen notes, Christ seemed to affect the hearts of his disciples so little, but when the Spirit came, their hearts were all aflame for him. 'And this is his work to the end of the world, – to bring the promises of Christ to our minds and hearts, to give us the comfort of them, the joy and sweetness of them.'[11]

All that said, Owen is aware that readers could view the Spirit as a mere impersonal force of God. Yet he is emphatic that, while the Spirit is sent out of the Father's love to communicate the Son's grace, still he comes of his own will. He is a real person, and as such can and must be related to: 'the Holy Ghost, being God, is no less to be invocated, prayed to, and called on, than the Father and Son'.[12] Thus, though he will never leave the elect, he will not in fact always console them, if, for example, they grieve or resist him (not, of course, that Owen believes the Spirit truly can be grieved 'or affected with sorrow; which infers alteration, disappointment, weakness, – all incompatible with his infinite perfections').[13]

Owen was clearly concerned that the Spirit was being ignored by many (especially by the rationalists of the day). But he saw the consequences as terrible: first, if the Spirit does not really enter believers, then believers have no real union with Christ and so no real consolation; secondly, if people do not really have the Spirit, then they must have a spirit of bondage instead, 'casting them into an un-son-like frame of spirit'.[14]

To conclude:

> The emanation of divine love to us begins with the Father, is carried on by the Son, and then communicated by the Spirit; the Father designing, the Son purchasing, the Spirit effectually working: which is their order. Our participation is first by the work of the Spirit, to an actual interest in the blood of the Son; whence we have acceptation with the Father.[15]

---

11. Ibid. p. 237.
12. Ibid. pp. 229–230.
13. Ibid. p. 265.
14. Ibid. p. 258.
15. Ibid. p. 180.

It is a powerful case Owen has built for being trinitarian. In unitarian worship one could never validly entertain such warm, close
thoughts of the Father, never have real union with the Son or
adoption by the Father. In other words, the Spirit would have no
comfort or assurance to give us.

The Doctrine of Justification by Faith

Something Owen had affirmed in *Communion with God* was that, in
order to fulfil the covenant of works, Christ had lived a life of active
righteousness. Thus when believers are justified, it is not merely that
their sins are dealt with by him on the cross; that active righteousness of his is also credited to them. Affirming that sparked off a
debate: was the active righteousness of Christ credited to believers?
Some felt that this undercut all motivation for believers themselves
to live lives of active righteousness.

Twenty years after publishing *Communion with God*, Owen
responded to his critics with *The Doctrine of Justification by Faith*. It
was more than a response, though; it was a massive exegetical,
doctrinal and historical argument for the fact that, since Christ is
one person, he has one righteousness, and since believers are part
of the body of Christ, that righteousness is theirs.

For all the skill of the argument, it is a difficult and badly
arranged work. And yet it has been significant: William Grimshaw,
the great eighteenth-century preacher, was converted upon reading
it and being confronted with Owen's question 'whether he will
trust unto his own personal inherent righteousness, or, in a full
renunciation of it, betake himself unto the grace of God and the
righteousness of Christ alone'.[16]

Christologia

After *Communion with God*, *Christologia* was a book Owen always had
to write, Christology being one of his two governing 'heads' of
doctrine (and Owen being so generally Christ-centred). Its main
point was to argue (against Socinianism, a heresy that, among
other things, denied the deity of Christ) that true faith is faith in

---

16. Ibid. p. 230.

the person of Christ. But Owen wanted to do more than argue that point: he wanted actually to build that faith in his readers. Such true faith, he believed, could only come about when someone came to apprehend and appreciate the love of Christ; thus 'the great end of the description given of the person of Christ, is that we may love him, and thereby be transformed into his image'.[17] In *Christologia*, then, Owen set out to fix his readers' eyes on Christ, to roll the truths about Christ around in their minds so that their affections begin to be warmed towards him. And it was, quite specifically, his readers' affections that he was reaching for through their minds: 'Affections are in the soul as the helm in the ship; if it be laid hold on by a skilful hand, he turneth the whole vessel which way he pleaseth.'[18]

Owen starts out by affirming that he will be Christ-centred and nothing else, for it is Christ (not Peter) who is the rock and promised cornerstone on which the church is built; it is he who, from eternity, was chosen by the Father to be head over all and Saviour of the elect. Indeed, Owen argues, we must be Christ-centred, for naturally 'we can have no direct intuitive notions or apprehensions of the divine'; only in Christ, the image of God, is God's inmost being shown to us.[19] Hence 'faith in Christ is the only means of the true knowledge of God'.[20]

Owen is quite unrelenting on the point. It is entirely possible, he says, to have the Scriptures themselves and still have no true knowledge of God, as the Jews prove. Faith in Christ, then, is foundational; when it is uprooted, the truth of every doctrine collapses. One can almost see Owen's head shaking for those who have only a 'notional knowledge' of the Scriptures.

Owen goes on to pile up proofs that it is only through Christ that God confers any benefit to us. What is unclear is whether he means that God blesses us only through the person of the *eternal* Son, or whether he means, more specifically, that God blesses us

---

17. Ibid. vol. 1, p. 27.
18. Ibid. vol. 7, p. 397.
19. Ibid. vol. 1, p. 65.
20. Ibid. p. 77.

only through the *incarnate* Son. On the one hand, he is clear that, even before the incarnation, the Father would send the Son to do his work (he quotes e.g. Zech. 2:8–9, where 'the LORD Almighty' says 'the LORD Almighty has sent me'). Later in the work and elsewhere he writes of 'Appearances of the Son of God under the old testament'.[21] But on the other hand, he compares God's being to the sun: if it

> itself should come down unto the earth, nothing could bear its heat and lustre . . . So is it with this eternal beam or brightness of the Father's glory. We cannot bear the immediate approach of the Divine Being; but through him, *as incarnate*, are all things communicated unto us, in a way suited unto our reception and comprehension.[22]

Quite apart from the question of why the humanity of Mary and Christ were not incinerated by the immediate approach of the Divine Being in the moment of conception, there seems to be a contradiction here. But that aside, his point is clear: God's blessings are to be found only in Christ.

In fact, Owen is so strong in his affirmation that God blesses only through Christ that he is forced to deal with the question of the Old Testament: Did God bless people without Christ then? Quite simply, no:

> the faith of the saints under the Old Testament did principally respect the person of Christ – both what it was, and what it was to be in the fullness of time, when he was to become the seed of the woman . . . this has been the foundation of all acceptable religion in the world since the entrance of sin. There are some who deny that faith in Christ was required from the beginning, or was necessary unto the worship of God, or the justification and salvation of them that did obey him. For, whereas it must be granted that 'without faith it is impossible to please God,' which the apostle proves by instances from the foundation of the world, Heb. xi. – they suppose it is faith in God under the general notion of it,

---

21. Ibid. vol. 17. pp. 215–233.
22. Ibid. vol. 1, p. 16; my emphasis.

without any respect unto Christ, that is intended. It is not my design to contend with any, nor expressly to confute such ungrateful opinions – such pernicious errors. Such this is, which – being pursued in its proper tendency – strikes at the very foundation of Christian religion; for it at once deprives us of all contribution of light and truth from the Old Testament.[23]

What Owen is fighting in all this is the practice of those 'who profess a respect unto the Divine Being and the worship thereof, [but] seem to have little regard unto the person of the Son in all their religion'.[24] Often that disregard for the Son is extremely subtle:

> Of all that poison which at this day is diffused in the minds of men, corrupting them from the mystery of the Gospel, there is no part that is more pernicious than this one perverse imagination, that to believe in Christ is nothing at all but to believe the doctrine of the gospel.[25]

In other words, he feared for those who worship 'God' ('under the general notion') and believe 'the gospel' but do not trust Christ.

After all this, we might wonder if Owen's Christ-centredness has become overwrought. Has the person of Christ effectively eclipsed or swallowed up the Father and the Spirit? Owen answers that the very reason we are called so to love Christ is because the Father loves him. 'And all love in the creation was introduced from this fountain, to give a shadow and resemblance of it.'[26] That is, our creaturely love for the Son is meant to be a reflection of that first love of the Father's. Thus to be lovingly devoted to the Son is not to disregard the Father. Far from it: 'therein consists the principal part of our renovation into his image. Nothing renders us so like unto God as our love unto Jesus Christ.'[27] Loving the Son we

---

23. Ibid. pp. 101, 120.
24. Ibid. p. 107.
25. Ibid. p. 127.
26. Ibid. p. 144.
27. Ibid. p. 146.

become like the Father. Also, trusting the Son we become like the Son, for we always become like what we trust. So, when we trust Christ, we become like what the Father loves. We are conformed into the image of God.

Christologia ends with a glance into the future. Having looked at Christ from eternity past as the beloved of the Father, the chosen Saviour, Owen now turns to examine the man Jesus' entry into heaven in the ascension, which 'is a principal article of the faith of the church, – the great foundation of its hope and consolation in this world'.[28] The man's presence before the Father is our consolation, for there he intercedes for us; but he is also our hope, for there his resurrected body is the head and beginning of the new creation. From the past to the future, then, Christ is the proper beloved of both God and man.

The overall effect of reading Owen's Christology can be summed up simply: it is like reading an invitation:

> Do any of us find decays in grace prevailing in us; – deadness, coldness, lukewarmness, a kind of spiritual stupidity and senselessness coming upon us? Do we find an unreadiness unto the exercise of grace in its proper season, and the vigorous acting of it in duties of communion with God, and would we have our souls recovered from these dangerous diseases? Let us assure ourselves there is no better way for our healing and deliverance, yea, no other way but this alone, – namely, the obtaining a fresh view of the glory of Christ by faith, and a steady abiding therein. Constant contemplation of Christ and his glory, putting forth its transforming power unto the revival of all grace, is the only relief in this case.[29]

Pneumatologia

While Owen believed that pneumatology was the second governing 'head' of doctrine, he was keenly aware that the person and work of the Spirit had always been badly neglected. In fact, he wrote, 'I know not any who ever went before me in this design of

---

28. Ibid. p. 235.
29. Ibid. p. 395.

representing the whole economy of the Holy Spirit.'[30] But such was the ambitious aim of *Pneumatologia*, to lay out a complete theology of the Spirit and his work.

In part, Owen was stung into writing by some views of the Spirit that he believed were threatening the health of the church. In the Roman Catholic Church, the Spirit had been replaced by the sacramental system; among the Quakers, the Spirit was being treated almost as a different God, delivering experiences and revelations entirely unconnected to Christ and the Scriptures; the Socinians thought of the Spirit as an impersonal force; and in far too many other places, the Spirit was simply forgotten or ignored.

After explaining the necessity of the task, Owen starts by looking at who the Spirit is. He is the spirit or breath of the Father and the Son, which means that, just

> as the vital breath of a man hath a continual emanation from him, and yet is never separated utterly from his person or forsaketh him, so doth the Spirit of the Father and the Son proceed from them by a continual divine emanation, still abiding one with them,[31]

However, while that speaks of the deity of the Spirit, it does not establish the fact of his 'distinct personality'. And it is this that he needed to prove against the Socinians. So Owen goes to Matthew 28:19, where God is named as Father, Son and Holy Spirit:

> Now, no man will or doth deny but that the Father and the Son are distinct persons. Some, indeed, there are who deny the Son to be God; but none are so mad as to deny him to be a person . . . Now, what confusion must this needs introduce, to add to them, and to join equally with them, as to all the concerns of our faith and obedience, the Holy Ghost, if he be not a divine person even as they![32]

---

30. Ibid. vol. 3, p. 7.
31. Ibid. p. 55.
32. Ibid. p. 72.

Moreover, the Spirit is said to have personal qualities: he understands, chooses, acts, teaches, he can be tested, grieved, blasphemed and lied to.

From there Owen goes on to look at the *work* of the Spirit, first of all in creation. The Spirit, he sees, essentially has a quickening, life-giving role in creation. That is, as a dove broods over her eggs, so the Spirit nourishes and imparts vital power into creation. In fact, this is his ongoing role, and not just what he did in the original act of creation: every year, after winter, it is the Spirit who causes everything to come to fresh life (Ps. 104:29–30). And so, in creation, the Spirit testifies to his proper work, which is the work of new creation.

Owen then shows the Spirit at work in the Old Testament, inspiring prophecy and the writing of Scripture, working miracles and enabling people (Samson to be strong, for example, and Bezalel to be a skilful craftsman). Indeed, 'we find everything that is good, even under the Old Testament, assigned unto him [the Spirit] as the sole immediate author of it'.[33] But, as in creation, his work there is preparatory for the work of new creation when, just as God once breathed (or 'spirated') life into Adam, so Jesus would breathe the Spirit onto his disciples.

On, then, to the Spirit's true work. This begins with his work on Christ's humanity, for he is the head of the new creation. The man Jesus, Owen shows, is the one so anointed with the Spirit that he does everything only as he is equipped and empowered by the Spirit. By the Spirit he is cast out into the desert, by the Spirit he himself then casts out demons, does miracles, offers himself as a sacrifice and so on.

Owen became uniquely strident in his eagerness to present Christ as the Spirit-anointed man. The eternal Son, he suggested, did not act directly in the man Jesus. 'The only singular immediate act of the person of the Son on the human nature was the assumption of it into subsistence with himself.'[34] After the Son had assumed human nature in Mary's womb it was the Spirit that acted

---

33. Ibid. p. 151.
34. Ibid. p. 160; cf. ibid. vol. 1, p. 225.

directly on the man. The man, then, did not have a divine nature he could wheel out in times of need; he had to trust entirely to the Spirit. Any other movements 'of the Son towards the human nature were voluntary', so that, when for example on the cross Jesus cried 'My God, my God, why have you forsaken me?', what happened was that 'the human nature complained of its desertion and dereliction by the divine', since at that point the divine nature was no longer consoling the human.[35] It is an intriguing theory that powerfully upholds the full humanity of Christ. One has to wonder, though: can we really talk here of the one incarnate person of Christ when God the Son only relates occasionally to the man Jesus, and normally relates through another person (the Spirit)?

From the work of the Spirit on Christ, the head of the new creation, Owen proceeds to the work of the Spirit on Christ's body, the church. By the Spirit, the Son gives *us* what the Father gave *him* by the Spirit. The Spirit, then, is the one who unites us to God so that, where we would merely have cowered before the Father as our Judge and Creator, now by the Spirit, with the Son we cry, 'Abba!' 'As the descending of God towards us in love and grace issues or ends in the work of the Spirit in us and on us, so all our ascending towards him begins therein.'[36]

This work in us begins with regeneration. Without the Spirit, we would be capable of altering ourselves superficially, though we could never actually be renewed. But the Spirit brings true and radical renewing, taking away our stony hearts and giving us new ones. Thus he gives life and light, as he did back in the dark, life-less original creation. This work of regeneration had in fact been done on all the elect under the Old Testament. 'The elect of God were not regenerate one way, by one kind of operation of the Holy Spirit, under the Old Testament, and those under the New Testament [by] another.'[37] After all, none can ever enter the kingdom without being born again of the Spirit. Yet regener-ation is, by its very nature, a new creation work, and is therefore

---

35. Ibid. vol. 3, p. 161.
36. Ibid. p. 200.
37. Ibid. p. 214.

particularly associated with Christ's coming to usher in the new creation.

With some, Owen felt it necessary to argue for our need of regeneration; but with others, it was more a case of clarifying what regeneration looks like. Against certain 'enthusiasts' he argued, 'regeneration doth not consist in enthusiastical raptures, ecstasies, voices, or anything of the like kind'.[38] Why? Because the Spirit is the Spirit of the Creator, and so does not work against his creation, but with it, by means of the faculties of his creatures. 'He doth not come upon them with involuntary raptures, using their faculties and powers as the evil spirit wrests the bodies of them whom he possesseth.'[39] That said, Owen was no rationalist, and was quite aware that 'many of those who have been really made partakers of this gracious work of the Holy Spirit have been looked on in the world, which knows them not, as mad, enthusiastic, and fanatical'.[40]

To show that belief in regeneration is necessary, but not mad, novel nor needing to entail enthusiastic excesses, Owen then looks through Augustine's account of his own spiritual pilgrimage and regeneration in the *Confessions*. He recounts how Augustine was ruled by his appetites and desires, incapable of choosing any differently. Then, *through the Bible*, God changed his heart with all its desires; and with his affections now won to Christ he was able for the first time to choose freely for the good. The lesson is clear: there were no raptures or ecstasies, but without that change in his heart Augustine would have remained a slave to his old ways.

After that initial, instantaneous work of regeneration, the Spirit then works progressively to sanctify those who are part of the new creation. This sanctification, Owen is most careful to argue, is never something we can do for ourselves (that would be mere moralism); it is a work of the Spirit. And the Spirit does it by exciting and affecting us by the gospel, making us acquire a taste for the Lord and his ways. In fact, 'holiness is nothing but the implanting, writing and realizing of the gospel in our

---

38. Ibid. p. 224.
39. Ibid. p. 225.
40. Ibid. p. 226.

souls'.[41] Thus true holiness is all about relating to Christ; it is not about giving something back to God as if to fulfil our end of some bargain.

Because growth in holiness is about the 'realizing of the gospel in our souls', it must happen in the same way as our initial salvation. That is, just as we are justified by the blood of Christ, so we are sanctified by the blood of Christ. 'The Holy Ghost actually communicates the cleansing, purifying virtue of the blood of Christ unto our souls and consciences, whereby we are freed from shame, and have boldness towards God.'[42] By faith, then, our consciences are freed from guilt and we are able to grow in heartfelt love for God, which is the essence of holiness.

Sanctification is the Spirit's work of renewing a sin-scarred creation, and that means conforming us into the image of God, as we were created to be. That being the case, it cannot be 'any one faculty of the soul or affection of the mind or part of the body that is sanctified, but the whole soul and body, or the entire nature, of every believing person'.[43] Sanctification is a work of complete healing, making believers beautiful and whole, a work that will be perfected in our resurrection. Thus holiness, Owen stresses, is an eternal thing, the beginning of the indestructible new creation.

There is another aspect to Owen's theology of sanctification, and it is one that starts to take over as he continues his examination of the subject. As he goes on, Owen relies more and more on Aquinas's view that in sanctification the Spirit infuses habits into us. By this infusion, the old habits of sin are starved, and new habits are formed in us, inclining us to 'the duties of obedience'.

This use of Aquinas reveals some interesting ambivalences in Owen. Aquinas's talk of habits was drawn directly from Aristotle (and Owen actually quotes Aristotle here with approval, showing he is quite aware of his sources), yet Owen was clearly in two minds about him. On the one hand, he could happily and repeatedly turn to Aristotle in his theology; on the other, he could refer

---

41. Ibid. pp. 370–371.
42. Ibid. p. 445.
43. Ibid. p. 417.

to his influence as a 'contagion' that was rightly 'vomited out' by the first Reformers, only to creep back in to pollute the Reformed churches 'like Greeks out of the belly of the Trojan horse'.[44]

And the use of Aquinas in his discussion of sanctification produces similar tensions. Before he spoke of habits, Owen spoke of the Spirit transforming us *from the inside out*, winning our hearts and in that way changing our behaviour; but in Aquinas's thinking, we become holy *from the outside in* as we work at developing virtuous habits. And this is how Owen can now sound: 'Frequency of acts doth naturally increase and strengthen the habits whence they proceed . . . They grow and thrive in and by their exercise . . . The want thereof is the principal means of their decay.'[45] In places it sounds as if the habits themselves (church attendance etc.) almost have an innate ability to sanctify, and in such instances, Owen's talk of holiness as being essentially about a heart won for Christ is exchanged for something less obviously relational, where at times it begins to look as if holiness is, after all, something we give to God: 'Without the holiness prescribed in the gospel, we give nothing of that glory unto Jesus Christ which he indispensably requireth . . . He saves us freely by his grace; but he requires that we should express a sense of it.'[46]

Owen finishes the work with an argument for the necessity of holiness. Almost every conceivable motivation is set forth, from the being of God to our goal of conformity to the image of God. One, perhaps surprising, major motivation is our election in eternity:

> It is the eternal and immutable purpose of God, that all who are his in
> a peculiar manner, all whom he designs to bring unto blessedness in the
> everlasting enjoyment of himself, shall antecedently thereunto be made
> holy. This purpose of his God hath declared unto us, that we may take
> no wrong measures of our estate and condition, nor build hopes or
> expectations of future glory on sandy foundations that will fail us.[47]

---

44. *Biblical Theology*, pp. 678, 680.
45. *Works of John Owen*, vol. 3, p. 389.
46. Ibid. p. 650.
47. Ibid. p. 591.

In other words, God *will* make the elect holy, and thus I must be sure that I am holy if ever I am to be sure that I am one of the elect. Christ, Owen held, died only for the elect, and so my assurance of salvation cannot be found in the cross if I am not one of the elect. 'Neither have we any ground to suppose that we are built on that foundation of God which standeth sure, unless we depart from all iniquity.'[48] This was commonly employed Puritan logic, and yet how it should be used was relatively controversial. Many Puritans wrestled with the extent to which it is right to rest our assurance of salvation on our works, and whether true holiness can be motivated thus.

Appendices

In the years that followed the publication of *Pneumatologia*, Owen produced a number of appendices for the work.[49] *The Reason of Faith* set out how, without having to rely on any pope, we can believe Scripture to be the Word of God. Owen believed that many Protestant writers were being overly rationalistic in how they dealt with the question, making faith in Scripture dependent on complex external arguments. While those arguments may be right, he argued, 'We believe the Scripture to be the word of God with divine faith for its own sake only; or, our faith is resolved into the authority and truth of God only as revealing himself unto us therein and thereby.'[50]

The Causes, Ways and Means of Understanding the Mind of God defended the Protestant view that all Christians have a right to interpret the Bible for themselves, and do not need to rely on the pope and his official interpretation. Owen therefore looked at the vital role of the Spirit (and the means he uses) in enabling us to understand scriptures that otherwise would be dead letters to us.

---

48. Ibid. pp. 593–594.
49. The original treatise of *Pneumatologia* makes up vol. 3 of Owen's *Works*. These subsequent appendices make up vol. 4, but are presented there as part of *Pneumatologia*, since they were intended to be a continuation of the work.
50. *Works of John Owen*, vol. 4, p. 70.

Having looked at how the Spirit enables us to read and trust Scripture, Owen then turned to examine *The Work of the Holy Spirit in Prayer*. Finally, a double-barrelled work completed the appendices: *The Holy Spirit as Comforter* dealt with much the same material as covered in *Communion with God*; and *Spiritual Gifts* looked at how the Spirit grants gifts for the building up of the church.

Hebrews

It would be rude to leave Owen without mentioning his massive, seven-volume commentary on Hebrews. The trouble is, commenting on commentaries can get very tedious, which is why I have avoided doing so in these introductions. But we can note the revealing significance of the work for Owen without bursting the bounds of this book.

It is not just that the commentary reveals Owen to be a first-rate linguist and exegete, capable of weaving together close textual analysis and doctrinal discussion; it is that Hebrews functioned in many ways as a complete theology for him. First, he believed it is a proclamation of Christ; but it is a message about him told through a comprehensive biblical theology that outlines the entire story and purpose of the Old Testament (especially the law), even managing to outline the history of the world from creation through to the millennium and final rest. It is yet more testimony to how Owen saw all things centred on Christ.

Going on with Owen

Owen, it has to be said, was pretty merciless towards his readers. He expected them to be serious and committed. He once wrote in a preface, 'Reader . . . If thou art, as many in this pretending age, a sign or title gazer, and comest into books as Cato into the theatre, to go out again – thou hast had thy entertainment; farewell!'[51] There are no gentle introductions, there is often little sense to the order of a book, and, bluntly, he does go on a bit. But all that is

---

51. Ibid. vol. 10, p. 149.

nothing to the way he writes. It feels as if Latin was his real native tongue, and so, when he tries to write in English, the result is uncomfortably constipated. Thus, trying to imbibe Owen in large doses can be a bit like drinking rather too much Horlicks. J. I. Packer's suggested medicine is to read Owen out loud, which can help a bit. But, to be honest, whether read, said, chanted or rapped, Owen is tough meat.

For all that, there is simply no substitute for going straight to the horse's mouth. Probably the easiest and most rewarding place to start is *Communion with God*. For a nicely accessible, modernized version, I recommend Kelly M. Kapic and Justin Taylor (eds.), *Communion with the Triune God* (Wheaton: Crossway, 2007), but it is also available in vol. 2 of *The Works of John Owen*, ed. William H. Goold, 24 vols. (Johnstone & Hunter, 1850–55; republished Edinburgh: Banner of Truth, 1965–91). After that, *Christologia* (*Works*, vol. 1) is well worth a read. *Pneumatologia* (*Works*, vol. 3) is best left to the more keen. These texts are all freely available on www.ccel.org, but really all Owen's works are too lengthy to be read on a computer screen. Last, the commentary on Hebrews: the seven volumes are obviously off-putting, but just a look at the short preceding articles in the first Hebrews volume (*Works*, vol. 17) is worth it.

After that, probably the best introduction to Owen's life is Peter Toon's now-classic biography *God's Statesman: The Life and Work of John Owen: Pastor, Educator, Theologian* (Exeter: Paternoster, 1971). As for his thought, try Sinclair Ferguson, *John Owen on the Christian Life* (Edinburgh: Banner of Truth, 1987).

John Owen timeline

1616	Owen born; William Shakespeare dies
1628	Enters Queen's College, Oxford; John Bunyan born
1637	Leaves Oxford for a private chaplaincy
1642	Civil war begins; moves to London and experiences assurance of salvation
1643	Becomes minister at Fordham; marries Mary Rooke
1646	Moves to Coggeshall and becomes a Congregationalist
1649	Charles I executed; Owen preaches to Parliament; to Ireland as Cromwell's chaplain
1651	Appointed Dean of Christ Church, Oxford
1652	Appointed Vice-Chancellor of Oxford University
1657	Steps down as Vice-Chancellor; *Communion with God* published
1660	Charles II crowned; Bunyan imprisoned as Puritanism begins to be repressed
1663–4	Begins to live and pastor in and around London
1668–84	Commentary on Hebrews published
1674	*Pneumatologia* published
1675	First wife, Mary, dies
1676	Marries Dorothy D'Oyley
1679	*Christologia* published; John Bunyan publishes *The Pilgrim's Progress*
1683	Owen dies in Ealing

10. AMERICA'S THEOLOGIAN

Jonathan Edwards

And if they had been taught aright,
Small children carried bedwards
Would shudder lest they meet that night
The God of Mr. Edwards.

Abraham's God, the Wrathful One,
Intolerant of error –
Not God the Father or the Son
But God the Holy Terror.
(Phyllis McGinley, 'The Theology of Jonathan Edwards')

For too long Jonathan Edwards suffered his reputation as the horrid old preacher of 'Sinners in the Hands of an Angry God'. As a two-dimensional caricature (little more than a starch collar and a snarl) he could be dismissed easily. But in recent decades Edwards has begun to be rediscovered as a theologian of the broadest concerns and the highest calibre, so that many now regard him as America's greatest.

Edwards's life

In fact, Jonathan Edwards was self-consciously British. Born in East Windsor, Connecticut, in 1703, more than seventy years before the American Revolution, he lived and died as an aristo-cratic member of a colony he thought was as English as Kent. Like Kent, New England felt uncomfortably close to the Catholic influence of France (the colony of New France was not far away to the north and west); the difference to Kent was that East Windsor was in frontier territory, prone to Indian attack.

Jonathan's father, the Reverend Timothy Edwards, was a minis-ter in the New England Puritan tradition (though we should not let the family's respectability fool us: Jonathan's 'grandmother was an incorrigible profligate, his great-aunt committed infanticide, and his great-uncle was an ax-murderer'[1]). Timothy Edwards was also a revival preacher, and this would prove key in the formation of Jonathan's mind. His preaching led to a short-lived spiritual 'awakening' in Jonathan when he was nine, making him intensely religious for a season. The fact that the phase soon passed would make him, as an adult, suspicious of religious enthusiasm as any sure guide to spiritual health.

Aged thirteen, he went to study at what was to become Yale University. That meant entering a rowdy world of rum, guns and riotous adolescent antics that was never Jonathan's scene. Bookish, hard-working and serious, he was not given to easy social banter and lounging, and so struggled to fit in. Coupled with that, a near-fatal illness triggered a period of spiritual turmoil that made him difficult company. Then, one day, reading 1 Timothy 1:17, 'a sense of the glory of the divine being' struck him in a way it never had before.[2] And this time it was no passing sense: over the months that followed he would wander alone through woods and fields (a lifelong habit), marvelling at the glory of Christ revealed

---

1. George M. Marsden, *Jonathan Edwards: A Life* (New Haven: Yale University Press, 2003), p. 22.
2. *Works of Jonathan Edwards*, 26 vols. (New Haven: Yale University Press, 1957–2008), vol. 16, p. 792.

there, or he would open his Bible to enjoy the beauty of Christ laid before him.

In the summer of 1722, aged eighteen, he went to assist the pastor of a small church in New York City. It was there that he began his habit of jotting down his thoughts in notebooks, and it was there that he compiled a list of seventy 'Resolutions', binding himself to live in specific, holy disciplines. For example, Resolution 4: 'Resolved, never to do any manner of Thing, whether in Soul or Body, less or more, but what tends to the glory of God; nor be, nor suffer it, if I can avoid it.'[3] He committed himself to reading them once a week, keeping a close eye on how well he scored each time. The result, his journal reveals, was that he was a yo-yo of spiritual highs and lows. He was spiritually alive at last, but struggling, relying too much on his own strength.

The next year his father engineered a pastorate for him in Bolton, back near East Windsor. It was a position he was uncomfortably shoehorned into, and so when Yale offered him a position as a tutor, he quickly left Bolton. The post was not Yale's only attraction, though: the thirteen-year-old Sarah Pierpont was also there. Within two years they were engaged, two more and they were married.[4] It was the beginning of what Jonathan would call an 'uncommon union' of affection (a union that was to bear eight sons and three daughters, all but one daughter living to adulthood). Through his love for the more approachable Sarah it becomes clear that while Jonathan was reserved in public, personally he was warm and affectionate. And that is important to notice: warm affections were crucial for Edwards.

At around the same time that Jonathan was getting married, his grandfather, the formidable Solomon Stoddard, had him appointed as his assistant pastor in Northampton, back up the Connecticut valley. Within two years, Stoddard had died and Edwards had succeeded him. However, Stoddard had been the pastor of Northampton for nearly sixty years, and had in that time

---

3. Ibid. p. 753.

4. Sarah was a young sweetheart and fiancée indeed, but this was not considered inappropriate at the time.

accrued an almost papal authority. Edwards would never escape his shadow. And that meant having to live with certain practices he disapproved of, such as giving communion to those who showed no sign of being converted (Stoddard had held that communion was able to convert them).

For five years Edwards pastored this sizable church of some thirteen hundred. Then, in 1734, he preached the funeral sermon for a young man who had died suddenly. It jerked many from their spiritual complacency and brought them, Edwards believed, to true conversion. A spirit of renewal began to sweep the town: people met to pray and sing hymns, and crowds came to his home for counsel. And with the conversion of a notorious 'company-keeper', the flames of revival intensified and spread to other towns. Edwards saw hundreds being converted, and extraordinarily, illness became unknown in the town.

All the while, Edwards was fuelling the revival with the message 'Despair, but for Christ!' Some, though, seemed only to hear 'Despair!' and after just over a year of awakening, Edwards's uncle committed suicide by slitting his throat. At that, things seemed to unravel. For months the town had seemed free of physical and mental illness, but at this, scores now seemed suddenly tempted to follow suit, hearing voices that urged them to commit suicide. Thus the revival left a curious legacy: on the one hand, Edwards recorded the events in *A Faithful Narrative of the Surprising Work of God*, a work that became the inspiration for revivals that soon began on both sides of the Atlantic; on the other hand, with the revival in Northampton over and lives returned to much the same as before, Edwards was left to reflect on how he had assumed genuine conversion too quickly in those touched by the awakening.

It was not as if Edwards gave up on the very idea of revival. Far from it: he prayed for it incessantly. Then George Whitefield, perhaps the main revival preacher in England, came to the colony, and in 1740 arrived in Northampton. With him came a new awakening, greater than the first. It would provide the background for the most notorious event of Edwards's life. The following July, with revival still coursing through the region, Edwards visited nearby Enfield, and preached the sermon 'Sinners in the Hands of an Angry God'. In contrast to George Whitefield, there were never any flashy theatrics to Edwards's preaching; it was his quiet intensity that seemed to make him so compelling. But before this sermon was done, 'there was a great moaning and crying throughout the whole house. What shall I do to be saved. Oh I am going to Hell. Oh what shall I do for Christ.'[5] Edwards asked for silence, but the shrieks and wails now drowned him out and he was forced to head down into the congregation to minister to individuals.

What the sermon *does not* show is *what* Edwards always sought to preach. Hell, after all, was just one truth Edwards believed in, and it would be extremely naive (and just plain wrong) to take the sermon on its own as representative of Edwards's overall thought. What the sermon *does* show is *how* Edwards always sought to preach. His aim was to preach every doctrine thoroughly and in such a way that his hearers felt the reality of the truths in question. What they were brought to feel in this case was the fearful danger of being a sinner in an unrepentant state; but in another sermon they would be brought to feel 'The Pleasantness of Religion' or the 'Safety, Fullness and Sweet Refreshment in Christ'.

After two years, this second revival also died down, and, as after the first, the people's old ungodly patterns of behaviour began to resurface. Only now, the people were no longer prepared to put up with being rebuked for their ways. Thus relations between Edwards and his parishioners (relations that had never really been warm) became progressively more strained. Then Edwards did the unthinkable: he proposed abolishing 'Pope' Stoddard's old practice of admitting the unconverted to communion. By this time Edwards had served Northampton as pastor for just over twenty years, but still the church was unable to countenance defiance of their old patriarch. The council moved swiftly to remove Edwards from the pastorate (though months of awkwardness remained as, for want of any other preacher, they asked him to preach most weeks).

Early the next year (1751), he took up an invitation to be the minister of Stockbridge, a mission station based among the

---

5. Stephen Williams, diary, 8 July 1741 (typescript), Storrs Memorial Library, Longmeadow, Massachusetts.

Mohican Indians. The evangelization of the Indians was a cause that had been growing in his mind for some time. Just a few years earlier, the missionary David Brainerd had stayed for four months with the Edwards family to recover from what turned out to be fatal tuberculosis. It shows what an impact Brainerd made that, almost as soon as he had died, Edwards began work on a biography, *The Life of David Brainerd*, which turned out to be one of the most influential accounts of mission ever. Other than fortifying Edwards's concern for the Indians, though, it is hard to know quite how much Brainerd actually influenced Edwards. It is easy, for example, to imagine the author of 'Sinners in the Hands of an Angry God' goggling at a comment Brainerd made of the Indians, 'It was surprizing [*sic*] to see how their hearts seemed to be pierced with the tender and melting invitations of the Gospel, when there was not a word of terror spoken to them.'[6] In fact, though, it seems that each found the other encouraging simply because of their sheer likeness of heart and mind. Certainly, Brainerd's striking comment is reflective of Edwards's own emphases.

Something that made Edwards's work with the Indians different from his previous ministry was the fact that the Bible had not been translated into their language. Edwards thus sought to teach them English. Interestingly, he was also eager to teach them to sing, for music, he believed 'has a powerful efficacy to soften the heart into tenderness, to harmonize the affections, and to give the mind a relish for objects of a superior character'.[7]

They were difficult years in Stockbridge: the English settlers were constantly feuding, and the tension was not helped by the perpetual threat of attack. The smallness and remoteness of the place did, however, give Edwards more time than he had ever had before. This he invested in writing. In particular, he wanted to write in defence of Calvinism.

The key work here was *The Freedom of the Will*, and Edwards saw it as foundational since (like Luther and Calvin before him) he believed the idea that we are self-determining (that we can

---

6. *Works of Jonathan Edwards*, vol. 7, p. 307.

7. Ibid. vol. 16, p. 411.

determine our own choices) cuts right against the gospel. Of course, he saw, I choose to do what I want to do, and in that sense my will is free. With complete freedom I choose to drink this cup of tea. But what I want is shaped entirely by what I love. I choose to drink tea and not sewage because I like tea and am less partial to sewage. Just so, we cannot ever choose God, for we do not naturally love him, and we only choose what we love. Thus, unless a divine and supernatural light breaks in to reorient our hearts to love God, we cannot choose to do so.

The other main apologia for Calvinism was *Original Sin*, a defence of the idea that our destinies are determined by another, since we inherit both guilt and corruption from Adam. But in his articulation of this old doctrine, Edwards made a unique move. So strong was he in his bid to annihilate any self-determination in the creature that he came up with the following: 'God's upholding created substance, or causing its existence in each successive moment, is altogether equivalent to an *immediate production out of nothing*, at each moment.'[8] Now, making God recreate all things out of nothing each new moment certainly stops the creature from having any self-determination, but at what cost? God is now (and at each moment) the creator of a fallen world.

While Edwards was completing *Original Sin*, revival broke out at the College of New Jersey in Princeton. And when they began looking for a new president, Edwards seemed the obvious candidate. Edwards, though, was reluctant. He had begun preparations for two 'great works' he was eager to complete, *A History of the Work of Redemption*, and *The Harmony of the Old and New Testaments*. They would be his final masterpieces, the encapsulation of his life's thought. At Princeton they were quite understanding, though, and so in January 1758 Edwards took up the post of president there.

A month later, Edwards had himself inoculated against the smallpox that was raging through New Jersey. The procedure went awry, though, and Edwards ended up contracting the disease in his

---

8. Ibid. vol. 3, p. 402, italics original. Edwards seemed to view each creative
   moment rather like a still on a film reel being played on the screen of God's
   mind. Played all together, the stills then give the effect of time and movement.

mouth and throat. It became impossible for him to swallow, and on March 22 he finally succumbed.

Edwards's thought

In order to grasp the overall shape and feel of Edwards's thought, we will look first at his *Religious Affections*, and then try to piece together the gist of his two projected 'great works', *A History of the Work of Redemption*, and *The Harmony of the Old and New Testaments*. Through them we will also get to sample a number of his other writings, such as *The End for Which God Created the World*.

Religious Affections

In 1746, shortly after the second (Whitefield-inspired) awakening in Northampton, Edwards published his *Religious Affections*. The aim was twofold: to show, against the critics of revival, that religious affections are necessary and important; and to show others, perhaps swept along by wonderful religious experiences, how such things could be misinterpreted. Again and again Edwards had been fooled into believing that a person was truly converted because of how they seemed, only to find them slipping back later into coldness towards Christ. So, while he realized that only God can know the heart for sure, he wanted to set out what are (and what are not) reliable indications that a person is truly converted.

What makes the *Religious Affections* such a striking read is not only the extraordinary penetration of Edwards's insights, but also the way he appeals to the reader. In all his preaching and writing, he always sought to have his audience feel the truths in question. It would therefore have been entirely incongruous, to his mind, to speak of religious affections in an unaffecting, lifeless way. The result is unforgettable.

Part 1: The nature and importance of the affections
In Edwards's society, most people would have had a theoretical knowledge of at least some Christian basics. But so do devils, thought Edwards. Mere knowledge of the gospel he thus saw as something entirely different from true conversion. Instead, he

argued, 'True religion, in great part, consists in holy affections.'[9] By this he meant that the true convert is palpably moved beyond indifference ('the motion of the blood and animal spirits begins to be sensibly altered') to love for Christ and joy in him.[10]

A whole understanding of what it is to be a person was implied. Edwards argues that it is our affections that drive everything we do: we seek money because we love it; we run from danger because we love our lives; and so on. Thus when we receive the Spirit (who is eternally the love between the Father and the Son), his work is to bring us to share that love for the Father and the Son. Love, then (by which he meant a real engagement of the heart), is 'the first and chief of the affections, and the fountain of all the affections'.[11] It is when we are brought to love Christ that other, Christian affections follow: we begin to be filled with joy and gratitude; we begin to hate sin; and so on.

This, Edwards says, is why God has ordained preachers. It is not that we might hear mere 'expositions on the Scripture' that do not rouse the affections. Rather, preachers 'stir up the pure minds of the saints, and quicken their affections' by setting the things of the gospel before them 'in their proper colors . . . And particularly, to promote those two affections in them . . . love and joy.'[12] This preachers do especially by presenting the cross, for the 'glory and beauty of the blessed Jehovah . . . is there exhibited in the most affecting manner that can be conceived of',[13] though in fact all God's ways of redemption are so arranged

> as to have the greatest, possible tendency to reach our hearts in the most tender part, and move our affections most sensibly and strongly. How great cause have we therefore to be humbled to the dust, that we are no more affected![14]

---

9. Ibid. vol. 2, p. 95.
10. Ibid.
11. Ibid. p. 108.
12. Ibid. p. 116.
13. Ibid. p. 123.
14. Ibid. p. 124.

In contrast, sin is about hardness or coldness of heart. Such a heart, because it has no true love for Christ, cannot produce any good. Edwards was thus highly wary of those in his day who, sceptical of affections, taught that religion is essentially about the intellect choosing the logically correct path:

> They who condemn high affections in others, are certainly not likely to have high affections themselves . . . The right way, is not to reject all affections, nor to approve all; but to distinguish between affections, approving some, and rejecting others.[15]

Part 2: Unreliable signs of conversion

Through bitter experience, Edwards had learned to be extremely wary of the complexities and deceitfulness of the human heart, and the second part of the treatise is simply devastating in how completely it dismisses so many apparent indications of conversion as mere false signs. It is not that Edwards is saying that there is necessarily anything wrong with them; merely that they are unreliable guides to the real state of a heart.

Essentially, Edwards's point here is that, for all sorts of reasons, it is quite possible for a person to get whipped up into a spiritual 'high' that is entirely superficial. The crowd's cries of 'Hosanna!' can quickly turn to 'Crucify!' As such, the zeal and enthusiasm people show may come, not from any fundamental change in their hearts, but from the mere froth of passing emotion. In pointing this out, Edwards has made an important distinction: true religion, in great part, does consist in holy affections, but those affections are deep, though palpable, changes in the very grain of the heart and its inclinations; they are not to be confused with passions of the moment, which come and go with blood sugar levels.

Yet these passing (or false) enthusiasms can be extremely convincing: I can appear to be loving, I can seem to be under a strong conviction of my sin, be zealously involved in church activities, delight in hearing the Scriptures preached, love talking about

---

15. Ibid. p. 121.

religion and the Bible; through such things I can even convince myself and others that I am truly converted.

The overall effect of the section is distinctly unnerving, and the reader is left hungry for the next.

Part 3: True signs of conversion[16]

What marks out the affections of the truly born again is that they come from the Spirit. The Holy Spirit makes the heart of the believer holy. Holiness, Edwards explains, 'is as it were the beauty and sweetness of the divine nature', and this is what the Spirit imparts to the believer.[17] He communicates the goodness of his nature so that Christians, 'by reflecting the light of the Sun of Righteousness, do shine with the same sort of brightness, the same mild, sweet and pleasant beams'.[18] Edwards talks much of the 'sweetness' of Christ and how he makes Christians 'sweet'. But it would be a mistake to imagine Edwards slipping into senti-mentality, for this 'sweetness' is no weak thing, but strength shown in the face of the natural slide into unpleasant viciousness.

In fact, Edwards sees that it is having a sense of the sweetness of God that is really what marks out the converted. He compares two men: one knows merely *that* honey is sweet; the other 'loves honey and is greatly delighted in it because he knows the sweet taste of it'.[19] So it is with conversion: it is not merely that I

---

16. Edwards lists twelve true signs of conversion, as he had listed twelve unreliable signs. However, boiling them down and presenting them one by one would border on cruelty to the reader! Instead I will simply try to present the gist of the section.

17. *Works of Jonathan Edwards*, vol. 2, p. 201.

18. Ibid. p. 347.

19. Ibid. p. 209. Stephen Holmes suggests that, since honey is more commonplace today, the illustration works less well than it would have done, and so provides his own illustration: 'I might have been told of a liquid that tastes of seaweed and peat smoke, and might even believe that this could be a pleasant experience, in the sense of giving intellectual consent to such a proposition, but only when I taste the whiskies of Islay will I really understand what is meant, and be seized by the desire

understand that God is sweet; it is that I now have a sense of and appreciation for that sweetness. I have tasted and seen.

This sense of the sweetness of divine things is essentially about enjoying the beauty of God. God, for Edwards, is distinguished from all other beings chiefly by his beauty, and it is beauty above all that stirs the affections and changes hearts. Thus true believers are impressed first by the beauty of God as he is in himself; they are not impressed primarily with what they gain from the gospel.

Seeing this enables Edwards to make some painfully piercing observations on Christian hypocrisy and hypocritical preaching of the gospel. The problems begin when the beauty of Christ is lost, for then the Christian message becomes nothing more than a cheap form of eternal fire insurance. But the hypocrite loves this, for the hypocrite most fundamentally loves himself and so is moved primarily by what God can do for him. That is, at root, the hypocrite does not love God, but himself, and simply likes the fact that he can be nicely served by God.

One way hypocrites can be unmasked is by the fact that, since their interest is essentially in themselves, they keep their eyes fixed not on 'the beauty of Christ, but the beauty of their experiences'; 'hypocrites, in their high affections, talk more of the discovery, than they do of the thing discovered'.[20] The worry is that, because of the self-love involved, such false affections tend actually to harden the heart in direct contrast to the true work of the Spirit, who makes believers always hungry to know and love God more, to hate sin more, and so on.

Hypocrites, because they have no true love for God, also misunderstand humility, thinking that it too is all about themselves. Instead of happily abandoning themselves for God, hypocrites

---

to discover more' (*God of Grace and God of Glory: An Account of the Theology of Jonathan Edwards* [Grand Rapids: Eerdmans, 2000], p. 162). Dare one quibble with such a fine illustration? Hardly, and yet to my knowledge there is one thing Islay whiskies lack that is important for Edwards's point: sweetness. But I stand prepared to be educated here.

20. *Works of Jonathan Edwards*, vol. 2, pp. 251, 252.

merely abandon certain things (e.g. wealth and pleasure), and do so only to fuel their own self-righteousness, selling 'one lust to feed another . . . a beastly lust to pamper a devilish one'.[21] And their lack of love for God becomes evident in the imbalance of their lives: claiming to love God but having no love for men, or loving people in church on Sunday but beating their wives on Monday.

Because true believers are affected by the Spirit, what moves them is nothing within themselves, but always the Spirit's revelation of the things of God in Scripture: 'Holy affections are not heat without light; but evermore arise from some information of the understanding, some spiritual instruction that the mind receives, some light or actual knowledge.'[22] It is by knowing God better that we love him more. Thus godly affections are not mere emotions, but are about having a taste or relish for the God revealed in Scripture. And this 'sense of the spiritual excellency and beauty of divine things, does also tend directly to convince the mind of the truth of the gospel' so that believers are no longer troubled by the truth of it, but bold to venture their all upon it.[23] The divine excellence of the gospel melts away prejudices against it. This is very different from those who place their faith fundamentally not on the gospel itself but on external attestations that the gospel is reliable. For them, the insufficiency of the evidence means that 'there will endless doubts and scruples remain'.[24]

Edwards ends the treatise by arguing that Christian practice is 'the chief of all the signs of grace', the best indication to others and to myself that I have been born again.[25]

> Christ is not in the heart of a saint, as in a sepulcher, or as a dead
> Saviour, that does nothing; but as in his temple, and as one that is alive
> from the dead. For in the heart where Christ savingly is, there he lives,

---

21. Ibid. p. 315.
22. Ibid. p. 266.
23. Ibid. p. 301.
24. Ibid. p. 304.
25. Ibid. p. 406.

and exerts himself after the power of that endless life, that he received at his resurrection.[26]

A History of the Work of Redemption

Before he died, Edwards was planning to write 'a great work, which I call *A History of the Work of Redemption*, a body of divinity in an entire new method, being thrown into the form of an history'.[27] It was to have started in eternity past, with a look at why God ever chose to create and redeem a world. It would then swoop down to tell the history of creation (heaven, earth and hell) from beginning to end. This, he believed, would be fittingly beautiful and entertaining, and thereby 'every divine doctrine, will appear to greatest advantage'. An ambitious plan indeed!

It might seem absurd to try to outline a work Edwards never wrote; however, he was clear that the first part would be based on his earlier work, *The End for Which God Created the World*, and the second part would be based on his earlier sermon series, *A History of the Work of Redemption*. So by getting to know those two earlier pieces we should get a good feel for what Edwards saw as the masterpiece that would encapsulate his theology.

The End for Which God Created the World

If *Religious Affections* reveals Edwards's pastoral insight, *The End for Which God Created the World* brilliantly displays the freshness of his mind and sheer creative panache. That said, it does not start well. A ten-page introduction is spent defining terms, the key ones being 'ultimate end' (something done for its own sake) and 'chief end' (the ultimate end most valued). But one can get along quite nicely without knowing exactly what Edwards is talking about here, and the section is best skimmed or skipped if you're feeling nervous.

Chapter 1: What reason tells us
Edwards does not believe that reason alone can establish what God's chief end or goal in creating the world was; that said, he

---

26. Ibid. p. 392.
27. Ibid. vol. 16, p. 727.

does think that what he is going to argue is rationally coherent, and that is what he sets out to show first. The reader needs to bear this in mind, for if the arguments of chapter 1 are read as logical proofs, they do look rather thin. For example, he will argue "Tis a thing infinitely good in itself that God's glory should be known by a glorious society of created beings."[28] In chapter 2 he will make a good, biblical case for this, but as it stands in chapter 1, the claim is not at all self-evident.

The argument begins by asserting that no rational account of God's goal in creation can suggest that God somehow needed creation. God, who existed before creation, cannot be dependent on creation. What, then, was his goal? It must have been what is most valuable; and that, of course, is himself. But what does that mean? Edwards looks at God's attributes or characteristics and says, 'If the world had not been created, these attributes never would have had any exercise.'[29] Certainly, this is unguarded language. Was the Father not good to the Son, for instance? At times in this section it can sound as if the God he is describing is a solitary being, not a Trinity of persons where, for example, the Son knows the Father: 'It seems to be a thing in itself fit and desirable, that the glorious perfections of God should be known, and the operations and expressions of them seen by other beings besides himself.'[30]

Then he comes to the nub of his argument: God's goal, he says, was 'to communicate of his own infinite fullness of good'.[31] God, he explains, is like a fountain of goodness, and delights to spread his own goodness and happiness, his knowledge of himself and joy in himself. None of this is to say that God is choosing to do any of this for his creatures as such. God had this delight before

---

28. Ibid. vol. 8, p. 431.
29. Ibid. p. 429.
30. Ibid. pp. 430–431.
31. Ibid. p. 433. The implications of this are profound for understanding God's judgment and hell. Since communicating his goodness is God's ultimate aim, Edwards held that damnation is God's strange work, done not for its own sake but for the great end of the plan of redemption.

he had even chosen to create. Rather, God's great aim is to express his goodness and happiness. But as soon as God decided to create, that aim meant that he would be all about communicating his goodness to his creatures. Thus 'God's acting for himself, or making himself his last end, and his acting for their sake, are not to be set in opposition'.[32]

With this, Edwards has brilliantly cut through a quandary. For if we say God's sole aim in creation is himself, we make God sound selfish, as if he is merely using us for his own purposes; but if we say God's sole aim is us and our good, we sound selfish, as if we were using God. But for Edwards, God's great goal *is* his own glory (God is not subservient to some higher purpose than himself); and yet that highest purpose is self-giving, not self-serving.

Edwards then turns to answer some potential objections. First, does this not actually make God dependent on creation, as if God needs creation in order that he might communicate his goodness? This is a position Edwards is determined to distance himself from. God, who is complete and happy in himself, is never about getting something from creation, but giving out of his natural, over-flowing goodness. His pleasure 'is rather a pleasure in diffusing and communicating to the creature, than in receiving from the creature'.[33]

On the other hand, does this not all make God out to be a selfish cosmic egotist? Such a view Edwards had equally little tolerance for. He would rail against those who imagined a God who 'has no proper love or fervent affection but only a cool purpose and that he has no true delight or happiness in his Creatures'. For Edwards, God is no self-serving applause-seeker; his aim is to communicate and share his goodness and happiness, and that is generous, not selfish: 'in seeking himself, i.e. himself diffused and expressed (which he delights in, as he delights in his own beauty and fullness), he seeks their glory and happiness'.[34]

---

32. Ibid. p. 440.
33. Ibid. p. 448.
34. Ibid. p. 459.

Chapter 2: What Scripture tells us

Edwards begins the second chapter by machine-gunning his readers with Bible verses to prove that God is the Alpha and Omega, the origin and goal of all things, that all things are from him and for him, and that the end of all things is to glorify God. To glorify God, he shows, was always Christ's aim, as it is the point of the Christian life.

So Scripture shows the glory of God as the chief end of creation and redemption. But (and here is the key question) what, precisely, does Scripture mean by 'the glory of God'? Sometimes it is a phrase 'used to signify the second person in the Trinity'.[35] And this fits with the fact that, as well as working for his glory, God repeatedly says he is acting for the sake of his name, and 'the Name of the LORD' is another phrase used of Christ. Commenting elsewhere on Isaiah 30:27 ('See, the Name of the LORD comes from afar, / with burning anger and dense clouds of smoke; / his lips are full of wrath, / and his tongue is a consuming fire'), Edwards says, 'God's name is evidently spoken of as a person.'[36] Christ is the name and glory of God.

But still, what could that mean? In Scripture, he says, the glory of a thing is its weight, majesty and essence. But the word also 'often signifies a visible exhibition of glory; as in an effulgence or shining brightness, by an emanation of beams of light. Thus the brightness of the sun and moon and stars is called their "glory".'[37] And thus we see Christ described as the brightness of the Father's glory shining out (Heb. 1:3). As it turns out, Edwards seems to view light as the most essential and revealing synonym for glory. The image of light is closely associated with enlightenment and knowledge. But light also shines forth, and that image of glorious beams of light shining out captures Edwards's understanding of glory:

> What God has in view in neither of them, neither in his manifesting his glory to the understanding nor communication to the heart, is not that

---

35. Ibid. p. 512.
36. Ibid. vol. 21, p. 377.
37. Ibid. vol. 8, pp. 514–516.

he may receive, but that he [may] go forth: the main end of his shining
forth is not that he may have his rays reflected back to himself, but that
the rays may go forth.[38]

God's glory is his going out (in Christ) to make known and available
his righteousness, wisdom, goodness and mercy. And this is why
creation exists, so that his people might enjoy him. God's glory, then,
is his grace (Edwards thinks the phrase 'according to the riches of
his *glory*' in Ephesians 3:16 is equivalent to 'according to the riches
of his *grace*' in Ephesians 1:7 [Authorized Version]). Thus Christ's
death is the hour he is glorified, for it is then that he is revealed in
his full graciousness, giving himself in love for his church. And thus
the church is the glory of Christ, for it is the fruit of his self-giving
grace.

Underneath the entire argument lie strong trinitarian foundations, which, although largely hidden, are worth being aware of.
Some of Edwards's language (God's 'love for himself', for instance)
can be quite misleading unless it is understood that Edwards is
thinking of the Father's love for the Son. In fact, the whole shape
of the work is trinitarian, especially in the second chapter. The
reason God creates is to express and communicate to others
the love that the Father has for the Son. And it is in that fellowship
that we will enjoy a never-ending increase of happiness as 'the
union will become more and more strict and perfect; nearer and
more like to that between God the Father and the Son'.[39]

A History of the Work of Redemption (sermon series)[40]

It was only fitting that Edwards should move on to this subject
next, for the history of redemption, in which God expresses and

---

38. Ibid. vol. 13, p. 496.
39. Ibid. vol. 8, p. 533. Edwards believed that both heaven and hell are
    progressive states, such that, as our love and union with God will ever
    develop in heaven, so hatred will ever worsen in hell.
40. This series of thirty sermons, preached in 1739, was put together as a
    book by others after Edwards's death (and appears as such in the two-
    volume Banner of Truth edition of his works); however, it should not

shares his love, *is* the end of creation. Edwards divides his history into three parts that correspond to the Old Testament, the New Testament and then subsequent church history up until Christ's return.

Part 1: From creation to incarnation

In *The End for Which God Created the World* Edwards had already begun his history with a look at God's intentions in eternity past. Back then, the Father had appointed the Son to be the redeemer. But then, as 'soon as ever man fell Christ entered on his mediatorial work'.[41] Immediately, the gospel was declared (in Gen. 3:15) and God began to show mercy to sinners and save them through Christ. Adam and Eve were even clothed with animal skins as outward signs of the righteousness of Christ with which they were now covered.

And redemption, Edwards is clear, was always through Christ:

> when we read in the sacred history [the Old Testament] what God did from time to time towards his church and people, and what he said to them, and how he revealed himself to them, we are to understand it especially of the second person of the Trinity. When we read after this of God's appearing time after time in some visible form or outward symbol of his presence, we are ordinarily if not universally to understand it of the second person of the Trinity.[42]

Judging by the time he gives to it in his writings, this was a point that clearly concerned Edwards. He devoted entire papers (e.g. 'In what sense did the saints under the Old Testament believe in Christ to

---

be confused with the 'great work' that he intended, but never managed, to write. The sermon series was to provide the foundations for the second part of that work, but in his preparatory notes he makes it clear that he intended to expand his history to include significantly more on the history of the papacy and more on the history of heaven and hell, angels and demons, 'the state of departed saints' and the new creation.

41. *Works of Jonathan Edwards*, vol. 9, p. 129.
42. Ibid. p. 131.

justification?') to arguing that it was 'plainly and fully revealed to the church of Israel' that Christ, the angel of the Lord, was a distinct person from the Father to be trusted, and in fact that the 'people of God trusted in this person to save them', knowing that he would come and make atonement for them.[43]

Then came the first revival, 'the first remarkable pouring out of the Spirit through Christ that ever was . . . in the days of Enos'.[44] This led to the salvation of men such as Enoch, who provided the first, important instance of a body being redeemed from death. It also set the pattern for the history to come: the work of redemption would be achieved mainly through great outpourings of the Spirit.

God also provided the church with prophecies and types (sacrifices as 'prototypes' of the cross etc.) to keep their hopes set on the coming redemption. But the 'greatest pledge and forerunner of the future redemption of Christ of any' was the exodus. It was not, though, as if the church was left with mere promises of the coming redemption. Christ himself was with them. It was he who wrought the exodus, appearing to Moses in the bush (which represented the human nature he would assume, being burned by the fire of God's wrath, but not consumed).

> Because this great mystery of the incarnation and suffering of Christ was here represented, therefore Moses says, I will turn aside and behold this great sight. A great sight he might well call it when there was to be seen represented God manifested in the flesh, and suffering a dreadful death, and rising from the dead.[45]

Then 'Christ went before 'em in a pillar of cloud and fire' and gave Moses the Ten Commandments with his own hand.[46]

More than the Ten Commandments, though, the whole law was a school of types so that 'the gospel was abundantly held forth to

43. Ibid. vol. 21, pp. 372, 389.
44. Ibid. vol. 9, p. 141.
45. Ibid. p. 175.
46. Ibid. p. 176.

that nation so that there is scarce any doctrine of it but is particularly taught and exhibited by some observance of this law'.[47] By this stage the reader should be clear that Edwards is very interested in types (something we will discuss more later). He believed that there are three sorts of types: *institutions*, of which the greatest were the sacrifices; *events*, of which the greatest was the exodus; and *individuals* who were themselves types, of whom the greatest was David (God's anointed who redeemed Jerusalem, the greatest type of the church).

David was also a prophet who sang of 'those great things of Christ's redemption that had been the hope and expectation of God's church and people from the very beginning'.[48] And as the time of Christ's coming approached, such prophesying increased, for God set up permanent schools of prophets so that there might be an unbroken succession of men who would proclaim Christ's coming. And to those prophets who would be most explicit (e.g. Isaiah, Daniel and Ezekiel) Christ himself would appear.

But with Solomon's slide into idolatry, things began to darken and, despite an outpouring of the Spirit in Ezra's day, the church generally declined into ignorant superstition. The lights of the types went out so that Christ the fulfilment might be seen as the only light: the temple was destroyed, the kings were removed; even prophecies eventually ceased as the time of the great prophet drew near. 'Thus the lights of the Old Testament go out on the approach of the glorious sun of righteousness.'[49]

But since the coming one would not just be the hope of Israel but the firstborn of the new creation, all creation went into labour to give him birth. History entered its most tumultuous stage as Babylon fell to Persia, Persia to Greece, and Greece to Rome. In those pagan empires, Satan was permitted to rise to his full strength in readiness for his final defeat. Also, heathen philosophy came to its height in Athens, permitted so that its insufficiency and the need for a divine teacher might be shown.

---

47. Ibid. p. 182.
48. Ibid. p. 210.
49. Ibid. p. 254.

At the same time the Jews began to be dispersed through the nations. This served to show the impracticality and so insufficiency of the temple's sacrificial system; more, it spread expectation of the Messiah through the world in preparation for the mass salvation of the Gentiles. And with some success, Edwards believed:

> Virgil the famous poet that lived in Italy a little before Christ was born, has a poem about the expectation of a great prince that was to be born and the happiness, time of righteousness and peace that he was to introduce, some of it very much in the language of the prophet Isaiah.[50]

The Scriptures were also translated into Greek, the language of the nations, 'making the facts concerning Jesus Christ publicly known through the world'.[51]

Thus the Old Testament (and, indeed, all world history) had prepared for the moment when Christ would come to purchase the redemption planned before creation itself.

Part 2: The purchase of redemption
Presumably, because the material is covered elsewhere, Edwards is remarkably brief in this second part, and its feel is much less historical and more abstract as he considers what Christ accomplished.

All Christ had done before his incarnation had been to prepare for this moment, but he could not actually redeem humans without becoming one of them himself. But from the moment of

---

50. Ibid. p. 257, referring to Virgil's *Fourth Eclogue* (something C. S. Lewis made a regular part of his Christmas reading). Through his life, Edwards became increasingly interested in the idea that the truths of the gospel had, in ancient times (especially Noah's day), been disseminated throughout the cultures of the world, there to be slowly distorted. See, for instance, Miscellany 1181, 'Traditions of the heathen, particularly the Chinese, concerning the Trinity, the nature of the Deity, the paradisaic state, the Fall, the redemption of the Messiah, the fall of angels, the nature of true religion' (*Works of Jonathan Edwards*, vol. 23, pp. 95–104).

51. *Works of Jonathan Edwards*, vol. 9, p. 258.

his conception, Christ began to purchase redemption. That meant humiliation, even from his birth, since while Mary and Joseph 'were both of the royal family of David, the most honorable family, and Joseph the rightful heir, yet the family was reduced to a very low state'.[52] And it meant almost immediate suffering, in his circumcision. Yet all this was necessary, for it was by such humiliation and suffering, even from conception, that he fulfilled the demands of the law and the covenant of works: 'the blood that was shed in his circumcision was propitiatory blood; but as it was a conformity to the law of Moses it was part of his meritorious righteousness'.[53]

It all culminated, of course, in the cross.

> Then was finished all that was required in order to satisfy the threatenings of the law, all in order to satisfy divine justice, the utmost that vindictive justice demanded, [the] whole debt paid. Then finished the whole of the purchase of eternal life.[54]

Part 3: From Pentecost to Christ's return

The last section looks at the subsequent spreading of that redemption through the world. Edwards held that God works in history primarily through extraordinary outpourings of his Spirit in revival. Thus he depicts the advance of Christ's kingdom happening in four great steps of awakening. Each time involves a growing degeneracy and opposition to the gospel; then God acts in judgment, the church is delivered and multitudes receive new life.

The first great step began with Christ's work on earth and ended with the destruction of Jerusalem in AD 70. In demolishing the temple (and so its whole sacrificial system), God thus judged the faithless Jews who were trusting in the types rather than their fulfilment. So redemption spread ever more to the Gentiles.

The second step involved the conversion of the Roman emperor

---

52. Ibid. p. 300.

53. Ibid. pp. 307–308. For the 'covenant of works', see p. 97, on John Owen, in this book.

54. *Works of Jonathan Edwards*, vol. 9, p. 331.

Constantine. This, Edwards is prepared to say, was 'the greatest revolution and change in the face of things on the face of the earth that ever came to pass in the world since the flood'.[55] Why? Because through it, pagan Rome, which had so oppressed the church, was destroyed. That effectively meant judgment on the entire heathen world, a judgment that was followed by the gospel being taken to such far countries as India and Ireland.

The third step concerns the destruction of papal Rome, an event so significant that the 'bigger part of the book of Revelation is taken up in foretelling the events of this period'.[56] After the conversion of Constantine, Satan succeeded in two great works: in the eastern half of the old Roman Empire he raised up Islam; in the western half he established the kingdom of Antichrist. Seated on seven hills, drunk with the blood of the saints, this of course was the Roman papacy.[57] But in the Reformation the fall of Antichrist began.

It all meant that it could not be long before Satan's kingdom was overthrown. And Edwards saw his own ministry to the Indians as proof of that. Satan, he believed, had first brought people to America so as to get them out of the reach of the gospel. But with the evangelization of even these remote people, it was clear that the ends of the earth were soon to be converted. He suggested that in their death throes Antichrist and Islam would make a final alliance against the church, only to be swiftly defeated. Then would come a time of unprecedented revival: 'the word of God shall have a speedy and swift progress through the earth';[58] Jew and heathen would convert en masse; then the earth, full of the knowledge of the Lord, would enjoy a thousand years of peace and prosperity.

Then (after a final apostasy) would come the fourth step in

---

55. Ibid. p. 396.

56. Ibid. p. 404.

57. Since the early days of the Reformation, it had been conventional for Protestant theologians to identify papal Rome as the persecuting whore of Babylon depicted in the book of Revelation.

58. *Works of Jonathan Edwards*, vol. 9, p. 466.

which Christ would return. In fact, the first three steps were all types of this one, for now Christ would judge the whole world and, not just spiritually now, but physically bring multitudes to new life. Then 'Christ's church shall forever leave this accursed world to go into that more glorious world, the highest heavens'; the world will be burned up, and the 'miserable company of wicked shall be left behind to have their cursed future executed upon 'em here'.[59]

There is undoubtedly material here that is problematic (e.g. the idea that this world is effectively to be discarded, not renewed); and yet we should probably be especially wary of our own reactions at this point. It is all too easy to snigger snobbishly when Edwards so directly connects events in his own day to events in Revelation. Those links might have been wrong, but our reaction reveals something much more worrying in us. That is, we moderns instinctively find it incredible that 'real' secular history should ever be connected to, let alone be driven by, God's cosmic plan of redemption. Edwards, on the other hand, rejected such dualism. He, at least, had a robustly Christian understanding of all history.[60]

The Harmony of the Old and New Testaments

This, Edwards's other projected 'great work', would, he said, have examined in more detail first, the Old Testament prophecies of the Messiah; secondly, Old Testament types of the gospel; and thirdly, 'the harmony of the Old and New Testament, as to doctrine and precept'.[61] Clearly, these were significant issues for Edwards, and yet, after a look at *A History of the Work of Redemption*, we probably have a good enough sense of where Edwards would have gone with this work. It would be made even more clear that the Old Testament is 'full of the gospel of Christ', and that 'Christ and his redemption are the great subject of the whole Bible'.[62]

---

59. Ibid. p. 505.

60. And not just history: his scientific notebooks (Ibid. vol. 6), for example, show how, even in the tiniest atomic details, Edwards refused to separate theology from the natural world and the discipline of science.

61. *Works of Jonathan Edwards*, vol. 16, p. 728.

62. Ibid. vol. 9, pp. 289–290.

That said, the question of types that he said he would examine here was more fundamental to Edwards than we have been able to see so far. For, the frequency with which God employed types in the Old Testament convinced Edwards that types were a regular means God used to communicate spiritual truths – and not just in Scripture. Indeed, Edwards held that since God had created in order to communicate himself, material reality naturally expressed and reflected the more substantial spiritual realities. Creation, he held, is a projection of the divine mind, and as such is entirely harmonious with the Creator, meaning that it is 'full of images of divine things, as full as a language is of words'.[63] To take one vital example: Edwards thought of the three persons of the Trinity constituting 'the supreme harmony of all';[64] their harmony provides the logic for all created harmony, such that singing in harmony (something Edwards loved to do with his family) reflects divine beauty:

> The best, most beautiful, and most perfect way that we have of
> expressing a sweet concord of mind to each other, is by music. When
> I would form in my mind an idea of a society in the highest degree
> happy, I think of them as expressing their love, their joy, and the inward
> concord and harmony and spiritual beauty of their souls by sweetly
> singing to each other.[65]

All this meant that, out walking amidst trees and rivers, Edwards would continue being instructed in and reminded of the gospel. The tiniest details around him poured forth knowledge. How he came to recognize these types in creation was controlled essentially by Scripture: when, for example, he observed that the 'rising and setting of the sun is a type of the death and resurrection of Christ' he was working from scriptural ideas of the Light of the World, the Sun of Righteousness and broader themes of light and darkness.[66] That said, he did not believe that Scripture listed every type to be found

63. Ibid. vol. 11, p. 152.
64. Ibid. vol. 13, p. 329.
65. Ibid. p. 331.
66. Ibid. vol. 11, p. 64.

in creation; rather, it taught the principles. So, for example, he could suggest that 'Children's coming into the world naked and filthy, and in their blood, and crying and impotent, is to signify the spiritual nakedness, pollution of nature and wretchedness of condition with which they are born.'[67]

Edwards's writings are remarkable for how richly (and how well) he illustrates his points by describing similar things in creation. Yet he did not believe that he was inventing his illustrations; it was rather that creation was specifically designed to represent truths about the Creator and his work of redemption. God's being and all his ways, thought Edwards, are a harmony.

Going on with Edwards

You should be able to feel quite relaxed about where to set off in Edwards's works. He is generally quite easy-going. An obvious starting point is *Religious Affections*, a work that leaves no reader unchanged. But if that feels too lengthy, you can get a swift taste of the same brew in 'A Divine and Supernatural Light' or 'Distinguishing Marks of a Work of the Spirit of God'. A little trickier is *The End for Which God Created the World*, but you can avoid the harder bits and get much the same reward by diving straight into chapter 2.

Banner of Truth provide *Religious Affections* and *A History of the Work of Redemption* (among a number of his other works) as handy, stand-alone books; they also produce a two-volume *Works of Jonathan Edwards*, which is the cheapest way to own all his most essential writings and sermons. It is not comprehensive, though, and if you find yourself really wanting to get stuck into Edwards, there is nothing to rival the definitive *Works of Jonathan Edwards*, 26 vols. (New Haven: Yale University Press, 1957–2008). You needn't break the bank, however: everything can be read online for free at Yale University's Jonathan Edwards Center (http://edwards.yale.edu). I say 'read', but perhaps 'sampled' might be better: reading

---

67. Ibid. p. 54.

Edwards's major works on a computer screen would be as harsh as licking caviar off an old sock.

There is one other 'must read': George Marsden's *Jonathan Edwards: A Life* (New Haven: Yale University Press, 2003). Gripping, insightful; bluntly, unsurpassable.

Jonathan Edwards timeline

1703   Edwards born in East Windsor, Connecticut
1716   Begins studies at Yale College
1721   Conversion experience
1722   Assistant pastor in New York City; writes 'Resolutions'
1723   Pastor in Bolton, Connecticut
1724   Tutor at Yale
1727   Assistant pastor in Northampton; marries Sarah Pierpont
1729   Solomon Stoddard dies; Edwards becomes senior pastor
1734–5 Revival in Northampton
1739   Preaches *A History of the Work of Redemption*
1740   George Whitefield sparks second revival in Northampton
1741   Edwards preaches 'Sinners in the Hands of an Angry God'
1746   Publishes *Religious Affections*
1747   David Brainerd visits and dies in Edwards's home
1750   Dismissed as pastor of Northampton
1751   Pastor of Stockbridge mission station
1755   Writes *The End for Which God Created the World*
1758   Installed as president of the College of New Jersey (now Princeton University); dies

11. THE FATHER OF MODERN THEOLOGY

Friedrich Schleiermacher

On 14 July 1789 an angry mob surged into the courtyard of the Bastille prison in Paris, sparking off the French Revolution. But the revolution and its reign of terror were only the most violent expressions of a general mood of the age against God and his appointed kings and authorities. Here was a generation profoundly grateful to all those philosophers who gave them grounds for religious scepticism. Then into the breach stepped the imposing intellectual figure of Friedrich Schleiermacher, who, with impressive artistry, set out to reconcile the Spirit of Christianity with the spirit of his generation.

Strangely enough, Schleiermacher himself remains largely unknown to English speakers, and yet his impact was such that we can hardly do theology today without his presence all around us. The day after he died, August Neander, Professor of Theology at the University of Berlin, said to his students, 'From him a new period in the history of the church will one day take its origin.' He was right, and that day did not take long to arrive. The spirit of Schleiermacher presided over so much of the nineteenth century, and soon it was clear that a new era in theology had begun: the era of liberalism.

Given Schleiermacher's status as the father of liberalism, one would expect him to be a magnet for the wrath of the conservatives. In fact, though, Schleiermacher was so Christ-centred in his thought that even conservatives have struggled to know quite what to make of him. 'He gave up everything that he might save Christ' is the sort of awkward praise heard instead of outright condemnation. Charles Hodge, that bastion of nineteenth-century Princeton conservatism, wrote that when he was in Berlin he often attended Schleiermacher's church. And the hymns sung there, he said,

> were always evangelical and spiritual in an eminent degree, filled with praise and gratitude to our Redeemer . . . [and] Schleiermacher, when sitting in the evening with his family, would often say, 'Hush, children; let us sing a hymn of praise to Christ.' Can we doubt that he is singing those praises now? To whomsoever Christ is God, St. John assures us, Christ is a Saviour.[1]

Certainly Schleiermacher loved Jesus; of that there can be no doubt. However, he was a deeply complex and original thinker, and it will take some more wrestling with him before we can discern whether or not he really thought of Christ as the living God. But Schleiermacher is worth the wrestle! In fact, dear reader, you should guard yourself now against the temptation to dismiss him with anything like disdainful swagger. Schleiermacher was a giant among theologians, and his influence upon the church has been immense. To ignore through haughtiness or impatience the persuasive power of his theology will mean failure to understand his legacy as it surrounds us today.

Schleiermacher's life

Fritz Schleiermacher, as his friends called him, was born in 1768 in Breslau (then part of the Kingdom of Prussia, now Wrocław in

---

1. C. Hodge, *Systematic Theology* (1871–3; repr. London: James Clarke, 1960), vol. 2, p. 440, n.

southern Poland). For generations, the men on both sides of his family had been Reformed preachers, and true to form his father Gottlieb became an army chaplain (though Freemasonry seems to have been dearer to his heart than the tenets of Calvinism).

Then, when Fritz was nine, the family moved near a Herrnhuter community. It was to prove a great turning point. The Herrnhuters (or Moravians) were Pietists who believed in the necessity of a living faith in Jesus and who reacted against the dry orthodoxy of the day, where doctrines, they felt, were treated like dead butter-flies, only to be collected, codified and catalogued. Expelled from Moravia, they had been given shelter at Herrnhut on the lands of Count Niklaus Ludwig von Zinzendorf, who became their bishop. The Schleiermacher family were profoundly impressed by this joyful community of living faith: Gottlieb was converted; and Fritz too, loving the experiential emphasis, soon underwent what he later referred to as his birth into a 'higher life'.

It was a good thing Fritz liked the Herrnhuters, for his parents gave their children over to be educated by them; and with his mother's death soon after and his father constantly on the move with the army, he never saw them again. The Herrnhuters thus became his new family, and shaped him permanently. And while he grew ever more frustrated with their doctrinal rigidity, he would always feel that true religion could not simply be taught but had to be experienced. Later in life he would define himself, saying, 'I have become a Herrnhuter again, only of a higher order.'

A 'Herrnhuter *again*. . .' So first there had to be a parting of the ways. It all began with a secret philosophical club Schleier-macher began at school. There, influenced by philosophers such as Rousseau, he began to question and then reject some of the Herrnhuters' doctrinal essentials (divine punishment for sin, the sub-stitutionary sacrifice of Christ on the cross, the eternal deity of the Son). Casting off these doctrinal chains, he felt he was getting closer to true Christianity, and yet the eternal Son's atoning sacrifice for sin was at the very heart of Herrnhuter piety: it could not be discarded without consequences. When he wrote to his father describing his new views, his father was so appalled he lashed out with the harshest rebukes and the father–son relationship broke down irretrievably.

Gottlieb did, however, agree for his son to go to the University of Halle, an establishment that would provide just the sort of atmosphere of free inquiry that Fritz longed to escape the Herrnhuter college for. Not that he would attend many of the lectures there: frustrated by their plodding mediocrity, he embarked on his own, vastly more challenging study projects. He immersed himself in the study of Kant, read large amounts of Plato and Aristotle, and found that he was beginning to work out an entirely original theology. The whole time at Halle he found quite depressing, though. His short, slight frame had never been in good health ever since his sister dropped him as a child and left him mildly hunched and misshapen; but now all the reclusive study really took its toll. And it wasn't just his health; his reading left him sceptical and his isolation left him lonely. All the social and spiritual warmth he had enjoyed with the Herrnhuters was gone.

Then, as was the custom of the time for a man in his position, he accepted a tutoring post in the aristocratic Prussian household of Count von Dohna at Schlobitten. And in the warmth of that large and happy family, the cold cynicism that had thrived in the ivory towers of Halle was melted away and feelings of love began to bud: love for Jesus, and a secret love for one of the young countesses. He was becoming a Herrnhuter again. He began preaching regularly and passionately, his sermons full of both moral challenge and Christ as our model and ideal. He said it was as if he had 'revelation from within', and it was by that intuition that his theology was now developing fast.

He left Schlobitten, took an assistant pastorate in Landsberg for a couple of years (where he grabbed every moment he could to read the pantheist philosopher Spinoza); then, in 1796, aged twenty-seven, he took up his first post of real responsibility, as chaplain of the large and dirty Charity Hospital in Berlin. For Schleiermacher, Berlin was a Prussian Eden, with salons overflowing with poets, philosophers and talk of Romanticism.[2] With its good society and

---

2. Romanticism, which was really more of a mood than a movement, was a reaction against the cold rationalism of the Enlightenment; it championed instead the individual and her feelings, self-expression, personal creativity

cultured repartee, it seemed to have the warmth of Herrnhut but with that longed-for 'higher order' of conversation.

It was also a world with little room for God. At least, it had little room for any God who might want to express himself in the world. Thus Schleiermacher came to write his first book, *On Religion: Speeches to Its Cultured Despisers*. In it he argued that true religion (of which Christianity is the highest form) is not about the dead letter of doctrine and the sort of historical events that Enlightenment scepticism pooh-poohed; it is about a living experience of the divine. In other words, Romantic 'cultured despisers of religion' need not trouble themselves with off-putting dogmas such as God and human immortality, for true religion was all about what it is to be human, about having an intuition, a feeling for the universe, a taste for the infinite. It was a vision of Christianity as the ideal for which Romanticism was really striving.

Thus Schleiermacher made his name, and thus he established the trajectory of his mature theology. But he also used language that he would later retreat from: he called the pantheist Spinoza a holy man filled with the Spirit, and spoke of the 'the World', 'the Universe' and 'the One' as the proper object of our pious adoration. Such pantheist language, he soon realized, would have to be softened.

In and out of the salons, Schleiermacher was naturally sociable and made easy and interesting company. Personally, though, he preferred to be with women. In fact, he once admitted to a female friend, he wished that he could be a woman (women, he felt, cherish feeling more). This led to some distinctly uncomfortable social situations, such as when, for example, he developed romantic attachments to two married women. One of them, Eleonore von Grunow, was in an unhappy marriage with a pastor, which

---

and mystery. Hear the heroic self-expression in a Beethoven symphony; think of the dark, questioning mystery of Mary Shelley's *Frankenstein*, of Wordsworth swooning over the ruins of Tintern Abbey or Turner's brooding washes of paint as he depicts some shipwreck – then you feel the spirit of Romanticism.

Schleiermacher concluded could be no true marriage. So he courted and secretly betrothed himself to her. Seeing the difficulty, Bishop Sack sent Schleiermacher far away to a tiny parish in Stolpe on the Baltic coast.

His time in Stolpe was a sobering one after the heady Romanticism of Berlin, but it was not long before he was summoned to the University of Halle as Professor of Theology and University Preacher. There he got his first taste of lecturing on the New Testament – and on everything else on the syllabus bar the Old Testament. But even the Halle days weren't to last long. A couple of years later, in 1806, Napoleon's Grand Army were marching through the streets and the university was shut down amid city-wide chaos.

But from the smoke and carnage now rose a new and more fiery Schleiermacher. Seeing Napoleon as a demonic figure, the enemy of freedom, Schleiermacher channelled his energy into volcanic sermons of patriotic resistance. There is something fascinating about the way his red-blooded nationalism sits next to his self-consciously feminine sensitivity; but in any case it stirred all Prussia. In 1808 he was back in Berlin, and now the whole city throbbed with his emotive, charismatic preaching and optimistic vision of God on the side of Prussia (and his legacy would continue: he later prepared a young Otto von Bismarck for confirmation).

The real reason Schleiermacher returned to Berlin was to assume the eminent pastorate of Trinity Church, where for the rest of his life he would preach nearly every Sunday to a packed congregation. And dalliances with the ladies would not be a problem this time, for he came with only one in mind: Henriette von Willich, the widow of a friend and some twenty years his junior. Soon they were married and their house was as packed as the church (she brought two children from her first marriage and they had four more together).

There was one other major demand on his time in this, his mature and settled phase. It was the creation and establishment of the new University of Berlin, and Schleiermacher was one of its key architects. Once it had been formed, he served as dean for many years, rector for a while, and lectured each day during the week, teaching New Testament, doctrine, church history and almost every theological discipline except the Old Testament.

As the founder of the theological faculty, he got to write the syllabus and so outline his vision of theology. It was something he then mapped out in his highly illuminative *Brief Outline of the Study of Theology*. There Schleiermacher argues that theology should be divided into three basic disciplines. The first is philosophical theology, which, he argued, should basically define the essence of Christianity. The second is historical theology, which should describe how Christianity has been spoken of down through history. Perhaps most revealing of all, historical theology he believed should include exegesis, which is simply an examination of the very first expressions of Christian experience (in the New Testament) and doctrine, which is how Christian experience is expressed today. In other words, the New Testament and Christian doctrine are mere historical and cultural expressions of Christian experience. The third basic discipline he believed should be practical theology, which then applies what has been learnt in the other disciplines to the church today.

His health did decline during those productive years in Berlin, and he found himself seeking any number of alternative remedies, even consulting a spiritualist friend of his wife's who lodged with them. Still, though, the end came quickly when a severe case of pneumonia struck in February 1834. He called the household together to celebrate the Lord's Supper, and during that he died. It was a small family ceremony, but all Prussia was struck by the death of their national prophet, and tens of thousands would follow his casket through the streets of Berlin to the cemetery.

Schleiermacher's thought

Schleiermacher's interests were broad and extensive: he produced a definitive translation of Plato, preached innumerable sermons, wrote New Testament studies, manuals of hermeneutics, a systematic theology, a life of Jesus and a church history. But underneath all these lay one foundational concern. He wanted to restate the

Christian faith in such a way that traditional Christianity could be made both credible and relevant to the modern age. In other words, he was, before he was anything else, an apologist. Even the bedrock of his theology would be formed (as he put it) by 'propositions borrowed from apologetics'.

In practice this meant pulling Christianity back beyond the range of any rational attacks from the Enlightenment. Christianity would be about religious experience so exclusively that any Enlightenment scepticism over doctrinal or historical details would simply be rendered irrelevant. In this way, not only would Christianity become intellectually unassailable; it would become much more available to modern people who need no longer abandon any modern belief in becoming a Christian.

The Christian Faith

This, Schleiermacher's *chef d'oeuvre*, written at the height of his powers during his mature Berlin years, became the seminal state-ment of liberal Protestantism, and is commonly ranked alongside Calvin's *Institutes* as one of the most important works of Protestant theology. It is, without doubt, a true masterpiece, dazzling in its originality and quite beautifully composed. In complete contrast to those systematic theologies that lurch from disconnected doctrine to disconnected doctrine, *The Christian Faith* is a coherent and organic whole which clearly shows the interrelation of various doctrines. And just that changed how theology must be done: after Schleiermacher, systematic theologies that present doctrines in a disconnected way just seem clunky and naive.

The work opens with a vitally important introduction, which is essentially the recipe for all that follows. The ingredients are listed and the method to be pursued outlined. The First Part then explains what philosophical principles and general religious premises Christians must presuppose. The Second Part then builds more specifically Christian thought on the foundations shaped by those presuppositions.

Introduction

The root and origin of everything to follow is Schleiermacher's description of the essence of piety. It is, he said, 'the consciousness of being absolutely dependent'.[3] He then proceeds to describe the history of humanity as the history of the development of this consciousness. Initially, this feeling of dependence was expressed only crudely through primitive fetishism and polytheism. But as religion developed it became more and more monotheistic until the religious impulse reached its zenith in Christianity.[4] Christianity, for Schleiermacher, is the purest form of monotheism and therefore the very highest stage of religious evolution. Judaism and Islam are weak approximations to the clean monotheism of Christianity, but are in themselves too bound up with the physical to be considered strictly monotheist (this is clearly not an argument that many Jews or Muslims, looking at the Trinity, would find very convincing). Schleiermacher was thus keen to distance Christianity from Judaism and Old Testament faith, for while he recognized Christianity has historical connections to the Old Testament, he believed that that faith was of a more primitive sort, with as much to do with Christianity as the philosophies of Plato and Aristotle (or perhaps less in practice).

In this history of religion there is no sharp distinction between true worship and idolatry. Instead, the religious instinct is a universally good thing, and simply expressed in different ways: 'we must never deny the homogeneity of all these products of the human spirit, but must acknowledge the same root even for the lower powers'.[5] The overall picture, then, is of a smooth, evolutionary

---

3. *The Christian Faith* (2nd ed. of *Der Christliche Glaube* [Berlin: Reimer, 1830–31]), ed. H. R. Mackintosh and J. S. Stewart (Edinburgh: T. & T. Clark, 1999), §4.

4. Schleiermacher's Berlin colleague, G. W. F. Hegel, quipped that if true religion really is simply the feeling of dependence, then 'the dog is the best Christian, for it has this most strongly . . . The dog also has feelings of redemption when its hunger is appeased by a bone' (quoted in K. Barth, *The Theology of Schleiermacher* [Grand Rapids: Eerdmans, 1982], p. 186). The critique is unfair, for while the dog may have feelings of dependence, those feelings would have to be of a higher and more developed order to qualify as specifically Christian.

5. Schleiermacher, *Christian Faith*, §8, postscript 1.

development of religion up to Christianity. Christianity here is the apogee of human searching, the ultimate civilization and triumph of the human spirit over nature.

It might seem surprising that Schleiermacher should have had a model of evolution so close to the heart of his system when writing a generation before Charles Darwin. However, Darwin's model of biological evolution emerged within an already existing evolutionary understanding of reality. One of Schleiermacher's colleagues at the University of Berlin was G. W. F. Hegel, the Professor of Philosophy, and a decade before Schleiermacher started compiling *The Christian Faith*, Hegel had put forth a massive argument for the evolutionary movement of all history towards – well, himself and his society.[6] Schleiermacher's model of the happy upward progress of religion thus sat well with the times.

It also dispensed nicely with any need for the supernatural. Christianity here was no longer so much about God intervening in salvation; it was more the culmination of a process. In fact, even the coming of Christ (what makes Christianity Christian) was for Schleiermacher more like an evolutionary step than God acting supernaturally in the world: Christ's purpose was 'gradually to quicken the entire human race into higher life'.[7]

The evolution model also set aside the problematic existence of so many different religions. For Schleiermacher, no longer were the different religions vying with each other to describe ultimate reality; all were simply expressions of the universal religious impulse. And though Christianity could be seen as the highest stage of religious evolution so far, it was not as if Christ is the final end of all. Even Christ might be superseded.

All this could be said by a Christian theologian because 'Christian doctrines are accounts of the Christian religious

---

6. 'Hegel's only real fault', wrote Robert Jenson, 'was that he confused himself with the last judge; but that is quite a fault' (R. W. Jenson, *The Knowledge of Things Hoped for: The Sense of Theological Discourse* [Oxford: Oxford University Press, 1969], p. 233).

7. *Christian Faith*, §13.1.

affections set forth in speech.'[8] (Courage, dear reader!) With this
key affirmation we can see an intriguing similarity to Jonathan
Edwards: both were writing in the face of Enlightenment critiques
of Christianity, both rejected the idea that Christian belief could
be boiled down to mere assent to a list of doctrines, and both
emphasized the importance of experience and religious affections.
But here Schleiermacher turned Edwards's theological universe on
its head, for where Edwards believed that holy affections arise
from doctrine, Schleiermacher argued that doctrines are the
product of our religious affections. It was a true Copernican
revolution in theology: religious affections were here moved to the
central place previously occupied by divine revelation. They would
now be the source of our theological knowledge. (And it takes
hardly a moment's thought to see how completely Schleiermacher's
revolution has triumphed today.)

For Schleiermacher, then, doctrine was not truth about (or
from) God as such: God is in reality ineffable, and language about
him could only then be a lisping attempt to describe indescrib-
able reality. Instead, doctrine is a cultural expression of the
deeper reality of religious consciousness, a communal attempt to
communicate religious experience. But this was an entirely happy
realization for Schleiermacher: no longer need Christians be
divided by their doctrinal differences. They could be unreservedly
ecumenical. And Schleiermacher was: Trinity Church in Berlin
became a united Lutheran–Reformed congregation, and he
worked and preached passionately for peace and unity in the
Prussian church.

In all this, he was unswerving in his belief that he was upholding the Reformation in his day. His greatest Reformation hero
was, unsurprisingly, Erasmus, the champion of doctrine–light
unity. But he also spoke most highly of Calvin and his concern for
religious affections. The very title *The Christian Faith* he thought
of as an evangelical, Reformation statement, for he would be the
theologian of 'faith alone'; that is, faith free of hard doctrine. He
would focus on 'faith' as a thing in itself. Yet the result of this turn

---

8. Ibid. §15.

to examine 'faith' in itself was that, where the eye of the Reformers was outward to God's revelation of himself, Schleiermacher's faith was forced to be an essentially introspective thing.

First Part

Having established that course for his theology, Schleiermacher then sets out the more basic religious presuppositions that must underlie more specifically Christian experience.

He begins with creation. Or perhaps it would be more accurate to say he begins with the existence of the world, for 'we have no consciousness of a beginning of being'.[9] That is, while our 'feeling of absolute dependence' does speak of the world as having its origin in God, it is simply not able to go so far as to say whether or not the world had a beginning. Thus 'the controversy over the temporal or eternal creation of the world . . . has no bearing on the content of the feeling of absolute dependence, and it is therefore a matter of indifference how it is decided'.[10] And we need to have the same sort of agnosticism towards the existence of angels, who, he says, are not only irrelevant, but only seem to have made an appearance in the New Testament as a sort of hang-over from the more primitive religion of the Old Testament. As for the Devil, that idea 'is so unstable that we cannot expect anyone to be convinced of its truth'.[11]

On, then, to the preservation of creation. Schleiermacher believed that a single, divine, eternal decree underlay the whole of creation. And, God being perfect, this decree so perfectly established creation that it exists without any need to depend on God in any direct, moment-by-moment way. Creation can operate like clockwork 'by the system of Nature'.[12] Furthermore, God being good, he has created a good universe, and as such there is no need for him ever to step in and correct things. What he created was good (and clearly nothing since – like a historical Fall of man – has

---

9. Ibid. §39.
10. Ibid. §41.2.
11. Ibid. §44.
12. Ibid. §47.

upset that). God, then, relates to the whole, but has no need to engage specifically with any individuals or any one part of creation. In fact, if he were to intervene or have any direct dealings with any particular part of creation, it would be an admission that he had not, in fact, created a good universe in the first place. No miracles, then, and no personal relationships with this God. (Cue the eerie sound of Luther, Calvin, Owen and Edwards turning ever faster in their graves.)

What then, asks Schleiermacher, can we learn about God from all this? (Given that God is ineffable and that doctrine is the product of our religious affections, Schleiermacher is of course unable to discuss the doctrine of God by itself. Instead, he spreads his doctrine of God throughout *The Christian Faith*, seeing what can be said about God from what is more immediately apparent to our 'feelings of dependence'.) The first thing to be said is that, since we feel absolutely dependent, God must be the absolute cause. And God being the cause of time and temporal being, he must therefore be eternal and absolutely above all time. But not just time: God causes all space, and thus must be omnipresent. In fact, he causes all that is finite, and thus must be infinite and therefore omnipotent. And since he causes all, he must know all and therefore must be omniscient. (There are some other less significant divine attributes, he informs us, but for now they can only be inferred from those more immediately obvious ones.)

Second Part

The remainder of the work is shaped around the themes of sin and grace (the examination of grace being where the overall argument finally becomes most explicitly Christian).

Sin, first of all, is essentially God-forgetfulness. It is the failure to have that 'feeling of absolute dependence', and is therefore the attempt to feel independent. But as I feel independent, I am simply deluding myself, imagining that somehow I am truly the author of my own existence. Forgetting God, then, renders me ignorant of myself (the knowledge of God and self being intertwined: one can hear Calvin's influence coming through clearly). And it renders me not only ignorant: thinking I am independent makes me feel unsupported and vulnerable. Thus scared and isolated, I begin to see myself in competition with others. Fearful, deluded and selfish: this is the 'flesh'.

Schleiermacher chose to open his examination of sin by looking at sin in us today, and this for good reason, since he did not believe in a historical fall of Adam. That the smooth progress of history could have been interrupted by a cataclysmic event that altered the very nature of the physical world had to be pure fantasy. Yet Schleiermacher wanted to affirm his belief in some sort of idea of original sin. What it could not mean was that sin and guilt are somehow inherited or received from some external source. How, exactly, could God-forgetfulness be inherited? It had to be that, since we are nurtured in a God-forgetful society, so we become forgetful of God ourselves.

Jettisoning belief in a historical Fall turned out to be a more significant step than Schleiermacher had perhaps first realized, though, and he quickly found himself struggling to account for sin. He would say, for instance, 'We are conscious of sin as the power and work of a time when the disposition to God-consciousness had not yet actively emerged in us,' which fitted the evolutionary progression idea well, but did this mean that our natural, created state was sinful?[13] His answer could only be confusing: sin's 'existence does not invalidate the idea of the original perfection of man, still we are bound to regard it as a derangement of our nature'.[14]

Next Schleiermacher turns to evil, which is the result of and punishment for sin. Evil is all about that sinful loss of God-consciousness. Something is evil when God is forgotten. But as such, evil is something that is relative: my family could be killed in a car crash, but if that did not disturb my God-consciousness, it would not be an evil. Only if the accident caused me to forget God would it be an evil. That being the case, God can be described as the author of evil in just the same way as he is the author of good, since those things we perceive as evil are only evil for us because of our God-forgetfulness. (Perhaps unsurprisingly, Schleiermacher

13. Ibid. §67.
14. Ibid. §68.

never ventures to discuss moral evil.) Our duty, then, is not to seek an end to evil as such, but an end to our God-forgetfulness.

What then, asks Schleiermacher, can we learn about God from this? First, it is clear that we need redemption, and thus we can say that God is holy. And since he ordains that evil be the consequence for sin, he must be just. Is he merciful, though? Here Schleiermacher gets distinctly nervous, because mercy implies God having a personal feeling and response, and such, he says, would be unworthy of God.

He moves instead to talk of his second major theme: grace. Grace, he argues, comes to us in much the same way as sin comes to us. That is, just as we forget God as a result of being reared in a God-forgetful society, so we can be brought to fresh consciousness of God in a God-conscious society. In a community of God-consciousness (the church) we can be weaned from God-forgetfulness and a new principle of God-consciousness can be infused into us.

But where has this community of God-consciousness come from? Ultimately, from Christ, and Schleiermacher now turns to considering him. Christ, he sees, was a man with perfect God-consciousness. In fact, this is the sense in which we can say God was 'in him': 'The Redeemer, then, is like all men in virtue of the identity of human nature, but distinguished from them all by the constant potency of His God-consciousness, which was a veritable existence of God in Him.'[15] Christ, then, was not the pre-existent and eternal Son, but a perfectly pious man – in effect, he was the first Christian. Not God become man but man become godly. Schleiermacher was quite aware that his view would entail a complete re-evaluation of the church's traditional teaching on the person of Christ. But he was eager for that. It would mean that off-putting and irrelevant doctrines could be stripped away, doctrines such as the virgin birth for which his system could find 'virtually no trace of a dogmatic purpose'.[16] In fact, if Christ's mere consciousness of God could amount to the very existence

15. Ibid. §94; cf. §99, postscript.
16. Ibid. §97.2.

of God in him, then even the doctrine of a personal God would have to be reformed completely.

Reeling from all that, it is easy to miss what is perhaps the biggest shock here. In everything, Schleiermacher has deliberately pursued a theology that is the product of religious affections. But now, at the heart of it all and underlying the very possibility of our having the God-consciousness we should have is this historically objective person. So which is it to be? An external redemption accomplished in history, or internal affections? Either our religious affections really are the source of all our doctrine (in which case the historical appearance of Christ has no place here and has been smuggled in illegitimately) or there are such things as objective historical and therefore doctrinal facts.

But back to Christ's God-consciousness. It was for him, says Schleiermacher, a state of such 'unclouded blessedness' that he could experience no evil.[17] Pain and suffering did not trouble him, nor could anything weaken his God-consciousness. (Christ's agony in Gethsemane and his cry of dereliction on the cross were moments Schleiermacher preferred to soften, if soften is the word.) And Christ's work of redemption consisted precisely in the impartation of this God-consciousness to others. 'Indeed, Christ's highest achievement consists in this, that He so animates us that we ourselves are led to an ever more perfect fulfilment of the divine will.'[18]

Clearly redemption, for Schleiermacher, is much more about the God-consciousness of Christ during his life than it is about his death. The idea of Christ as a substitutionary sacrifice on the cross is entirely rejected. What, then, of the cross? It was the moment when Christ proved that, come what may, his God-consciousness would not falter. 'His blessedness emerged in its perfect fulness only in that it was not overcome even in the full tide of suffering.'[19] Thus when we see Christ on the cross we can only be impressed by his blessedness and so be drawn into it ourselves.

---

17. Ibid. §101.
18. Ibid. §104.3.
19. Ibid. §101.4.

Schleiermacher deliberately omitted the resurrection and ascension, arguing that they are not integral parts of the Christian faith. Though he does not say as much here, this was almost certainly connected to his doubts as to whether Jesus really died on the cross. Schleiermacher leaned towards the idea that Jesus only seemed dead, but was then taken down and revived.

One cannot really speak of God's mighty acts of salvation here, but once again this all fits Schleiermacher's story of the steady evolution of man. It is not even an evolutionary jump that Christ brings about, for his God-consciousness is really only a more potent version of something we all have. It is more that Christ is an enabler, pulling us up to a more perfect or complete stage in the history of humanity. Schleiermacher speaks of Christ as the redeemer, but since there is no Fall to be redeemed from, perhaps it would capture his thought more accurately to speak of Christ here as our perfecter.

Something else worth spotting about Christ's God-consciousness here is that it does not really amount to a personal relationship with God. That is not, after all, something Schleiermacher sees as being possible with God. The result is that Christ himself begins to look more like a principle than a person (perhaps we shouldn't be too surprised, given how awkward the presence of a historical person is in this system). Christ's kingly office, for example, is not portrayed as being anything to do with his personal rule; it 'consists in the fact that everything which the community of believers requires for its well-being continually proceeds from Him'.[20] It is as if Christ could be a pleasant smell, imparting to us, not a relationship, but the universal presence of the Infinite.

Next Schleiermacher turns to look at the effects the grace of Christ has on believers. Above and beyond anything else, of course, redemption for the individual will mean being brought to share in Christ's God-consciousness and blessedness. Regeneration is finding our God-consciousness awoken; sanctification is the deepening of that God-consciousness. But Schleiermacher also talks

---

20. Ibid. §105.

about our justification. Justification, for Schleiermacher, clearly cannot mean anything like a divine declaration that I, personally, am now righteous before God. God does not deal with individuals like that. No, God has 'only one eternal and universal decree justifying men for Christ's sake'.[21] Justification is an eternal decree for humanity as a whole. So my own justification must be about my appropriation of that decree to myself.

But what could that mean? With complete consistency, Schleiermacher has asserted that there is no such thing as divine wrath: such a primitive idea suggests an irritable (personal) God. In fact, there does not seem to be such a thing as actual sin and actual guilt; it is simply that we sense these things. We have been created good, after all, and merely perceive guilt in order that we might be spurred on to do better. Forgiveness of sins, then, cannot be about God forgiving me, but about my conscience being cleansed from guilt (though it is hard to see quite how this could work and what pastoral comfort it could give when guilt is not real and there is no actual divine pardon to be had).

His readers' nerves notwithstanding, on moves Schleiermacher then to reconceive the church. The church, he feels, began when Christ influenced his disciples with his blessedness and so established a community of God-consciousness. The disciples then influenced others, so becoming the foundations of a new community where, instead of sharing our God-forgetfulness, as happens elsewhere, we share our God-consciousness. This community, being about the perfection of human God-consciousness, is the future of humanity, and as such must be an ever-expanding community that will one day include all, even if only after death: 'everyone still outside this fellowship will some time or another be laid hold of by the divine operations of grace and brought within it'.[22]

Importantly, Schleiermacher now introduces us to the Spirit – the Spirit which once so filled the man Jesus of Nazareth, and which is now the common spirit of this new community. This Spirit is not a person or even a supernatural force; indeed, this Spirit is now

---

21. Ibid. §109.3.
22. Ibid. §118.1.

'no longer personally operative in any individual, but henceforth manifests itself actively in the fellowship of believers as their common spirit'.[23] In other words, the Spirit is the common disposition to God-consciousness that the community of the church shares. This Spirit is what binds the community together, undoing the isolation of sin and so making us more perfectly human, as we were created to be.

In this new community we foster each other's God-consciousness particularly through the witness of the New Testament and preaching Christ. 'Faith comes from preaching' he says with all the resolve of a traditional evangelical.[24] For it is when we remember Christ's blessedness that we desire to be rid of our God-forgetfulness. But why open the New Testament rather than simply share our religious affections? It was not that the New Testament needed to be reliable or authoritative; it was that it records the experience of the earliest Christians, and thus influences and inspires us. The New Testament does these things, but of course the Old Testament, as the expression of a legalistic, pre-Christian faith, could not. 'Even the noblest Psalms always contain something which Christian piety is unable to appropriate as a perfectly pure expression of itself.'[25] Thus Schleiermacher considered the Old Testament 'a superfluous authority'.[26]

After then explaining how we are received into the church through baptism and regularly strengthened by remembering Christ in the Lord's Supper, he comes to a revealing analysis of prayer. Given all that he has said about how God does not interact with or deal with individuals, we should not be surprised to read his warning against petitionary prayer. Praise is appropriate, but we cannot think that we can affect or interact with God. Petition should be reserved for our fellow men, particularly fellow believers, that they might be united, and Schleiermacher ends with a passionate appeal for church unity.

---

23. Ibid. §124.2.
24. Ibid. §121.2.
25. Ibid. §132.2.
26. Ibid. §27.3; cf. §12.

Before moving on, though, Schleiermacher inserted an import-ant appendix to this section on the church. In it he argues that, while there have been people who have shared their God-consciousness with each other ever since the beginning of the human race, the church began with the man Jesus of Nazareth. 'Christ could not have exerted any redeeming influence' on any who lived before him – in fact, he could not have exerted it on those, such as Simeon, who knew him only as a child.[27] Schleiermacher realized that he was stepping out on a limb here:

> The Confessions [the creeds and confessions of orthodox faith] . . .
> assume that faith in Christ existed before His personal action [the
> incarnation], but we make such faith conditional on, and derive it from,
> His personal action.[28]

His suggestion was that before the incarnation, instead of trusting Christ, people trusted in promises. And those promises were neces-sarily vague. Indeed, had they been specific, Christ need not have come; all he brought through the incarnation would already have been made clear through the promises.

Schleiermacher's last main subject for discussion is what he calls 'the consummation of the church'. He chose his words carefully, for he would now take language usually understood as referring to future events and explain how really they are 'a pattern to which we have to approximate'.[29] The fact is, if doctrine is an expression of our own experience, then we cannot speak of the future, since we have no experience of it. Schleiermacher maintained that we can make only logical inferences about the future. For example, we can deduce that the notion of eternal damnation is a false one, since it is incompatible with the eternal blessedness that Christ is disseminating throughout humanity.

How, then, should we understand such New Testament ideas as the return of Christ? Not literally. Rather, it is essentially about

---

27. Ibid. §156.1.
28. Ibid.
29. Ibid. §157.

'the reunion of believers with Christ'.[30] And that is both a present and a future experience. The last judgment, similarly, is about the separation of the church from the world. What we can vaguely sense, though, is that, since the infinite and immortal divine unites with the human in Christ, there must be some sort of continuation for us beyond death, even an 'organic life which has links of attachment to our present state'.[31] Then we will share Christ's 'unclouded blessedness' (though, given that Christ's 'unclouded blessedness' included having nowhere to lay his head, thirst, tiredness and the cross, this is probably not a fate that will excite every Christian).

Finally, asks Schleiermacher, what can we learn about God from this whole understanding of the theme of grace? Essentially, what we have seen is that 'the Supreme Being imparts Himself', and thus we can conclude that he is wise (so arranging things that he can impart himself) and loving.[32] It seems rather ambitious to equate something imparting itself with love (after all, the smell of sewage can impart itself), but then this is the tightrope Schleiermacher tries to walk: he wants to speak of God as loving, but not as personal.

Talk of God's love brings us at the very last to the Trinity, 'the coping-stone of Christian doctrine'.[33] Having seen 'the union of the Divine Essence with human nature, both in the personality of Christ and in the common Spirit of the Church', we can conclude that we experience God as a Trinity.[34] That is not to say that Schleiermacher thought of Father, Son and Spirit as three divine persons: the Spirit, certainly, is not a person, and the idea of personhood generally, he felt, impugned God's infinity.

The result is a discussion of the Trinity that looks like a rather incongruous and useless third nipple on the torso of his overall system and understanding of God. And it is so because Schleiermacher's God is fundamentally impersonal and

---

30. Ibid. §160.2.
31. Ibid. §161.3.
32. Ibid. §166.1.
33. Ibid. §170.1.
34. Ibid.

non-relational. He does not interact with us, and we cannot interact with him. Schleiermacher asserts that 'the consciousness of
being absolutely dependent' is the same thing as being in relation
with God.[35] But is it? I am dependent on air, but I don't have a
relationship with air in the same way I have a relationship with my
wife, or even my dog (on whom I do not depend). Talk of the
love of the Father for the Son, the love of God for the world or
our love for God simply cannot arise from the system of *The
Christian Faith*.

But once again, Schleiermacher knew he was reinventing traditional Christianity for his time. He was quite prepared to admit
that the Trinity was something of an appendix for him. He was
eager to question conventional ideas, such as

> that both the Second and the Third Person in the Trinity were implicated
> even in the creation of the world, while the Second Person was also the
> subject thereafter of all the Old Testament theophanies, and it was from
> the Third Person that the whole prophetic movement of the Old
> Testament received its impulse.[36]

For, while he felt he must speak of the Trinity at the end of *The
Christian Faith*, he was quite consciously striving for 'a thoroughgoing
criticism of the doctrine in its older form'.[37] In fact, the 'position
assigned to the doctrine of the Trinity in the present work is perhaps
at all events a preliminary step towards this goal'.[38]

Going on with Schleiermacher

Schleiermacher is not an easy (or, ironically, heart-warming) read.
But still he is usually less painful to approach than the bulk of the
secondary literature on him, which tends to be extraordinarily

---

35. Ibid. §4.
36. Ibid. §170.3.
37. Ibid. §172.2.
38. Ibid. §172.3.

dusty and confusing. *The Christian Faith* (ed. H. R. Mackintosh and J. S. Stewart) is still in print (2nd ed. of *Der Christliche Glaube* [Berlin: Reimer, 1830–31]; Edinburgh: T. & T. Clark, 1999); and Keith Clements's *Friedrich Schleiermacher: Pioneer of Modern Theology* (London: Collins, 1987) provides a useful selection of some other key texts, along with a good introduction and notes.

Two other books worth pursuing are J. Gresham Machen's *Christianity and Liberalism* (New York: Macmillan, 1923), an almost painfully penetrating critique of Schleiermacher's liberal heritage; and from the opposite point of view, James Barr's *Fundamentalism* (London: SCM, 1977) is an equally thought-provoking condemnation of conservative theology for, among other things, what Barr sees as an almost universal capitulation to Schleiermacher's legacy.

Friedrich Schleiermacher timeline

1760	Count Niklaus von Zinzendorf dies
1768	Schleiermacher born in Breslau (modern Wroclaw, Poland)
1770	G. W. F. Hegel born
1776	American Revolution
1783–7	Attends Herrnhuter schools at Niesky and Barby
1787–9	University at Halle
1789	French Revolution
1790–93	Tutor to von Dohna family in Schlobitten
1794–6	Assistant pastor in Landsberg
1796–1801	Chaplain, Charity Hospital, Berlin
1799	*On Religion: Speeches to Its Cultured Despisers*
1802–4	Pastor in Stolpe
1804–6	Professor of Theology, University of Halle
1806	Napoleon Bonaparte invades Prussia
1808	Pastor of Trinity Church, Berlin
1809	Marries Henriette von Willich; Professor of Theology, University of Berlin
1811	*Brief Outline of the Study of Theology*
1821–2	*The Christian Faith*
1834	Schleiermacher dies

12. THE BOMBSHELL IN THE PLAYGROUND OF THE THEOLOGIANS

Karl Barth

Karl Barth towers above the theological landscape of today. Is it just because he is so close to us in time that he seems so titanic? Certainly, it is harder to be objective about a giant close-up, but either way he was a giant, dominating the theology of the last century. And, like all giants, Barth scares people: the thirteen hefty volumes that make up his colossal (but unfinished!) main work, the *Church Dogmatics*, are enough to send most people scurrying for the secondary literature or some sound bite by which to understand him. Thus you hear Barth described as 'neo-orthodox', or some such tag. The tags are usually neither accurate nor helpful. And yet, scared of approaching Barth himself, slogans are often all that students are left with. In fact, it is not just the students: even the most respected theologians have been known to have created Barths of their own imagining. This was something that clearly frustrated the man himself:

> Am I deceived when I have the impression that I exist in the phantasy of far too many . . . mainly, only in the form of certain, for the most part hoary, summations of certain pictures hastily dashed off by some

person at some time, and for the sake of convenience, just as hastily
accepted, and then copied endlessly, and which, of course, can easily be
dismissed?[1]

He had good reason to feel unjustly dealt with, for he himself was
capable of highly respectful and intricate readings of those with
whom he disagreed (such as Friedrich Schleiermacher).

Who, then, was this colossus?

Barth's life

In 1886 Karl Barth was born in Basel, Switzerland, to a family of
pastors who, unusually for the times, were by and large theologically conservative. Tensions quickly developed then, when, aged
eighteen, he set off to Germany to study under the greatest liberal
theologians of the day: Adolf von Harnack in Berlin and Wilhelm
Herrmann in Marburg. Before long he was known as a rising star
of liberalism, and though he would soon utterly renounce that
theology, those years were influential. Herrmann especially, who
was very much a disciple of Schleiermacher, profoundly affected
Barth with his transparently genuine and profound love for Jesus.

His studies completed, he moved to become an assistant pastor
in Geneva, and there plunged into Calvin's *Institutes* for the first
time. He even found himself preaching from Calvin's old pulpit,
though later he would write, 'I'm afraid Calvin would hardly have
been very pleased at the sermons which I preached in his pulpit
then'.[2] But it was only a few years later, after he had become the
pastor of the little village of Safenwil, between Zurich and Bern,
that the wheels really began to come off his liberalism. Telling
people to be religious, it was becoming clear, was not helping them.

---

1. Karl Barth, 'Foreword to the English Translation', in Otto Weber, *Karl
   Barth's Church Dogmatics* (London: Lutterworth, 1953), p. 7.
2. Letter to F. J. Leenhardt, 14 February 1959, cited in E. Busch, *Karl Barth:
   His Life from Letters and Autobiographical Texts* (Philadelphia: Fortress;
   SCM: London, 1976), pp. 53–54.

Then, in 1914, war broke out, and Barth was shocked to find his liberal teachers supporting it. All his confidence in them and their theology was rocked as he saw their total accommodation of the gospel to the culture. And so 'I gradually turned back to the Bible', and found a 'strange new world' there. As with Luther, it began with Romans: in the summer of 1916, 'I sat under an apple tree and began to apply myself to Romans with all the resources that were available to me at the time . . . I began to read it as though I had never read it before.'[3] It forced him to repudiate all his old theological inheritance and reach out for a new way of thinking.

The notes he made on Romans were published early in 1919, and immediately caused outrage. And no wonder: instead of the old liberal, critical method of filtering the text through the dust of a historically reconstructed context, Barth wanted to use 'the old doctrine of Verbal Inspiration' and let the text speak directly.[4] It was with this cheek that he began:

> Paul, as a child of his age, addressed his contemporaries. It is, however, far more important that, as Prophet and Apostle of the Kingdom of God, he veritably speaks to all men of every age. The differences between then and now, there and here, no doubt require careful investigation and consideration. But the purpose of such investigation can only be to demonstrate that these differences are, in fact, purely trivial.[5]

So what Paul said about Jewish attitudes to the law, for example, applied to the liberal view of religiosity. That is, liberalism treated religiosity as a ladder to God. Without any help from God, liberalism believed, we can speak of and know him.

In place of all that, Barth increasingly wanted to argue that there is in reality a 'dialectical' relationship between God and humanity.

---

3. K. Barth, *The Theology of Schleiermacher* (Grand Rapids: Eerdmans, 1982), p. 264.

4. K. Barth, *The Epistle to the Romans* (London: Oxford University Press, 1933), p. 18.

5. Ibid. p. 1.

In other words, God is absolutely other. Man and God, time and eternity, are so qualitatively different that we are simply unable to speak of God. If we try, we find only ourselves speaking about ourselves (in a loud voice, as it were). This great gulf between God and us can be crossed only by God himself, and this he does in his word. Thus only in his revelation of himself can we know God.

In 1921 Barth was appointed to the chair of Reformed Theology at Göttingen, where his teaching duties forced him to do his own crash course in Reformed theology and history. And with this newfound knowledge of Calvin, Zwingli, the Reformed confessions and Schleiermacher he was beginning to amass a truly awesome theological arsenal with which he could wage war on liberalism.

Four years later he moved to teach at Münster, and in 1930 moved again: to Bonn. It was around that time that he was reading Anselm, and Anselm seemed to clarify things for him. From Anselm's maxim 'faith seeking understanding' he saw that theology must consist not of working things out by our own independent logic, but of thinking and understanding by faith, in the light of what God has said.[6]

In the 1950s the Swiss Roman Catholic theologian Hans Urs von Balthasar argued that around 1930 Barth's theology underwent an important change of direction: where previously Barth had argued for that dialectical relationship between God and man, from then he began to see that relationship as analogical (that there is in fact a correspondence ordained by God between God and humanity).[7] Barth himself (though aware of it) never disagreed with von Balthasar's theory, and thus the argument held sway for the decades to come. However, partly because of a major re-examination of that early stage of Barth's thinking by Bruce

---

6. Those who have read my introduction to Anselm in *The Breeze of the Centuries* (Nottingham: IVP, 2010) may notice that I have understood Anselm rather differently from the way Barth did.

7. H. U. von Balthasar, *The Theology of Karl Barth: Exposition and Interpretation* (San Fransisco: Ignatius, 1992).

McCormack,[8] and partly because of the recent publication of much previously unpublished material by Barth from the 1920s, that theory of a real change of direction now looks too crude. His 'dialectical' theology was not just a passing, immature phase. What happened around 1930 was a clarification: what Barth had more abstractly called 'the Word' was from then on quite clearly the specific person of Jesus Christ – who is the only way we can know God.

By the early 1930s, Barth had become Europe's leading Protestant thinker, and was ready to begin the project that would fill almost all of his remaining life: the writing of the *Church Dogmatics*. Yet no sooner had he started than Hitler came to power in Germany, changing everything. Much of German Protestantism swiftly bowed the knee; Barth, however, did not, seeing that capitulation as just the latest political expression of a theology derived from outside God's Word. For this he would soon lose his job. But it is what he did in the meantime that is most telling: quite apart from spearheading the creation of a confessing church that would resist accepting Nazi theology, Barth got down to the task of theology with even greater fervour. What Barth saw was that, instead of its being a time to abandon deep theology for quick response, now was the time to do theology all the more intensely in order to recover and safeguard the gospel.

As soon as he was dismissed from his teaching post in 1935, he was snapped up by Basel, and so found himself back in his native Switzerland. He did what he could to keep up pressure on the Nazis, but his time now was focused on the production of the *Church Dogmatics*.

The tough times, hard work and monumental reputation could easily lead one to miss something vital in Barth, and that is his Alp-climbing, pipe-loving sheer humanity. Endlessly curious and interested, he had a near mania for Mozart that was very revealing of him – Mozart surely appealed for how he shared Barth's own characteristic, twinkling, often impish, playfulness. And that,

---

8. B. McCormack, *Karl Barth's Critically Realistic Dialectical Theology: Its Genesis and Development, 1909–36* (Oxford: Oxford University Press, 1995).

Barth thought, was just how a theologian should be: 'The theologian who has no joy in his work is not a theologian at all.
Sulky faces, morose thoughts and boring ways of speaking are
intolerable.'[9]

In 1964 his health declined sharply, leaving him unable to work
with anything like the ability he had had before. The end came in
December 1968. He penned the words 'God is not a God of the
dead but of the living' for a lecture he was due to give the next day,
then folded his hands to pray. And that was how his wife, Nelly,
found him – with, of course, Mozart playing in the background.

Church Dogmatics

The very title of Barth's magnum opus still shocks today. In direct
and deliberate contrast to his nemesis, Schleiermacher, who wrote
of the Christian's *faith* and experience, Barth wanted to write about
absolute God-given truth – dogma.

After that, it is the gargantuan bulk and unfamiliar style that
terrifies. Much of that fear can be quickly dispelled by coming to
understand Barth's manner of writing (for the length of the work
is really just a consequence of that manner). Barth believed that
the task of theology is the same as the task of preaching, and thus
preaching is just what he does in the *Church Dogmatics*. But preaching is not about merely conferring information: it is about winning
hearts, and thus involves the sorts of persuasion and repetition
that take time. Points must be reinforced, the readers won. The
result is that Barth can be deeply moving to read. It also means he
is peculiarly resistant to being quoted. Context is needed, and this
is why, when he is quoted, he usually sounds impossibly complicated and so off-putting. Perhaps most important of all, though,
the fact that Barth writes in such a sermonic, almost story-telling
style actually means the reader can relax. Failing fully to grasp a
few pages really will not matter, for the sweep of the argument is
larger than that. Looking for the bigger picture is the main thing.
Colin Gunton put it like this:

---

9. *Church Dogmatics* (Edinburgh: T. &. T Clark, 1956–75; hereafter *CD*) II/1,
   p. 656.

> Barth is an aesthetic theologian. Barth worshipped before he
> theologized. His love for Mozart is to be noted here. The structure of
> Barth's theology is assertive, it is not argumentative; it can be considered
> as a sort of music. In the sense that Barth is not concerned to argue any
> more than Mozart is concerned to argue, Mozart just plays. I think that
> is Barth's aim: to play on the revelation of God so that its truth and
> beauty will shine.[10]

Of course, that does all mean that Barth demands you give him time. He will not dish out theological fast food. But giving him time does make one a more thoughtful theologian. Even in this little introduction, I hope, Barth should get you thinking and wondering, for agree or disagree with him (and you will almost certainly do both at different points), he is both stretching and stimulating. And as much as anything, that is probably because of another of his stylistic traits: he is deliberately (often infuriatingly) provocative.

Unfortunately, the mountainous proportions of the *Church Dogmatics* mean that this short sketch of them is going to have to be the most cartoon-like of all. Time dictates that we must fly past the intricacies of his argument and all those intriguing small print detours on everything from laughter to Leibniz. We must content ourselves with a bird's eye – no, satellite's eye – view.

There are four 'volumes' or main sections in the *Church Dogmatics*: *The Doctrine of the Word of God*, *The Doctrine of God*, *The Doctrine of Creation* and *The Doctrine of Reconciliation*. A fifth volume, *The Doctrine of Redemption* (on the Spirit and eschatology), was planned but never written (and Barth left no indication of what it would have looked like). In fact, even the fourth volume was cut short by Barth's death. Each 'volume' is divided up into part-volumes (each one an entire book), so that you have Volume I, part 1 (I/1), Volume III, part 2 (III/2) and so on.

Volume I: The Doctrine of the Word of God
I/1 In Barth's day, two practices had become conventional in writing complete works of theology like the *Dogmatics*. The first

---

10. C. E. Gunton, *The Barth Lectures* (London: T. &. T Clark, 2007), p. 63.

was to begin by asking if it is possible for God to be known. Straightaway Barth disobeyed that rule, beginning his work by arguing that the very question had things the wrong way round. Why ask about some abstract possibility when God has actually made himself known? The question, he believed, dangerously overlooked what God has in fact done.

The second convention was to do with the Trinity. Since Schleiermacher had shunted the Trinity into an appendix at the end of his *The Christian Faith*, it had become the most dust-covered of all theological subjects. Again Barth rebelled and instead put the Trinity at the very beginning of his theology, making it (and not some general principle or view of God) the foundational presupposition, the grammar for everything to follow.

What was even more revolutionary, though, was that Barth combined the two subjects of revelation and Trinity. And thus his theology begins with the God who makes himself known – that is, the self-revealing Trinity. Because God is triune, he reveals himself in a threefold word. First, there is Christ, the revealed word of God; secondly, that revelation is attested to in the written word of God, the Scriptures; and thirdly, those Scriptures are preached or proclaimed, and so the world hears the one word of God. However, it is not as if revelation is the mere giving of information; it is God himself coming to us, making himself known. God the Father is the revealer; God the Son is the revelation; God the Spirit is the 'revealedness', the one who enables us to perceive the revelation.

Barth was seeking to apply the old Reformation banner of 'grace alone' to the doctrine of revelation. He wanted to reject all Pelagianism in our knowledge of God (i.e. actually contributing to it ourselves) to show that our knowledge of God is a divine gift, unsupported by any presuppositions we may bring to it. Thus we cannot decide in advance what God is like and then let his revelation simply add another storey to the structure we have made. We cannot even know what 'God' truly means without revelation. Thus Barth rejected all 'natural theology'.

He is commonly misunderstood here. He was not rejecting a theology of creation, as we will go on to see; nor was he denying that God speaks to us through creation: 'God may speak to us through Russian Communism, a flute concerto, a blossoming shrub, or a dead dog.'[11] The point was that we can come to know God only in his Word; and once we have done that, we can appreciate the true meaning of his revelation of himself elsewhere. Natural theology proceeds in the opposite direction by first constructing its own theory of the possibility of knowing God, and then using that as a yardstick by which to measure what may or may not be true. In effect, it places the knowledge of God, and so our faith, on a foundation other than God's revelation.

From revelation, Barth then goes on to focus on the triune nature of this God. As Father, God reveals himself as the *creator*; as Son he reveals himself as the *reconciler*; as Spirit he reveals himself as the *redeemer*. Thus Barth shows his intent to have the very structure of the *Dogmatics* shaped by the triune being of this God: after looking at the doctrine of the word of God (vol. I) and the doctrine of God as a whole (vol. II), his aim was to examine creation (vol. III, appropriated to the Father), reconciliation (vol. IV, appropriated to the Son) and redemption (vol. V, appropriated to the Spirit).

There was just one area of traditional trinitarian thought that, he believed, needed to be re-expressed. The language of the three 'persons' of God he felt was misleading. God, he argued, is one divine person or subject, not three; and, rather than speaking of the three 'persons' of God, it would be more accurate to speak of God existing in three 'ways of being'. This was not the old heresy of modalism, he averred, and yet many today feel that he had at least slipped in that direction.

I/2   The second part-volume on the word of God really serves to flesh out that main theme of the triune God and his revelation of himself. He begins with Jesus the revealed word of God, and here we probably come closest to Barth's theological heartbeat. 'A church dogmatics', he wrote, 'must, of course, be christologically determined as a whole and in all its parts.'[12] Christ is the revelation of God, and thus the Bible and all good theology must be about

---

11. *CD* I/1, p. 55.

12. *CD* I/2, p. 123.

pointing to and looking to him. Barth's favourite image (and one he had hung above his desk) was Grünewald's Isenheim altarpiece, where the prodigious pointing finger of John the Baptist directs viewers so clearly to the crucified Christ. For Barth, that summed up the task of the church and all its dogmatics.

From there he goes on to describe the Spirit as the one who enables us to receive the revelation of God. Under the heading of the Spirit, he then deals with Scripture, which, like the pointing finger, exists to bear witness to Christ, the revealed word of God. Barth never meant by this that Scripture is not itself the word of God. He scrupulously affirmed that.[13] His point was that the Bible is not an alternative way of knowing God next to Christ; it proclaims him.

Barth was so sensitive to the danger of studying the Scriptures without looking to Christ that he hit out hard against any tendency to raise the Bible to the place where Christ alone belongs. He would speak, for instance, of Scripture 'becoming', not 'being' the word of God to us. Fearful of the idea that we might view Scripture as a deposit of information that we now have at our disposal as the means by which we can work out our own know-ledge of God, he preferred to speak of Scripture only becoming the word of God to us by God's grace through the Spirit. In other words, we never have the word of God at our disposal; we always depend on him in his grace to encounter us.

Even more strongly, for some of the same reasons he argued that, in the same way that Jesus, being human, had the potential within him for sin, so too the Scriptures, having human authors (as well as a divine author), have the potential to contain error. Those who hold to the infallibility of Scripture are surely right to be nervous about such statements, and our nerves are hardly helped by Barth's rhetoric here, when, for example, he speaks of Scripture's 'capacity for error'.[14] Yet while evangelicals have cause to be uncomfortable with some of Barth's formulations of biblical inspiration, it would be decidedly foolish simply to stop our ears

13. Ibid. 'Scripture as the Word of God', pp. 473–537.
14. Ibid. p. 509.

against him. The irony would be that we would leave ourselves deaf to one of Barth's most emphatic messages: that we submit all our thinking to Scripture as our absolute authority, as he himself always sought to do. Perhaps the way to get the most rounded understanding of Barth's view of Scripture is to see, not just what he says about it, but how he actually treats it in one of the many small-print exegetical sections of the *Dogmatics*. Of course one cannot expect to agree with his every point, but there one sees a theologian entirely shaped by the desire to hear and yield to Scripture.

From the word of God written he then moves to the word of God proclaimed. The church is to listen to the word of God and speak it. And this is where the practice of theology comes in: dogmatics summons the church to listen to the word of God afresh and so proclaim it faithfully.

Volume II: The Doctrine of God

II/1   By now readers need hardly be told that Barth will truck no belief in any 'God in general' unshaped by Jesus. Thus here now we will 'have to learn to say "God" in the correct sense'.[15] How? Not by asking 'What might or must God be like?' but by asking 'What has God actually shown himself to be like?' Everything to be said about knowledge of God really stems, for Barth, from the central fact that 'God is known only by God.'[16] That is, God knows himself in Christ, meaning that the sending of Christ was God's sharing of his own self-knowledge. But more: 'God is known *only* by God' and thus we can know God *only* in Christ.

What, then, do we learn about God from his revelation? Clearly, in Christ we see a God who seeks to create fellowship with us. Thus he is a God who loves. But God's revelation is truly revealing of who he is, and so it is not simply that God happens to love us, as if love could be some random blip in God. God has revealed himself to *be* a loving God. As Father, Son and Spirit, God is eternally loving without needing anything else to love. Furthermore,

---

15. *CD* II/1, p. 3.
16. Ibid. p. 179.

we do not see in Christ a God who needs to be in fellowship with us: we see in Christ a God who has life in himself, but who comes to share that life with us out of pure love. Thus we see a God who 'loves in freedom'. Unconstrained by anything, this God can be who he is: a freely loving God.

With that foundation in place Barth can examine what are traditionally called the divine attributes (though Barth prefers to call them divine 'perfections', 'attributes' suggesting that somehow we might have attributed these characteristics to God, instead of simply recognizing them in how he has revealed himself to be). Essentially, they are an unpacking of what it means for God to be 'the one who loves in freedom', and the result is a strikingly coherent picture. Instead of just giving a list of disconnected divine characteristics, Barth shows the interrelationship between God's perfections.

First, the perfections of God's love: we see God is gracious and holy, gracious in establishing fellowship with us, and holy in refusing to allow evil to remain as he seeks that fellowship. Similarly, he is merciful and righteous; he is also patient and wise, patient in even allowing his creatures to exist, and wise in so arranging things that they can.

Secondly, the perfections of God's freedom: God is one and omnipresent, constant and omnipotent, eternal and glorious. At first glance, this could look like a standard description of some 'God in general', but the actual content is quite specific. For example, instead of the traditional idea of God's immutability, which Barth feared could mean impersonal, abstract changelessness, he preferred to speak of God's constancy. And what, say, might omnipotence mean for this God?

> Jesus Christ the Crucified . . . is Himself the power of God. This is true in just the same sense as that the power of God is the power of His wisdom. It is in Him as the Crucified that all this is revealed and can be learned. The first lesson this teaches us is that we must really keep before our eyes God's reconciliation along with His revelation, that we must really understand His reconciliation itself as His revelation.[17]

---

17. Ibid. p. 607.

II/2   Next in the doctrine of God comes election. It comes here because Barth saw that election is essentially about God electing himself. He wanted to rid the doctrine of what he saw as the baleful influence of Augustine, who had taught a doctrine of election that seemed to have little to do with Christ.[18] Of course, the idea that what really underpins our salvation is some unknown divine decision and not Christ himself was intolerable for Barth. It not only pushed Christ aside; it suggested that God has not revealed his very self in Christ.

Instead, for Barth, there is no depth of God or salvation behind Christ; there is no decision in eternity other than him. Jesus Christ, then, is the one elected by God. And with Jesus' election, humanity in him is elected. Thus it is in Christ that God is gracious to humanity. In fact, not only is Christ the chosen one; on the cross he became the rejected one, taking on himself God's rejection of sinful humanity. Thus the only ones who remain rejected now are those who – perversely and against the truth – refuse the fact that God is for them.

Election for us, then, is being caught up into God's choice of Jesus Christ. But what should that relationship to which we have been called look like? It is to that question that Barth now turns. In choosing us, he says, God has freed us to choose him. God has been gracious and loving to us, freeing us to be gracious and loving. In other words, we have been freed by God to be Godlike. As God loves in freedom so we are freed to love (love of Christ being the only freedom).

Significantly, Barth strews all his ethics through the *Dogmatics* like this because he did not believe that ethics is a discipline that can be practised separately. Ethics can flow only directly from doctrine. Just as he shunned any doctrine that was abstracted from Christ, so he shunned any abstract ethics. So, for example, he would argue that the goodness of any action is determined by how Godlike (how gladly gracious) it is.

---

18. Barth preferred Athanasius here (and, in fact, more generally). Largely because he saw how profoundly shaped by Neoplatonism Augustine's theology was, he called it *süsses Gift* – 'sweet poison'!

Volume III: The Doctrine of Creation

III/1   There was much to recover in the doctrine of creation, Barth felt. Theologians had weakly allowed themselves to be pushed out of any serious study of creation by the natural scientists, meaning that the doctrine of creation had become a mere study of origins, losing what is specifically Christian about creation.

And creation is a specifically Christian doctrine, Barth held. It is an article of faith. God is a personal being, not merely an abstract principle that caused the world to be that any philosophy might be able to imagine. In fact, the creator is God the Father, and so the creator cannot be known other than through the Son. And it is not just the creator; the very creation itself can be understood only in the light of God's purposes revealed in Jesus Christ. That is because creation is all about the covenant relationship between God and humanity. Creation exists for the sake of that relationship. And that relationship is not therefore just a response to the Fall; it is the reason God created in the first place. Creation, therefore, simply cannot be understood without Christ, the one who brings about that relationship.

The act of creation happened when the internal goodness of God was turned outwards. The result is a creation that is itself good; not that that is self-evident, however (one could hardly conclude that by merely looking around us), but through revelation we learn the truth about creation: that it is good, and that light is stronger than darkness. And since creation is good, it can have a very real existence.

Note Barth's characteristically counter-intuitive logic in all this: we do not believe in a creator because we know about creation; rather, it is only because we know that God really exists that we can believe that creation really exists. Commenting on this, Colin Gunton observed that it is only under the influence of Christianity 'that the world has been affirmed in its full reality. In Platonism it isn't; in Hinduism it isn't – only where the Christian gospel has run have people believed that the world concretely exists.'[19]

III/2   Having argued that the relationship between God and

---

19. *Barth Lectures*, p. 252.

humanity is the reason for creation, Barth's next step is to look
at humanity itself. Here we get to see how far Barth would carry
his rejection of natural theology. Having argued that we are unable
to know God without revelation, Barth now maintains that we are
unable even to know what it is to be human without God revealing
it to us! Only when we look at Jesus Christ can we know God's
purposes for us, and so know who we are. 'Who and what man is,
is no less specifically and emphatically declared by the Word of
God than who and what God is.'[20]

In fact, Christ reveals to us what it is to be human because in a
sense he is the first human. How? Because Christ shows that, in
essence, 'to be a man is to be with God', and he is pre-eminently
the one with God and the only one through whom any other can
be with God.[21] It is not, though, that Christ is simply modelling to
us what it is to be human; in Christ, man is with God and God
with man. Thus sin, which is an attempt to be godless, is an
attempt at the impossible – it is an 'impossible possibility'.[22]

Barth is strong in his use of such language, so strong that many
have wondered if he is as a result promoting universalism, the idea
that everyone will be saved. Barth repeatedly denied this, and yet
even if the man himself did not want to go to that conclusion, the
weight of a good deal of his theology certainly does seem to tip
towards at least an extremely optimistic hope for all humanity.

III/3   Tying together the themes of the previous two part-
volumes, Barth now examines how the creator is Lord over his
creation. In other words, Barth looks at the doctrine of providence. Unsurprisingly, he wants an account of God's providence
that is explicitly Christian. He is not interested in how, theoretic-
ally, a supreme being might relate to his creation; he wants to see
specifically how this God acts.

God's lordship, he explains, is a fatherly lordship, and is expressed in the relationship between himself and Jesus Christ. His
will for creation, and especially humanity, is really the outworking

---

20. *CD* III/2, p. 13.
21. Ibid. p. 135.
22. Ibid. p. 146.

of his will for Jesus Christ. His, then, is the most caring, preserving lordship!

So what of evil in creation? Barth defined evil as 'nothingness'. By that he was not even remotely implying that evil does not exist (having lived for so long in the shadow of Adolf Hitler, he was very aware of the reality of evil); it is that evil is what God has willed not to exist. God did not create it, and so it has no real being, but like a hole in the creation, it spoils what God has declared good and committed himself to. Like darkness, it is a lack that is and will be refuted and abolished by the shining of Christ, the Light of the world.

III/4 Barth finishes his account of creation with a look at what ethics flow from what has been seen. First, the ethics of creation cannot in any way be neutrally 'non-Christian' or generic. Far from it: 'the one command of the one God who is gracious to man in Jesus Christ is also the command of his Creator and therefore already the sanctification of the creaturely action and abstention of man'.[23] The Creator in his fatherly lordship calls humanity to himself, and that means our very existence is under command: to be human means we are called to confess and know him.

This has repercussions for the whole of life. Under the command of the Father, we are directed not only to him, but to each other. Our every relationship, from relations with our closest family to relations to those most distant from us are the outworkings of that basic obedience and enjoyment of him. And, since he affirms our existence, so too must we affirm our own lives 'and that of every other man as a loan, and to secure it against all caprice, in order that it may be used in this service and in preparation for this service'.[24] To be against life would mean being against the God who affirms it.

Volume IV: The Doctrine of Reconciliation
The fourth volume of the *Dogmatics* consists of three part-volumes (the third divided into two in the English translation: IV/3i and

---

23. *CD* III/4, p. 3.
24. Ibid. p. 324.

IV/3ii) and some posthumously published fragments of a fourth part-volume. The structure here is a little different: instead of being a sequential argument, this volume is more like a tapestry, with themes interwoven with each other. Doctrines that traditionally are kept separate (such as the person and the work of Christ) are here intertwined. This is because Barth was eager to show that it is wrong to divorce the person of Christ from what he came to do. What he does shows who he is; he is who he is in what he does.

Instead of arranging doctrines in some systematic order, Barth uses the volume to tell a story. The basic structure of that story is taken from the parable of the prodigal son. It starts with 'The Way of the Son of God into the Far Country' (not that the Son of God is wicked like the prodigal, but that he leaves his Father for a place that has become unclean), and it turns, triumphantly, into 'The Homecoming of the Son of Man'.

In order to appreciate what Barth is doing (and how elegantly he has arranged things), it is really necessary to read the three parts of 'The Doctrine of Reconciliation' alongside each other. The following table lays out how the various themes are picked up and treated in each part of Volume IV.

Part 1: Jesus Christ, the Lord as Servant	Part 2: Jesus Christ, the Servant as Lord	Part 3: Jesus Christ, the True Witness
§59 The Obedience of the Son of God	§64 The Exaltation of the Son of Man	§69 The Glory of the Mediator
§60 The Pride and Fall of Man	§65 The Sloth and Misery of Man	§70 The Falsehood and Condemnation of Man
§61 The Justification of Man	§66 The Sanctification of Man	§71 The Vocation of Man
§62 The Holy Spirit and the Gathering of the Christian Community	§67 The Holy Spirit and the Upbuilding of the Christian Community	§72 The Holy Spirit and the Sending of the Christian Community
§63 The Holy Spirit and Christian Faith	§68 The Holy Spirit and Christian Love	§73 The Holy Spirit and Christian Hope

IV/1   The first part tells the story of 'The Way of the Son of God into the Far Country', how Christ the Lord became a servant.

It concerns Jesus as God, coming to be God with us, humbling himself even to the cross. Typically, Barth reverses our expectations yet again: Jesus' humiliation and lowly servanthood are not associated with his humanity but with his divinity. And that reveals something infinitely profound about the very nature of God. It is that the humility of Jesus is not something strange and alien to God; the self-emptying of Jesus reveals that God's glory is his humble self-giving. That is what God in his lordship is like.

The lowest depth of the Son's obedient self-humbling was on the cross, when he became 'The Judge Judged in our Place'. There in our place he suffered under the death-dealing wrath that God's rejected love had become. And in so doing, he won a complete victory: 'The man of sin, the first Adam, the cosmos alienated from God, the "present evil world" (Gal. 14), was taken and killed and buried in and with Him on the cross.'[25] The old humanity was destroyed so that he might be the new Adam of the real humanity God always intended.

True to form, Barth thought it quite impossible for us sinners to know naturally what sin is:

> Men preoccupied with themselves have no eyes to see this or categories to grasp it . . . Access to the knowledge that he is a sinner is lacking to man because he is a sinner . . . This is revealed in the fact that he does not see beyond the natural inward contradiction of his existence, in face of which he is capable of remorse and pity and melancholy, or even rueful irony, but not of genuine terror, in face of which he can always quieten and excuse himself, remaining obstinately blind and deaf to the contradiction which is his guilt and the breach which is his need. He sees and thinks and knows crookedly even in relation to his crookedness.[26]

It is only in Christ's judgment of sin (here especially on the cross) that sin is exposed and unmasked for what it is. And the divine humility of Jesus Christ here shows sin to be its rebellious polar

25. *CD* IV/1, p. 254.
26. Ibid. pp. 360–361.

opposite: it is pride. Reviling self-giving humility, I wish to be the lordly judge myself. Indeed:

> man only wants to judge. He thinks he sits on a high throne, but in
> reality he sits only on a child's stool, blowing his little trumpet, cracking
> his little whip, pointing with frightful seriousness his little finger, while
> all the time nothing happens that really matters. He can only play the
> judge. He is only a dilettante, a blunderer . . .[27]

But then, Christ is the answer to that, too. Not only was he judged in our place, but he is the judge in our place; meaning we can abandon our silly conceit.

Throughout his whole doctrine of reconciliation, Barth weaves the traditional designation of Christ as prophet, priest and king. Here Christ is seen to be our priest, achieving reconciliation between God and humanity, and in particular, achieving our justification.

Then, finally, he looks at the Holy Spirit's role in forming the body of Christ, the church, the gathering of those he makes willing through faith to live under God's condemnation of the proud old humanity.

IV/2   The story now does a U-turn as we see 'The Homecoming of the Son of Man' and Jesus Christ the servant's being Lord. It describes Jesus as the man (the new and true man) who is exalted to be with God in his resurrection and ascension. And, as his humility was associated with his divinity, now his humanity is associated with his exaltation. Jesus is now depicted as the Son of Man in his kingly office, enthroned by God. In him, man is now with God and we see what we are meant to be as human.

This exaltation further exposes sin as the sloth that miserably refuses to join Jesus as he goes to his Father. In the resurrection of the Son of Man, then, we see his (defeated) antithesis:

> the man who would not make use of his freedom, but was content
> with the low level of a self-enclosed being, thus being irremediably and

---

27. Ibid. p. 446.

radically and totally subject to his own stupidity, inhumanity, dissipation and anxiety, and delivered up to his own death.[28]

However, in his resurrection and ascension, Jesus has brought man to be with God, and so made it possible for us to reject our sloth and be sanctified. In establishing what it is to be truly human, truly alive and with God, he frees us from our pretentiousness to be for God and for our fellow man. Liberated to be truly human, we are thus liberated to be Godlike, loving.

Finally, Barth turns to look at how the Spirit builds up the body of Christ into the maturity of Godlike love. So empowered, the church can then represent to the world the freedom and humanity Christ has brought.

IV/3   The third part deals with Christ as prophet. By that, Barth does not mean that Christ is about proclaiming some message other than himself: unlike all other prophets, in everything he does he announces himself as the mediator, the one who unites God and humanity in himself. 'Revelation takes place in and with reconciliation. Indeed, the latter is also revelation. As God acts in it, He also speaks. Reconciliation is not a dark or dumb event, but perspicuous and vocal.'[29] Barth's preferred image here is of the light of life: Christ's life-giving reconciliation is light-giving.

This light of truth exposes sin as a perverse self-condemning lie, an attempt to hide from the truth of Christ and grasp life on man's own, sinful terms. But Christ calls and awakens us to know the truth and then proclaim that truth to the world. He therefore gives us his enlightening Spirit to overcome the deceit in us, to cause us to hope in him and call all people to know that hope.

IV/4   A fourth part, which Barth never lived to complete, would have looked at our faith-response to this reconciliation, and how, as we are baptized with the Spirit, we are called to be baptized with water as the 'first step of this life of faithfulness to God'.[30]

---

28. *CD* IV/2, p. 378.
29. *CD* IV/3i, p. 8.
30. *CD* IV/4, p. 2.

Going on with Barth

There is no end of books, articles and websites on Barth. Yet there is really very little that is genuinely accessible and helpful for the beginner, and all the 'Barth-speak' can feel like razor wire designed to keep out the uninitiated. A couple of books stand out as good next steps, though: for an overwhelmingly positive introduction and assessment, try John Webster's *Karl Barth* (London: Continuum, 2000); or, for a delightful and more critical review, get Colin Gunton's *The Barth Lectures* (London: T. & T. Clark, 2007). The latter will also give you the joy of getting to know the late, great Colin Gunton and some of his theology.

But by now, readers should not be surprised that I recommend going straight to read the man himself. Armed with the knowledge of his narrative style, you can. Really you can jump into the *Church Dogmatics* wherever appeals, but many find little III/1 a good place for a first visit. Or, if the *Dogmatics* still just seems too much, go for his short *Evangelical Theology: An Introduction* (Grand Rapids: Eerdmans, 2004), or perhaps his *Dogmatics in Outline* (London: SCM, 1949).

Karl Barth timeline

1886	Barth born in Basel
1904	Theological studies in Berne, Berlin, Tübingen and Marburg
1909	Assistant pastor in Geneva
1911	Pastor in Safenwil
1914	Barth's liberal teachers endorse the First World War
1916	Studies Romans
1919	Commentary on Romans published
1921	Professor of Reformed Theology in Göttingen
1925	Lecturer in Münster
1930	Professor of Systematic Theology in Bonn; begins writing *Church Dogmatics*
1933	Adolf Hitler becomes Chancellor of Germany
1934	Co-authors the Barmen Declaration for the Confessing Church in Germany, rejecting Nazi theology; writes *No!* against Emil Brunner's openness to natural theology
1935	Dismissed from his teaching post and appointed Professor of Theology in Basel
1939–45	Second World War
1940	Volunteers for the Swiss Army
1962	Retires from professorship
1968	Barth dies

13. THE PURITAN THEOLOGIZER

J. I. Packer

The room was crammed with Christian luminaries when the nervous young assistant walked in. Against all desire, she had been told to wait there. None paid her any attention. None save one, who came over and made her warmly welcome. He was Jim Packer; she is now my wife.

That was a little moment that captured something pivotal in Packer's character and ministry: thoroughly unpretentious, he has given himself to making every Christian feel welcome – welcome, that is, in the inner sanctum of theology. As such he has been a key figure in transforming evangelicalism from the theologically stunted thing it was in the early twentieth century to being a theological force with which to be reckoned. Indeed, one can only really make good sense of modern evangelicalism with a knowledge of Packer.

Packer's life

James Innell Packer was born in Gloucester, UK, on 22 July 1926, the son of a clerk for the Great Western Railway. It was very nearly a short life, never to be noticed by the history books: aged seven, young Packer was chased out of school onto a busy road and knocked down by a bread van. His head was so damaged it left a sizable dent that could be seen for the rest of his life. Kept, as a result, away from boyish games and friends, the accident came to reinforce his natural introversion and bookishness. Then, for his eleventh birthday, he was given not the bicycle most boys received but a typewriter. It soon became his pride and joy, and for the rest of his life – even into the age of computers – he would write his works on a typewriter.

From school in Gloucester Packer went up to Oxford to study classics. Until that time he had had almost no contact with what he would call 'true Christianity'. He was familiar with the name George Whitefield, an alumnus of his old grammar school with a house named after him, but the Packer family was only nominally Anglican, and no place for spiritual answers. Yet conversations with a Unitarian friend had got him wondering about Christianity, and he had begun reading his grandmother's Bible with interest. Then, early in his first term as an undergraduate student, on Sunday, 22 October 1944, he went to an evangelistic service at St Aldate's Church. At first the elderly preacher's exposition left Packer cold, but then came the preacher's account of his own conversion: it made Packer realize that he was not yet, as he had thought, a Christian, and that he needed to 'come in'. That night he gave his life to Christ, just yards from where George Whitefield had done the same in 1735.

In the next couple of years as a student Packer would go through three theological moves that would set the course of his new life as a Christian. The first was the undoing of the liberal view of the Bible he had grown up with. Reading Scripture, he had always taken it to be nothing more than a ragbag of human writings about religious experience, something helpful but fallible. Yet hearing it preached, six weeks after his conversion, he became convinced (with surprise) that the Bible is the very Word of God.

The second shift came about during the first Christmas vacation. He decided to read a biography of his fellow alumnus, George Whitefield. Here, he found, was an Anglican who refused to be confined by denominational lines, an evangelist with the heart of a Puritan. Packer would share those emphases for the rest of his life.

The final move had to do with 'Keswick theology', the triumphalist teaching that promised bliss and victory over sin to all who would simply 'let go and let God'. At the time, such talk of perfect peace through perfect surrender was in vogue among the students in Oxford, but for Packer it was an infuriating mirage. He longed for the deliverance it offered, but found it a will-o'-the-wisp, ever out of his grasp, however many times and however desperately he reconsecrated himself.[1] Then, in a cluttered basement, he found an uncut set of the works of John Owen. Intrigued by the titles in volume 6 – 'On Indwelling Sin in Believers' and 'On the Mortification of Sin' – he opened and read. In delicious contrast to the Keswick teaching, Owen had a realism about the ongoing problem of sin in believers, and the need for every Christian, however mature, to battle with it daily. The whole harrowing experience would mark Packer for life in two ways: first, having been burnt by Keswick theology, he would always carry a special and heartfelt emphasis on the importance of sanctification and battle with sin. Secondly, his experience of Owen had given him an appetite for the Puritans that would only grow.

After graduating, he moved to Oak Hill College in north London for a one-year appointment to teach Greek and Latin. There he discovered his aptitude for teaching, and that honed his intentions for the future: he wanted to enter ordained ministry in the Church of England, but now he saw that that might well mean teaching in a theological college. Also that year, attending Westminster Chapel on Sunday evenings, he got to know Martyn Lloyd-Jones, and suggested to him the idea of 'The Puritan Conference'. The conference, as it ran over the next two decades, would itself be deeply formative for British evangelicalism, proving how spiritually and pastorally enriching robust theology could be.

---

1. See his later, damning critique of this Keswick teaching in '"Keswick" and the Reformed Doctrine of Sanctification', *Evangelical Quarterly* 27.3 (1955), pp. 153–167.

Then it was back to Oxford, first for ordination training at Wycliffe Hall, and subsequently for doctoral studies on the Puritan Richard Baxter (who would influence him profoundly).[2] With the research stage of his doctorate complete, in 1952 he moved to a suburb of Birmingham to serve as curate at St John's, Harborne, while writing up his thesis. The same month as the move, he proposed to a young Welsh lady named Kit Mullett: they would marry some nineteen months later.

His experience as a curate convinced him that he was more of an academic teacher than a preacher, and so after two years he moved to a lectureship at Tyndale Hall in Bristol, there to be received warmly by the students. Three years later he had published his first book, *'Fundamentalism' and the Word of God*. It served as a morale-boosting rallying cry for evangelicals with a high view of the Bible, it raised the level of sophistication and nuance with which they could think about Scripture and it established Packer as a theological leader of the movement.

In 1961 he moved to become Warden of Latimer House, Oxford, a research centre dedicated to strengthening the evangelical cause theologically in the Church of England. It would be the beginning of a more difficult time for Packer. It was not simply that he missed the energizing cut and thrust of the classroom: the winds of controversy were beginning to blow. In 1966, at the National Assembly of Evangelicals, Martyn Lloyd-Jones made a plea for evangelicals to leave the Church of England and gather instead in a purely evangelical fellowship of churches. John Stott immediately stood and opposed the idea. The issue had been one of gathering disagreement between Lloyd-Jones and Packer, and now Packer found himself (with Stott) on the other side of a very public dispute.

But relations with Lloyd-Jones and the (especially nonconformist) evangelical constituency were only about to deteriorate. A campaign had got underway to unite the Church of England with the Methodist Church, and Packer's manner of opposing this would

---

2. The thesis was eventually published as *The Redemption and Restoration of Man in the Thought of Richard Baxter* (Carlisle: Paternoster, 2003).

lead to a final break with Lloyd-Jones, and with that an end to the Puritan Conference they had co-led. Seeing that this Anglican–Methodist merger would involve sitting light on a host of doctrinal issues, Packer and another evangelical, Colin Buchanan, teamed up with Anglo-Catholics Eric Mascall and Graham Leonard to oppose it. Together they wrote *Growing into Union*, an argument that Anglo-Catholics and evangelicals could stand and cooperate in a common cause. But the nature of that common cause worried many evangelicals: both Stott and Lloyd-Jones expressed their concern about doctrinal compromise with Anglo-Catholicism, Lloyd-Jones especially worried by the book's 'lack of clarity concerning justification by faith only'. Packer was removed from the board of *The Evangelical Magazine* and the committee of a Bible conference.

That same year (1970) Packer was appointed to be the new principal back at Tyndale Hall. It would provide no immediate let up for him, though, as the House of Bishops was merging theological colleges at the time, leaving Bristol a morass of bitter politicking. Tyndale was soon incorporated into the new Trinity College, Bristol, where Alec Motyer would be Principal and Packer Associate Principal. It did soon mean, though, that he had more time for writing again, and the following year *Knowing God* was on the shelves, giving him – to his great surprise – an international profile far greater than he had had before.

At the same time, he was setting his sights overseas more than before. In 1977 he became a founder member of the International Council on Biblical Inerrancy, and the following year attended the summit meeting in Chicago that produced the Chicago Statement on Biblical Inerrancy, a document that helped a generation of evangelicals hold to biblical inerrancy with clarity and confidence.[3]

The year after that he left England for good, settling in Vancouver, to teach at Regent College. Ever since, the question has been asked, did he jump or was he pushed? The truth is that it was probably a bit of both. The move happened because the Principal of Regent, James Houston (Packer's friend from undergraduate days), asked

---

3. The document can be viewed online at http://library.dts.edu/Pages/TL/ Special/ICBI_1.pdf.

him to come – and the teaching position, lacking administrative burdens, was immensely attractive. He would have more space for writing; he could remain an Anglican; and in North America he was in obvious demand. But since *Growing into Union* and the split with Lloyd-Jones, he was also feeling unwelcome – and unfulfilled – in England. The move was not simply an escape, but it was revealing of the state of evangelicalism in Britain: a brain drain had begun, and British evangelical talent was finding it could be more fruitful abroad.

Packer stayed teaching at Regent until his official retirement in 1996 – and then he simply continued to teach part-time. In that time, as well as travelling and producing a steady stream of books, chapters and articles, he became a contributing editor – really a theological advisor – to *Christianity Today*. Then, in 1998, he was appointed General Editor of the English Standard Version, a fully hands-on work that he later reckoned was perhaps the most important thing he ever did for the kingdom of God.

Controversy had refused to stay behind in England, though. In 1994 Packer almost repeated the events of 1970 by endorsing the document 'Evangelicals and Catholics Together' (ECT). Rather like *Growing into Union*, this was an ecumenical paper designed to pave the way for individual Catholics and evangelicals to work together in a common Christian mission. But once again many evangelicals felt that the theological waters were being muddied, especially around the area of justification. The document stated, 'We affirm together that we are justified by grace through faith because of Christ.'[4] The trouble, according to the critics, was that evangelicals and Catholics would mean quite different things by that, and the suggestion that this is a point of agreement simply pretends that the Reformation never happened. As he had been back in 1970, Packer would be severely censured by many evangelicals for his endorsement of ECT.

The other main controversy of his later years involved the Anglican Church of Canada (ACC). Packer was a convinced and

---

4. http://www.firstthings.com/article/1994/05/evangelicals--catholics-together-the-christian-mission-in-the-third-millennium-2.

lifelong Anglican, but in 2002 his increasing frustration with the liberalizing of the ACC came to a head. When his diocesan synod approved the blessing of same-sex unions, he and some other evangelical clergymen walked out, explaining

> this decision, taken in its context, falsifies the gospel of Christ, abandons the authority of Scripture, jeopardizes the salvation of fellow human beings, and betrays the church in its God-appointed role as the bastion and bulwark of divine truth.[5]

Then, in 2008, his church of St John's Shaughnessy, where he had served for over two decades as Honorary Assistant Minister, voted to leave the ACC and come under the alternative episcopal oversight of the Province of the Southern Cone. An Anglican he remained, though harried from church to church.

Packer's thought

Packer himself once wrote

> I would ask you to think of me as a Puritan: by which I mean, think of me as one who, like those great seventeenth-century leaders on both sides of the Atlantic, seeks to combine in himself the roles of scholar, preacher, and pastor, and speaks to you out of that purpose.[6]

It was a self-aware and highly revealing comment, for Packer has been a modern-day Puritan in many ways, and not only as a scholar, preacher and pastor who has straddled the Atlantic. Shaped by a constant and grateful engagement with the Puritans ever since he picked up that copy of Owen as an undergraduate, his theological convictions and emphases are all Puritan: he is a thoroughgoing

---

5. http://www.christianitytoday.com/ct/2003/january/6.46.html.
6. 'Inerrancy and the Divinity and Humanity of the Bible', in *Honouring the Written Word of God: The Collected Shorter Writings of J. I. Packer*, vol. 3, p. 162.

Calvinist; he has the highest regard for theology; he refuses to allow the thought that theology should ever be an ivory-tower game; and he is deeply concerned about Christian holiness and the reformation of the church.

His self-description as a Puritan is also indicative of his keen broader historical consciousness. Like C. S. Lewis before him, Packer has a strong instinct always to consult – and never to neglect – the wisdom of the past. Thus it is with these words that he introduced his quintessential work of doxological (and Puritan) theology, *Knowing God*:

> 'Stand ye in the way and see, and ask for the old paths, where is the good way, and walk therein, and ye shall find rest for your souls' (Jeremiah 6:16). Such is the invitation which this book issues. It is not a critique of new paths, except indirectly, but rather a straightforward recall to old ones, on the ground that 'the good way' is still what it used to be.[7]

Despite being recognized as a competent scholar in his fields, Packer's pastoral concern has meant that he has tended to concentrate on writing devotional works accessible to every thinking Christian. Alister McGrath concluded, 'Some would say Packer is a great theologian; it would probably be more accurate to say he is a great "theologizer" – someone who knows, loves and thinks about God, and is able to communicate that passion in his books.'[8]

Has this meant a failure on his part to maximize use of the theological talent and knowledge at his disposal? Certainly that was the view of Martyn Lloyd-Jones, who, in his 1970 letter that called an end to the Puritan Conference, wrote to him:

> You have known throughout the years not only my admiration for your great gift of mind and intellect but also my deep regard for you. I had expected that long before this you would have produced a major work in the Warfield tradition, but you have felt called to become involved

---

7. *Knowing God* (London: Hodder & Stoughton, 1973), p. 8.
8. *To Know and Serve God: A Biography of James I. Packer* (London: Hodder & Stoughton, 1997), p. 280.

in ecclesiastical affairs. This to me is nothing less than a great tragedy and a real loss to the Church.[9]

It was a criticism that would be repeated by many others in the years that followed. Packer did, in fact, once sign a contract (with Tyndale House Publishers) to write a full systematic theology, but eventually decided against it, reasoning that

> there are already quite a number of evangelical systematic theologies written by professors . . . We have as many of them as we reason and thus I see no need to add to their number because, as a mainstream Reformed thinker, I haven't anything fresh to say that these people haven't already said. On the other hand, if I am given more time, I would like to survey the whole of Christian doctrine at what I call the 'higher catechism level' – the level which one addresses thoughtful laypeople who are not technically educated in theology but who want to know their faith accurately and to have a solid grounding in Christian basics.[10]

Again, it was a revealing comment: Packer's freshness has always lain in the clarity of his communication, not his content. He is, essentially, a catechist – a teacher of Christian essentials – not a theological pioneer.

The lack of a grand systematic theology also fits with his life-long inclination to prefer theology that is more or less immediately useful. He has often described theologians such as himself as the sewage specialists and water engineers of the church, in that they are the ones who are meant to remove the theological sewage, ensuring God's people drink pure spiritual water.[11] As such, Packer has tended to be an occasional writer, writing in response to the needs and threats he sees around him.

---

9. Letter from Lloyd-Jones to Packer, 7 July 1970, http://banneroftruth.org/uk/resources/articles/2010/the-end-of-the-puritan-conference.

10. http://theresurgence.com/files/pdf/reformation_and_revival_2004-10_james_i_packer_interview.pdf.

11. *Hot Tub Religion* (Wheaton: Tyndale House, 1987), p. 13.

Those few things said, introducing Packer's thought is no straightforward task. To start with, I realize that I am writing far too close in time to be able to evaluate him with any serious objectivity. On top of that, and in contrast to every other theologian in this book, Packer writes in modern English, and with such clarity that he needs no interpretation. I will therefore confine myself to attempting to give a broad and rounded picture of his output.

But then again we hit a snag, for, long lived and ever industrious, Packer has been dauntingly prolific. Which of his many works should we choose? I suggest that five themes have dominated his thought and writing: the Bible, the Puritans, knowing God, the cross and sanctification. We will therefore look at five works, one representative of each theme (around those, other works can cluster and be mentioned). They are, in order, *'Fundamentalism' and the Word of God*; *A Quest for Godliness/Among God's Giants*; *Knowing God*; 'What Did the Cross Achieve?'; and his introduction to Owen's *On the Mortification of Sin*.

'Fundamentalism' and the Word of God

As first books often do, Packer's first book revealed something foundational in the author's thought. The themes it touched would echo through all his works, and would surface repeatedly in his career: in his classic expression of the evangelical doctrine of Scripture, *God Has Spoken* (1965); in the careful nuance of the Chicago Statement on Biblical Inerrancy; and in his work as General Editor of the English Standard Version.

However, this work was also characteristic in being (in good part, at least) a response to current events. In the 1940s and 1950s liberals had developed the tendency to tar evangelicalism with the contemptuous label 'Fundamentalism', a tendency that was given forthright expression in A. G. Hebert's *Fundamentalism and the Church of God* (1957). Evangelical belief in biblical inerrancy they dismissed as 'new, eccentric and in reality untenable'.[12] Packer, who at the time was seeking to write up a talk he had already given on Scripture,

---

12. *'Fundamentalism' and the Word of God* (London: Inter-Varsity Fellowship, 1958), p. 11.

decided that Hebert's book needed an evangelical response. The result was a positive and persuasive evangelical doctrine of Scripture combined with a blistering attack on liberalism. Feisty, boldly assertive, confident and clear as crystal, *'Fundamentalism' and the Word of God* had all the rhetorical swashbuckling that would be characteristic of Packer's earlier writing.

Packer starts by showing that the term 'Fundamentalist', like the terms 'Puritan' or 'Methodist', was serving as a vague, pejorative label – in this case used to enable easy dismissal of the evangelical position. For the reality was that this 'Fundamentalism' was simply historic evangelicalism, not a new heresy; merely old orthodoxy. The label suggested that, where liberalism was marked by intellectual honesty and freedom, evangelicalism was an intellectual ostrich. According to Packer, the 'fundamentalist' epithet was mere gamesmanship: the real question at issue was not closed- or open-mindedness, but the question of authority in the church:

> We shall argue that subjection to the authority of Christ involves subjection to the authority of Scripture ... Types of Christianity which regard as authoritative either tradition (as Romanism does) or reason (as Liberalism does) are perversions of the faith, for they locate the seat of authority, not in the Word of God, but in the words of men.[13]

To support the evangelical position, Packer then goes on examine the attitude of Jesus, the apostles and the early church towards Scripture, finding in each case that they treated it as their supreme authority. Having its origin in God, it is the truthful and truth-revealing word of God, and as such the very ground of our faith. It is, Packer argues, both infallible and inerrant: '"Infallible" denotes the quality of never deceiving or misleading, and so means "wholly trustworthy and reliable"; "inerrant" means "wholly true".'[14]

How, then, should faith and reason relate? 'The true antithesis here', he writes, 'is not between faith and reason (as if believing and thinking were mutually exclusive), but between a faithful and a

---

13. Ibid. 21.
14. Ibid. 95.

faithless use of reason.'[15] Reason *should* be used to receive the word of God, then apply the word of God to life, then finally to communicate it to others. It *should not* be thought of as the source of all truth (quite the opposite: unless enlightened by the word of Christ, reason *will* misfire). Making exactly this mistake, thinking that the human mind is the best and final arbiter of truth, rational secularism attempts to 'correct' faith by reason, bringing it into line with secular ideas. Liberalism also has reason 'correct' faith. But in Christianity, faith seeks to challenge and correct secularism in the light of revealed truth.

Throughout the book one hears the distinct echoes of Calvin, Owen and B. B. Warfield; towards the end the spirit of Gresham Machen presides, as Packer delivers his final judgment on liberalism. 'Liberalism is subjectivism trying to be Christianity.'[16] That is, it listens to men and women, but not to God; it discounts the authority of Christ, it denies the rule of the Creator over his world, and it refuses intellectual repentance. And since it is so captive to current prejudice, one has to say that it is liberalism, not evangelicalism, that narrows the mind.

A Quest for Godliness/Among God's Giants

The bulk of the material for this book (published in the UK under the title *Among God's Giants*, and in the US as *A Quest for Godliness*) was assembled from previously published articles and chapters, but as a work it represents a core theme for Packer: the Puritans. A huge number of introductory essays and articles could have been included, for Packer has been an avid Puritan scholar and student for six decades. But there is something especially appropriate for the book in how it represents Packer's thought, for the presence of John Owen dominates.

The book also provides an important clue as to *why* the Puritans would have such a magnetic appeal for Packer, and for *how* he would tend to view them. In the introduction he writes, 'As Redwoods attract the eye, because they overtop other trees, *so the*

---

15. Ibid. 140.
16. Ibid. 153.

mature holiness and seasoned fortitude of the great Puritans shine before us as a kind of beacon light.'[17] In other words, ever since those days of greatest existential crisis for him, as a student, when reading John Owen released him from the lure of a Keswick view of sanctification, the Puritans had appealed to him *as champions of holiness*. Of course, their theological seriousness and orientation were essential ingredients, but for him it is their theology and practice of holiness that have given them their X factor. As a result, Packer has been inclined to view the Puritans largely through that lens, meaning that the serious theological differences that often divided the Puritans tend not to be mentioned in his writing. In his afterword to the book, for example, when introducing the Puritans as a body, he writes:

> On matters of liturgy and order in the church, in particular, agreement on what needed to be abolished far outstripped agreement as to what should be brought in instead. But in seeking to honour and please God by the methodical holiness of mortifying sin, vivifying habits of grace, keeping the Sabbath, governing one's family, mastering the Bible, working hard in one's calling, practising purity, justice, and philanthropy in all relationships and keeping up communion with God by regular, constant prayer, the Puritans were all at one, and all the more so because these were the things that their preachers most stressed.[18]

All of which is quite true, but it does give the misleading impression that the Puritans were basically agreed on all essentials, bar a few matters of liturgy and church practice. (None of which is really a criticism: a man may specialize where he chooses – and the devotion of the Puritans is no bad place to specialize – but Packer is so influential an advocate for the Puritans it is worth being aware of where he does, and does not, focus.)

It would be rather pointless and very tiresome to summarize each chapter, but in his introduction Packer lists seven ways the

---

17. *Among God's Giants: The Puritan Vision of the Christian Life* (Eastbourne: Kingsway, 1991), p. 11, my emphasis.

18. Ibid. 434.

Puritans have shaped him, and these are worth seeing: (1) 'John Owen helped me to be realistic (that is, neither myopic nor despairing) about my continuing sinfulness and the discipline of self-suspicion and mortification to which, with all Christians, I am called.'[19] (2) Owen helped him see 'the sovereignty and particularity of Christ's redeeming love', a fact that 'has marked my Christianity ever since'.[20] (3) Richard Baxter convinced him of the importance of regular meditation, of preaching to yourself and then turning that truth into praise. (4) 'Baxter also focused my vision of the ordained minister's pastoral office.'[21] (Packer had in mind Baxter's *The Reformed Pastor* in particular, a work for which he provided an introduction.[22]) (5) The Puritans taught him to see how passing this life is:

> the Puritans' awareness that in the midst of life we are in death, just one step from eternity, gave them a deep seriousness, calm yet passionate, with regard to the business of living that Christians in today's opulent, mollycoddled, earthbound Western world rarely manage to match.[23]

(6) The Puritans fostered in him a holistic view of reformation, not separating orthodoxy from personal life, church structure, morality in wider society, mercy in social witness, and so on. (7) The Puritans 'made me aware that all theology is also spirituality, in the sense that it has an influence, good or bad, positive or negative, on its recipients' relationship or lack of relationship to God'.[24]

Packer uses the book to show the Puritans as deeply reflective and prayerful worshippers; as warriors; as hopers; as spiritual giants with no privatized faith but a strong sense of responsibility

---

19. Ibid. 12.
20. Ibid. 12–13.
21. Ibid. 13.
22. *Richard Baxter, The Reformed Pastor* (repr., Edinburgh: Banner of Truth, 1974).
23. Ibid. 14.
24. Ibid. 16.

to the wider church. Undoubtedly, their influence helped shape him in all these ways – and to make him the powerful influence he has been on evangelicalism.

Knowing God

It is entirely right that *Knowing God* should be the work for which Packer is best known: it reveals the heart of the author as well as presenting God. Never less than richly theological, never less than strongly devotional, it is a noticeably 'Puritan' book that urges contemplation, prompts prayer and leads to praise. The book's statement of intent is the man's life purpose: 'The conviction behind the book', he writes, 'is that ignorance of God – ignorance both of his ways and of the practice of communion with him – lies at the root of much of the church's weakness today.'[25]

The book started life as a series of articles written for *The Evangelical Magazine* in the 1960s. Each article developed the line of argument, and each needed to conclude with an application of the theological truth learned to the life of the reader. After a little editing and rewriting these were put together, and surprisingly (not least for the author) a major bestseller was born. Having been assembled from a series of articles, it 'is at best a string of beads', as Packer put it in the introduction.[26] It is not the easiest read, nor is it a 'how-to' book. But it offers something every Christian yearns for: a closer, more intimate knowledge of the living God.

Knowing God is not a systematic theology, or even a comprehensive examination of the doctrine of God. The triune nature of God, for example, is mentioned, but it does not very obviously shape the picture of God presented (though it strongly shapes the nature of the gospel as Packer describes it). Thus God's majesty, love, jealousy, and so on, are outlined, but without the trinitarian logic behind them being unpacked or referenced.

Instead, *Knowing God* is a journey – a journey towards God. More than helping readers to know *about* God or godliness, it

---

25. *Knowing God*, p. 6.
26. Ibid. 5.

seeks to lead readers to know and trust God personally, and so
have an energy and boldness *for* him and a contentment and
delight *in* him. This means two things: we must study who God is,
and we must appreciate how he relates to us in the gospel. This is
because when someone comes to know something of the majesty
and holiness of God, they begin to see themselves aright in that
light: as a wicked sinner. They need then to know that they can
throw themselves upon his mercy and find themselves accepted
for Jesus' sake. Then, and only then – knowing God and knowing
that they can approach him – they can exult in the adequacy of
God. That is the goal of the work:

> Where has all this led us? To the very heart of biblical religion. We
> have been brought to the point where David's prayer and profession
> in Psalm 16 may become our own. 'Preserve me, O God, for in Thee
> I take refuge. I say to the Lord, "Thou art my Lord; I have no good
> apart from Thee."'[27]

'What Did the Cross Achieve?'

Appropriately for this 'theologizer', 1973, which saw the publication of *Knowing God*, also saw Packer deliver the scholarly Tyndale
Biblical Theology Lecture. He chose the title 'What Did the Cross
Achieve? The Logic of Penal Substitution'. Methodically and
meticulously Packer set out to defend what he called 'a distinguishing mark of the world-wide evangelical fraternity', a notion that
'takes us to the very heart of the Christian gospel'.[28] That is, the
penal substitutionary 'model' of atonement.

Quite apart from being so commonly misunderstood and carica-
tured (even by its proponents), Packer believed that Reformed
articulations of penal substitution had tended to be overly rationalistic and defensive. He sought therefore to provide a biblical case

---

27. Ibid. 313.
28. 'What Did the Cross Achieve? The Logic of Penal Substitution', *Tyndale
    Bulletin* 25 (1974), p. 3. This is now more readily available in J. I. Packer
    and Mark Dever, *In My Place Condemned He Stood: Celebrating the Glory of
    the Atonement* (Wheaton: Crossway, 2007).

that preserved the mystery of the gospel without the pretence that it had exhausted the truth of the atonement.[29]

If we are to know anything of the mystery of the cross, he said, we must look to the Bible and the thought models given to us there. There we see that Christ's death was clearly substitutionary: Christ died *for us*, he became a curse *for us*, he gave his life as a ransom *for many*. In establishing this point, he explains that there

---

29. This idea of 'mystery' has itself been something of a hallmark in Packer's theology. It can be seen most clearly in his *Evangelism and the Sovereignty of God* (London: Inter-Varsity Press, 1961), where he proposes we see the sovereignty of God and our responsibility as an 'antinomy'. By this he means there is an apparent contradiction between the two that no amount of investigation will solve, but which nevertheless finds perfect resolution in the infinite God, if not in our finite minds. To this, John Piper later offered a brief but robust response: 'I would like to ask where Packer gets the idea that this so-called antinomy between the sovereignty of God and the responsibility of man is "inexplicable" to our finite minds? Does he simply have an intuitive feeling that we can't understand the unity of these two truths? . . . There is not one sentence that I know of in the New Testament which tells us the limits of what we can know of God and his ways. I might just say in response to much silly talk about the dangers of exhausting the mysteries of God, that my conception of God makes such a thought ludicrous. If we may compare God's wisdom to a ragged mountain and our growing understanding of it to a slow assent [*sic*], I do not have the slightest fear that during some midnight meditation I may (by the grace of God) attain some new ridge and all of a sudden find I am on the peak of the mountain with no more cliffs to climb. On the contrary, for every newly attained height of insight there stretches out an ever more glorious panorama of manifold wisdom. And one can only pity the poor souls who, for fear of finding out too much, never approach the sacred mountains but stand off and chirp ironically about how one should preserve and appreciate mystery' (John Piper, 'A Response to J. I. Packer on the So-Called Antinomy Between the Sovereignty of God and Human Responsibility', http://www.desiringgod.org/articles/a-response-to-ji-packer-on-the-so-called-antinomy-between-the-sovereignty-of-god-and-human-responsibility).

have been three basic understandings of the cross in church history, each reflecting a particular view of God, sin and salvation:

- The first sees the cross affecting us, whether by revealing God's love for us, causing hatred of sin, or simply by giving us an example of self-sacrificial godliness. It assumes 'that our basic need is a lack of motivation Godward and of openness to the inflow of divine life; all that is needed to set us in a right relationship with God is a change in us at these two points, and this Christ's death brings about'.[30]
- The second sees the cross as a victory over hostile spiritual powers. 'The assumption here is that man's plight is created entirely by hostile cosmic forces distinct from God.'[31]
- 'The third type of account denies nothing asserted by the other two views save their assumption that they are complete. . . . On this view, Christ's death had its effect first on God, who was hereby *propitiated* (or, better, who hereby propitiated himself), and only because it had this effect did it become an overthrowing of the powers of darkness and a revealing of God's seeking and saving love.'[32]

The second stage of the argument seeks to demonstrate that this substitution of Christ on the cross was *penal* in character. That is, that what Christ bore for us in our place (and exhausted) was nothing less than God's penal judgment on us. Packer is quite clear that penal substitution does not encompass the totality of our salvation (e.g. it is a way of speaking about the cross only, not the resurrection), but it does reveal to us the core of the gospel and give us the deepest insight into the triune love of God.

One other comment he makes here reveals something broader in his thought: his understanding of Christian motivation. 'To affirm penal substitution', he says, 'is to say that believers are in debt to Christ specifically for this, and that *this is the mainspring of all*

---

30. 'What Did the Cross Achieve?', p. 19.

31. Ibid. 20.

32. Ibid., emphasis original.

their joy, peace and praise both now and for eternity.[33] It is an important and noteworthy difference of emphasis from what we have seen in Jonathan Edwards (though it is not necessarily a contradiction): gratitude, rather than the enjoyment of God for his own sake, is held out as 'the mainspring of all their joy, peace and praise'.

Introduction to John Owen's On the Mortification of Sin

This last work might well be thought too insubstantial to be worth mentioning, but it is in fact highly *representative* of Packer, not only for being a short introductory piece (and on his 'first' Puritan, John Owen), but also for its content. It is a micro-treatise on that lifelong concern of his: sanctification.[34] And it shows his sources very clearly, that through Owen Packer developed a theology of sanctification with deep roots in the Reformation.

The first aspect of this Reformational view of his can be seen in his stunning but (tragically) little-read 1957 introduction to Luther's *The Bondage of the Will*. There he explained that, in complete contrast to Erasmus, who felt that we have some natural ability to improve ourselves before God, Luther viewed sin as a humanly incurable disease. The problem, explains Packer, is this: the fallen man '*wants* only to sin, and his choice ... is thus always sinful'.[35] The problem, in other words, is with our heart desires: we naturally *want* what is wrong. That is significant for our conversion: our very hearts and their desires must be turned (something that, wanting wrongly, we can never do for ourselves).

---

33. Ibid. 25, my emphasis.
34. Packer wrote a good number of works on sanctification and holiness, most obviously (and note well the title) *A Passion for Holiness* (Cambridge: Crossway, 1992). In fact, a number of his other works, while often ostensibly about some other subject, concern themselves in large part with sanctification. *Keep in Step with the Spirit* (Old Tappan, N.J.: Revell; Leicester: Inter-Varsity Press, 1984), for example, is more given over to the question of sanctification than any other aspect of the Spirit's work.
35. J. I. Packer and O. R. Johnston, 'Historical and Theological Introduction' to Martin Luther, *The Bondage of the Will* (Cambridge: James Clarke, 1957), p. 50, my emphasis.

But the same truth also pertains to our sanctification, and this is what Packer picks up in this introduction to Owen:

> In Scripture, and in Owen, desire is the index of one's heart, and the motivation is the decisive test of whether actions are good or bad. If the heart is wrong, lacking reverence, or love, or purity, or humility, or a forgiving spirit, but instead festering with pride, self-seeking ambition, envy, greed, hatred, sexual lust or the like, nothing that one does can be right in God's sight, as Jesus told the Pharisees time and time again . . . [W]hen Scripture tells Christians to mortify sin, the meaning is not just that bad habits must be broken, but that sinful desires and urgings must have the life drained out of them.[36]

That is how the Spirit exercises his life-changing and life-giving power in our sanctification: he wins our hearts to desire differently, to want God and want like God.

This theology of desires is not merely the fruit of Packer's own particular temperament: it springs from what he saw in Scripture, and from what he saw being upheld by the great Reformers and Puritans. Nevertheless, it helps us to see that Packer, for all his cerebral bookishness, is a red-blooded, jazz-loving man of hearty passions and desires. Witness this window on his soul:

> C. S. Lewis' first and, for my money, most dazzling Christian book was his Bunyanesque allegory, *The Pilgrim's Regress* (1933). There he traced the lure of what he called Sweet Desire, and Joy: namely, that tang of the transcendent in the everyday . . . revealing itself ultimately as a longing not satisfied by any created realities or relationships, but assuaged only in self-abandonment to the Creator's love in Christ. . . . I can speak of the sight of trees, waterfalls, and steam locomotives, the taste of curry and crab, bits of Bach . . . Louis Armstrong . . . Lewis himself, and Williams, and (you saw it coming) seraphic Baxter, dreamer Bunyan, and elephantine Owen.[37]

---

36. *Introduction to John Owen, The Mortification of Sin* (Tain: Christian Focus, 1995), pp. 14–15.

37. *Among God's Giants*, pp. 16–17.

Being human means that we are creatures of passion. We love
and yearn. What Packer saw in Scripture and in Owen was that the
essence of sanctification involves deliverance from *sinful* passions
as we look to Christ and come to share his *holy* passions.

'Set faith at work on Christ for the *killing* of thy sin,' [Owen] writes.
'His blood is the great sovereign remedy for sin-sick souls. Live in
this, and thou wilt die a conqueror; yea, thou wilt, through the good
providence of God, live to see thy lust dead at thy feet.'[38]

Going on with Packer

'I love pregnant brevity,' he once wrote, 'and some of my material
is, I know, packed tight (Packer by name, packer by nature). I ask
my readers' pardon if they find obscurity due to my over-indulging
this love of mine.'[39] Packed tight his writings usually are, but few
could find them obscure: he has an orderliness of mind and clarity
of expression much akin to C. S. Lewis. Most of his work is (and
was intended to be) accessible for the thinking layperson.

The place to start is, rather obviously, *Knowing God* or any of the
works introduced here. I would, however, add one personal –
perhaps whimsical – plea: that more people pick up and read his
introduction to Luther's *The Bondage of the Will*. It is hard to beat as
a marriage of sparkling content and style. For a more in-depth
analysis of the man and his thought, Leland Ryken's biography
J. I. Packer: An Evangelical Life (forthcoming, Crossway) is now, to
my mind, the most up to date and definitive.

---

38. Ibid. 16.
39. *God's Words* (Downers Grove: InterVarsity Press, 1981), foreword.

J. I. Packer timeline

1926	Packer born in Gloucester, UK
1944	Enters Corpus Christi College, Oxford
1948	Tutor, Oak Hill College, London
1949	Ordination training, Wycliffe Hall, Oxford
1950	Doctoral research
1952	Curate, St John's, Harborne
1954	Marries Kit Mullett
1955	Lecturer, Tyndale Hall, Bristol
1958	*'Fundamentalism' and the Word of God*
1961	Warden of Latimer House, Oxford
1966	Martyn Lloyd-Jones and John Stott divide
1970	*Growing into Union*; end of the Puritan Conference; appointed Principal of Tyndale Hall, Bristol
1972	Associate Principal, Trinity College, Bristol
1973	*Knowing God*
1978	Chicago Statement on Biblical Inerrancy
1979	Moves to Regent College, Vancouver
1994	'Evangelicals and Catholics Together'
1998	General Editor, English Standard Version
2008	Leaves Anglican Church of Canada

BACK TO THE SOURCES!

The lovely landscape of thirteenth-century Italy was studded up and down with ancient and crumbling remains. It was hard to miss the fact that here had once been a glorious and imperial civilization. In practice, though, all those arches, pillars and heaps of marble blocks were seen to be useful only as free quarries: the stone could be taken and used for new building projects, the marble turned into agricultural lime and spread round farms. Unappreciated for what it was, the past was being raped.

Then somehow the mood changed and people began instead to look more to that classical past for inspiration. 'Back to the sources!' was the new cry. And with that, there was an explosion of creativity. There was Renaissance. Rebirth. Under the influence of a rediscovered past, the worlds of art, literature, science, philosophy (and soon, theology) were seized with freshness and energy. Even the new buildings looked quite different; not because more stone was being pilfered from old ruins, but because now the very style of classical architecture was inspiring a taste for beautiful proportion and clean lines.

The refreshment of the past

Of course, it is quite possible to revel in the past in such a way as to become a reactionary or a romantic. But the Renaissance shows that we can also be refreshed by it. In fact, is that not what roots are for? The healthiest trees in a forest are those with the most extensive roots, for it is by using their roots that trees thrive and blossom. If a tree is to grow great, its roots must go deep. It is when those roots are cut that they die. It is no different in the church: without good roots into the past, we will be blown around by the assumptions of our generation, overly sensitive to petty changes in our immediate environment, ever more pinched and puny, our gospel all puckered and sour. But simply try this experiment at home: trot out some insight from Edwards or Athanasius, don't name your source, and people will think you dazzlingly original and fresh. Worrying? Maybe. But clearly, what is old can be new.

Go on!

That, at least, has been the aim of this utterly unoriginal book: to explore and appreciate roots, to sense some of the refreshment (and challenge) available. Has it worked? It has certainly been but a tiny effort, and for all the inclusion of some theologians, the necessary constraints of space have sadly meant the exclusion of so many. Oh to have spent time with others, perhaps feisty Tertullian or Bernard of Clairvaux. But my real fear now is that readers will go away with the wrong idea. Reading the greats ought to breed modesty, and he who spends time with these giants should sense what a clod he is. The reality, though, is that even the vaguest familiarity with a celebrity can induce the most cockeyed egotism. Thus if somehow I have left any reader feeling that he is a match for even one of these theologians, I apologize now. The attempt to introduce simply can convey the impression that the subjects are simple. But to have mastered an introduction to a theologian is not to have mastered a theologian.

That is why this is not a conclusion, for the whole point of this book has been, not to bag and collect, but to introduce, to lead on. And if you have managed to wade this far through the introductions, then getting to know the men themselves will be a delight. Great theologians are usually infinitely more interesting than the things said about them. So go on: back to the sources!

also by Michael Reeves

The Unquenchable Flame

Introducing the Reformation
Michael Reeves

ISBN: 978-1-84474-385-8
192 pages, paperback

Burning pyres, nuns on the run, stirring courage, comic relief: the story of the Protestant Reformation is a gripping tale, packed with drama. But what motivated the Reformers? And what were they really like?

In this lively, accessible and informative introduction, Michael Reeves brings to life the colourful characters of the Reformation, unpacks their ideas, and shows the profound and personal relevance of Reformation thinking for today.

'With the skill of a scholar and the art of a storyteller, Michael Reeves has written what is, quite simply, the best brief introduction to the Reformation I have read. If you've been looking for a book to understand the Reformation, or just to begin to study church history, this little book brings history to life.' Mark Dever

'A lively and up-to-date account of this important event in Christian history that will stir the heart, refresh the soul and direct the mind towards a deeper understanding of our faith.' Gerald Bray

Available from your local Christian bookshop or **www.thinkivp.com**